To: Ann
Join me into the
Your True
Miriam
Oct 27-2012

High Point of Persistence: The Miriam Richards Story

Damara Paris
Miriam Richards
Hilary White

Cover Photo: Photo of Miriam Richards was taken by Hilary White on top of Mt. Elbert in Colorado.

Library of Congress Cataloging-in-Publication Data:

Paris, Damara; Richards, Miriam; White, Hilary

High Point of Persistence: The Miriam Richards Story

ISBN 978-1-4303-1324-3

Library of Congress Control Number: 2007905664

Published by www.lulu.com

Some names are withheld in this book to protect certain parties, unless permission to use names was obtained in advance.

Miriam's Personal Record of Summits

This is a chronological order of the summits that Miriam achieved over ten years. On the far right side, "F" means that Miriam climbed the summit with a friend. "G" means she climbed with an experienced guide. "S" means that she climbed the summit solo.

Date	Summit	Height (Feet)	F,S or G
1. July 7, 1997	Guadalupe Peak, Texas	8,749	F
2. May 22, 1999	Mt Hood, Oregon	11,239	G
3. July 30, 2000	Mt. Whitney, California	14,494	F
4. August 19, 2000	Borah Peak, Idaho	12,662	F
5. August 26, 2000	Mt. Sunflower, Kansas	4,039	F
6. August 27, 2000	Mt. Constable, Nebraska	5,426	F
7. August 30, 2000	Mt.Elbert, Colorado	14,433	S
8. October 1, 2000	Brasstown Bald, Georgia	4,784	S
9. October 1, 2000	Sassafras Mountain, S.Carolina	3,560	S
10. October 1, 2000	Mount Mitchell, N.Carolina	6,684	S
11. October 2, 2000	Mount Rogers, Virginia	5,729	S
12. October 2, 2000	Black Mountain, Kentucky	4,145	S
13. October 3, 2000	Clingmans Dome, Tennessee	6,643	S
14. October 15, 2000	Driskell Mountain, Louisiana	535	S
15. October 15, 2000	Magazine Mountain, Arkansas	2,753	S
16. October 16, 2000	Taum Sauk Mountain, Missouri	1,772	S
17. October 16, 2000	Woodall Mountain, Mississippi	806	S
18. October 16, 2000	Cheaha Mountain, Alabama	2,407	S
19. October 16, 2000	Britton Hill, Florida	345	S
20. February 1, 2001	Mauna Kea, Hawaii	13,796	F
21. June 13, 2001	Timm Hill, Wisconsin	1,951	F
22. June 13, 2001	Mount Arvon, Michigan	1,979	F
23. June 14, 2001	Eagle Mountain, Minnesota	2,301	F
24. June 16, 2001	Hawkeye Point, Iowa	1,257	F
25. June 18, 2001	Charles Mound, Illinois	1,235	F
26. July 21, 2001	Mount Davis, Pennsylvania	3,213	F
27. July 21, 2001	Backbone Mountain, Maryland	3,360	F
28. July 21, 2001	Spruce Knob, West Virginia	4,863	F
29. July 22, 2001	Campbell Hill, Ohio	1,550	F
30. July 22, 2001	Hoosier High Point, Indiana	1,257	F
31. July 23, 2001	Tower Hill, Delaware	448	F
32. July 23, 2001	High Point, New Jersey	1,803	S
33. July 24, 2001	Mount Frissell, Connecticut	2,380	S
34. July 24, 2001	Mount Greylock, Massachusetts	3,491	S
35. July 25, 2001	Mount Marcy, New York	5,344	S
36. July 26, 2001	Mount Mansfield, Vermont	4,393	S

Date	Summit	Height (Feet)	F,S or G
37. July 27, 2001	Mt. Washington, N. Hampshire	6,288	S
38. July 28, 2001	Mount Katadin, Maine	5,268	S
39. July 30, 2001	Jerimoth Hill, Rhode Island	812	F
40. June 16, 2002	Black Mesa, Oklahamo	4,973	F
41. July 4, 2002	Boundary Peak, Nevada	13,143	S
42. August 7, 2002	Kings Peak, Utah	13,528	S
43. August 14, 2002	Granite Peak, Montana	12,799	G
44. August 17, 2002	White Butte, North Dakota	3,506	F
45. August 20, 2002	Harney Peak, South Dakota	7,242	F
46. Sept. 23, 2002	Humphrys Peak, Arizona	12,633	S
47. July 5, 2003	Mt Wheeler, New Mexico	13,161	F
48. August 14, 2004	Gannett Peak, Wyoming	13,804	G
49. August 19, 2005	Mt Rainier, Washington	14,410	G
50. June 2006	Denali, Alaska	20,340	G

Acknowledgements

I thank God for giving me the opportunity to climb each mountain I have climbed. I appreciate my many wonderful friends who prayed and supported my dream:

My sponsors: Balance Bar Grant, Sprint, Mid-Valley Interpreters, ASL Forever Performing Group (Debi, Jeffrey, Mark, Dan), ASL Club of Western Oregon University, DWOW (Deaf Women of Oregon and Washington).

I want to thank my Canadian and US friends who donated toward my climb, friends who donated their time to make and purchase "I Love You" ornaments, my ASL students, Corvallis residents, and Hilary White's relatives who consider me part of their family. I commend Hilary for writing the essay on my behalf that made it to the finals for Energizer's "Keep-Going" promotion. I want to thank all those who voted for me as one of ten finalists for the Energizer's Hall of Fame.

I appreciate all the professionals who understood my need to climb in spite of my MS: Dr Linda Fox, Dr Connie Graham, Dr Betsy Anderson, Dr Ronald Wobig, Dr Cecilia Keller, Nurse Patti, Laura Hoffman, my physical therapist, and Jenny Miller, my personal trainer. Thank you to Scott, Laura, Amy and Dennis who encouraged me as a motivational speaker and MS advocate. Thank you Susan Kenyon, for volunteering to review my manuscript. Thank you Tiffany Brown, for patiently photographing me during my good times and bad times. Thank you Michaela Hammer, for scanning my photographs.

I want to say thank you to the people who offered me hospitality during my travels: Sheila Farcy, Kelly Butterworth, Hilary White's step sister Sarah, Jim and Lyn, Brian's family, Arlita, Rita and Kathleen, Carla Garcia, Henri Grau, Ken Litherland, Debbie Richards, Allison Hamstreet, Julia Allen, and Lindy Deane.

Thank you to my friends who were excited to climb with me: Hilary White, Robert White, Nathan, Stacey, Allison Hamstreet, Ken, Carol, and Christina Litherland, Leslie and George Beilstein, Brian, Ellen, Anna and Peter Smith, Debbie Richards, Richard Blake, Lindy Deane, and Kelly Butterworth.

Thank you to my canine companions who accompanied me during my hiking and backpacking excursions: Rocky, Tilly Jane, Sadie, Cheeva, Rose, Dixie, Maddie, Geena, and Sierra.

Thank you for safely guiding me on my journeys: Kathy Cosley (Cosley & Houston Alpine Guides), Joel and Mark with Alaska Mountaineering School, Rainier Mountaineering, Inc., Timberline Mountain Guides, Jackson Hole Mountain Guides and the Boy Scout Leader and his troop on Kings Peak. Thank you to those who assisted in my rescue off Mt Hood, both mountain rescuers and Life Flight and military helicopters.

I want to say a very special thank you to my parents. My father accompanied me on my first state highpoint summit success: Texas, and encouraged me in my endeavors. I want to especially thank Mum, who drove the RV and waited patiently for me to return from some risky climbs. Although Mum did not want me to face danger, she finally gave in to accepting my determination to complete my goals. My parents sacrificed their own priorities by coming to my bedside during my worst episode of Multiple Sclerosis.

I want to say a unique thank you to my friend Hilary White who gave her time to help me write my book, promote my cause, travel with me and for "being there for me." And thank you to Damara Paris for writing, editing, formatting and sharing her knowledge with book publishing.

A special thank you to all the humble people whose names I have forgotten to add, but helped me along my way and remain with me in my heart.

Miriam Richards

Table of Contents

Foreword

I most recently spent time with Miriam Richards on her Denali attempt in June, 2006. But I first met her in 1999, when she joined an expedition to Aconcagua, which I was hired to help guide, along with my husband Mark and two other guides. She and her deaf friend Heidi, with gentle patience and humor, taught me as much ASL as my feeble brain could retain—enough to communicate with them on the climb.

When a violent snow-storm turned the group back short of the summit, Miriam had the satisfaction of knowing that she had tried as hard and gone as far as anyone in the group. She was just beginning her journey as a climber at that time, and she had "the bug." She knew that climbing mountains held great meaning for her, and she determined to do as much of it as she could.

I have made a life-long career out of helping other people reach summits of mountains, and I know that climbers motivations vary greatly; some desire more to "have climbed" a mountain, than they enjoy actually climbing it! Deep desire and aspiration can overcome great obstacles; more casual motivation drops away once serious obstacles arise. It was clear to me that Miriam's motivation was deep and her aspirations high. I didn't know her well enough at that time to know what I now believe is true: that this is the way she approaches all the aspects of her life.

Mountain climbing offers the same rewards as any other endeavor that is intensely involving, physically and/or emotionally arduous, and of uncertain outcome: a feeling of engagement with life, of adventure, satisfaction, and growth in self awareness and self reliance.

Because mountaineering is so demanding, it requires and develops many useful character traits. Faith in oneself; patience and fortitude in the face of uncertainty and disappointment; the persistence to keep on trying; the judgment to weigh risks and opportunities, to accept the facts when it is clear that further effort will not be enough to win through-all this as well as physical qualities: fitness, strength and stamina, and a high threshold for pain and discomfort! Fortunately, the very qualities needed to do well in the mountains are valuable in and of themselves. So even if we don't reach all our hoped-for summits, we need never come home un-rewarded.

Over the years that I have followed Miriam's progress in her quest to reach the 50 high points, I have seen these personal qualities in her. She is undaunted by long and often tedious effort, inclement weather, long hours of boredom sitting out storms in tents, physical discomfort and even pain. The prospect of having to get up and try again doesn't discourage her. Her cheerfulness and happiness to just to be in the mountains help ease the hardships for her companions as well.

Not least of Miriam's helpful qualities is her ability to strike a healthy balance between ambition and acceptance of disappointment. Mountain climbers must give their all, but they also must strive to come home safe and sound. Persistence is no longer a virtue when it becomes a refusal to admit defeat or to change course when going on poses unreasonable risks.

But as impressed as I have been by Miriam in the mountains, I have to say I admire her equally for other qualities I came to see in her in other contexts. She has a strong desire to share her passion for the outdoors with her friends in the deaf community. Her achievements in exploring and climbing make her a good role model for others who may not have her experience or her innate can-do confidence.

Also, although my own contact with the deaf population is essentially limited to my acquaintance with Miriam, I have always felt very much welcomed and encouraged by her to learn and to use my primitive level of communication in ASL. She opened a door for me on a world I would otherwise never have known, and she showed the same open friendliness with the many people we interacted with on Denali and on Aconcagua. Being a hearing person was never an obstacle to talking with Miriam. Again and again, other parties on the mountain would stop to say hello, to see how she was doing, to encourage her and cheer her on. They showed interest in her, not just because her situation was special, but because she is so outgoing and nice to talk to.

Finally, I admire her courage and persistence in the face of her Multiple Sclerosis. She knows and shows the importance and the value of staying active with this condition.

I will always remember Miriam's voice behind me on the rope, as she struggled through deep, soft snow in the stifling heat of the midday Alaskan sun, saying over and over "*I can! Come on!*" I'm sure we can all do more than we think possible, if we can just summon that same voice.

Kathy Cosley
Colsey & Houston Alpine Guides
www.cosleyhouston.com

An Important Introduction

I was fortunate to meet Miriam Richards in 2003, during a time that we both taught American Sign Language (ASL) courses part-time at Western Oregon University. I have always admired her friendly spirit, and her ability to touch people with her enthusiasm for life.

Last year, Miriam approached me about the possibility of writing a book regarding her quest to reach the high points of state here in the USA. I was honored to be trusted with an important piece of her life. At that time, while I had experience as an author and a publisher, I had very little understanding of high point climbing.

What I learned was that high point climbing, or highpointing is actually the sport of finding and visiting a point with the highest elevation within a county, state or even each country. It is believed that the first pioneers of this sport began in the 1900s, when conditions were more arduous, with far less tools available to assist with climbing.

In Miriam's case, she picked a goal of highpointing the highest point (also called summit) within each state. Some of these high points can be reached by car, or a short walk. Others are treacherous, and have dangerous elements such as snow, deep cold or inclement weather.

There are no official rules to highpointing, but the general principles of this sport are:

1. The goal is to stand upon the highest natural point, regardless of what kind of man-made structure is placed on top.

2. Some of the high points are on private property. It is always good to research these sites in advance to see if you need to call or write for permission to access the high point.

3. Any route to the top - walking, climbing, riding a cable car, or driving - is a valid means of attaining the high point. The goal of highpointing is reaching the high point, and whatever means to reach the high point is a personal choice.

Originally, this book was to be written as a biography. Later, we decided that Hilary, Miriam and I would all contribute to writing this book. While this is essentially Miriam's journey, there are close friends and family members who accompanied Miriam during her highpointing. Their perspectives, written subjectively, so enhanced the quality of this book we were reluctant to reduce them to more objective prose. As a result, you will notice that the flow of the chapters will change periodically from third person to first person narratives of various trips to summits.

It has been a blessing to work with Miriam and Hilary over the past year. Miriam's story deeply moves and uplifts me. I believe that after you read this book, you may be encouraged to complete your own personal goals—be they new or long forgotten.

Damara Paris, MS CRC

Prologue

.....My guide and I had to climb through another deep passage. I was feeling a little exhausted so I signed to Peter to find a place to sit and rest for a short time. But Peter motioned to keep going a little bit. I remember taking one step, looked up, then all of a sudden ice was breaking in front of us. What happened next was erased from my memory.

Later I learned the details. As I was nearing the summit, only 100 feet from the top, the ice I had planted my ice axe in had been melting as a result of the hot sun that unusually warm day in February. A large area of ice gave way, sending me down the mountain with it, only to be stopped by the quick hand of Peter Keane who immediately dug his ice axe into the mountain.

Initially he was able to hold onto me. However, the powerful impact of my plunging down was enough to dislodge Peter's axe. As Peter was pulled downwards, he plunged his ice axe back into the ice. He was so trained and experienced. My unconscious body still on his rope, swung into the mountain where the sharp ice cut into my face, breaking some bones in my chin. Again, the swinging jerking motion dislodged Peter's ice axe. As he fell, for a third time, Peter plunged his axe into the mountain and held on as long as he could, however his hold gave way and he plunged after me for the remaining portion of my fall.

An onlooker from another climbing team described my last free fall as cart-wheeling down with my legs bending in positions not normal for the human body. My helmet protected my brain even though the total fall was 1,000 feet into Devil's Punchbowl.

Miriam Richards plunged 1,000 feet while attempting the first mountain on the list of her highpointing goals. How does one recover from severe injuries, and later a devastating disease, to go on and attempt all 50 state summits? To understand this, and who Miriam is, turn the page to read more about her childhood, her challenges and her triumphs.

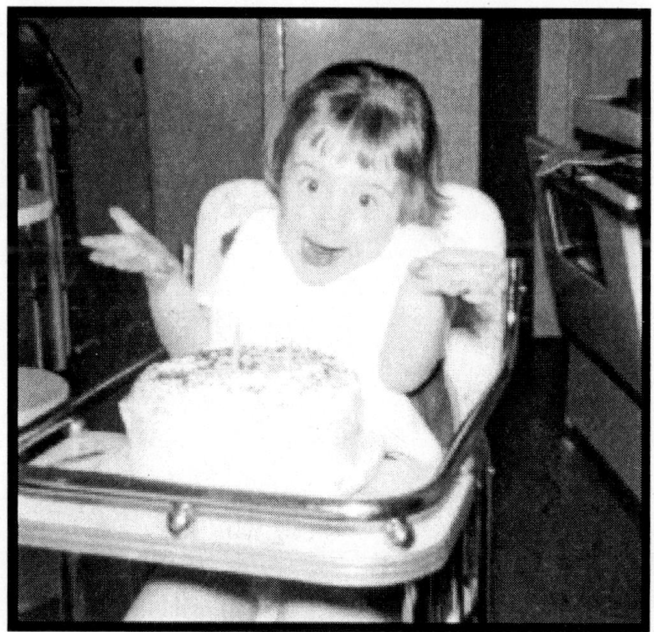

Miriam, during her third birthday, hams it up for the camera

Miriam Richards: The Early Years

Miriam was born in Victoria, British Columbia, Canada. She was born into a Canadian family that values their simplicity and privacy. Her mother, Marjorie Robson, was a nursing student at the time she met Miriam's father, Hugh Richards, on a blind date that was arranged by her mother's group of nurses and co-workers. Hugh was a dockyard apprentice machinist at the time they met. He continued to work for the H.M.C. (Her Majesty's Canadian) Dockyard as a civil servant machinist for 36 years until his retirement.

The Richards were married November 1, 1958. Miriam's mother decided to stop working at the hospital a year after their marriage and focus on the household. Miriam was born February 2, 1965 at 10 AM at St. Joseph's Hospital near her childhood home after nine hours of labor. She weighed 7 pounds, 6 ounces.

By all accounts from family members and childhood friends, Miriam was a happy, bright, energetic child. Early photos show Miriam as a smiling toddler, hamming it up for the camera with a mischievous twinkle in her eyes.

At approximately age two, Miriam's mother noticed that her daughter was not using her voice and did not seem responsive to noise. Since most children are born into families that are predominantly hearing, it is not surprising that Miriam was not tested for hearing loss during her infancy. Until recently, states or provinces did not require hearing tests on infants.

Miriam spent two days at Vancouver General Hospital undergoing a variety of tests, including auditory tests. It was a surprise to find that Miriam was born deaf, and to date, she is the only family member who is deaf, other than the work-related hearing damage Miriam's father obtained from firing guns while repairing them on Navy ships without ear protection. One interesting thing to note is that Miriam's doctor discovered her quick wit and responsiveness to her environment. In fact, he warned Miriam's parents that she would be a handful considering her intelligence. Miriam's mother recalled an incident that emphasized her introspective nature:

> "*When Miriam was about 3 years old, our family went on a camping trip across Canada. It was very difficult to communicate with Miriam at this time as none of us knew any sign language, so it was mostly pictures and pointing out things to her. She was familiar with the Indian people who lived around the Vancouver Island area and had seen teepees at the museum. When we arrived in Quebec, New Brunswick, Nova Scotia and Prince Edward Island, she immediately related to the steepled churches (which were all white and a church in every village) as teepees, and promptly asked (through motions and pointing), " Is that where the Indians live?"*
> *(Marjorie Richards,January 2007)*

Yet, despite her intelligence, Miriam also displayed a sweet naivety as a child. With communication difficult between her and her family members, Miriam would sometimes misunderstand or depend on her visual acuity to interpret the world around her. Marjorie fondly remembers one cute incident when Miriam was young:

> "*When Miriam was a very young girl, she loved to have whipped cream on her desserts. One day, she saw her father shaving in the bathroom and he had shaving cream all over his whiskers ready to shave. She thought that he had whipped cream on his face and so she climbed on a chair and took her finger and wiped off some of the shaving cream and put it in her mouth thinking it was whipped cream. The look on her face when she discovered it was really shaving soap was*

absolutely astounding, something we will never forget!
(Marjorie, interview January 2007)

Both Miriam and her parents recall the first time Miriam went to Disneyland and Knotts Berry Farm when she was around four or five years old. Miriam vividly remembers the long trip from Canada to Anaheim, California and her reaction upon seeing Disneyland:

> *"I remember getting into the car from Canada and my parents tried to explain Disneyland to me. I didn't quite understand where we would be going. It was a long drive to Disneyland and I was getting very impatient! Finally, we arrived at the amusement park. I remember walking with my family to the front of Disneyland, through the gates and then saw the magic castle. It suddenly dawned on me where I was! I was so excited that I immediately took off for the castle waving my arm beckoning my parents "Come on!" My parents were behind me trying to get me to slow down!"*
> *(Miriam Richards, May 2006)*

Right after Disneyland, Miriam and her family went to Knott's Berry Farm where several other amusing incidents occurred. Miriam recalled:

> *"At that time, Knott's Berry Farm had a real monkey and an organ grinder. I went up to the monkey and he took one look at the bag of popcorn I held, grabbed it and ran off with it! I was so upset!*
>
> *One really funny incident happened when we were on the train that took us around the amusement park. I was seated on the train and looked outside to see two cowboys*

> *having a shootout. One of the cowboys was shot and fell down dead! I was taking this in when the shooter boarded the train. Apparently he had crawled under the train and came through the old-fashioned gates on the train, shoving them aside and then marched up to me and stuck his guns at me. I really thought he would shoot me next. Panicked, I immediately stood up with my hands in the air! My parents started laughing and then I saw through the window the cowboy on the ground getting up. I realized then that this was a show and felt embarrassed afterwards!" (Miriam Richards, January 2007)*

These incidents, while funny, also concerned family members that they were not communicating adequately with Miriam. Her mother decided to contact John Tracy Clinic in California for advice. She received materials by mail that included pictures with appropriate signs. For a few years, her mother faithfully worked with Miriam on learning rudimentary signs for communication at home.

Miriam vividly recalls how difficult it was to sit still watching her "Mum" teach her signs. The youngster was so active and antsy, there was so much to explore, she could not bear to sit at the table. Marjorie in her desperation somehow communicated to Miriam that she would be rewarded with swim lessons if she paid attention until the end of the lesson. As the doctor had forewarned Miriam's parents, she was crafty and weaseled her way out of the sign language lessons but continued with swim lessons. She had no patience with sitting.

Arriving at the pool, Miriam saw a swim teacher in a brightly colored swimsuit and headed in her direction. But another instructor in a dull black swimsuit with a zipper waved Miriam towards her. Miriam frowned at the black swimsuit and looked pleadingly with her smile in the direction of the instructor wearing the colorful swimsuit who smiled and gestured. Miriam ran quickly toward her but jumped into the deep water and took off, churning up the water. All the onlookers watched in amazement as this bold and brazen child showed she was ready to swim.

Ballet lessons made no sense at all to Miriam. She'd been told it would make her look pretty. She did not see any point to ballet and the fairy-like poise.

Miriam was sent to the Pearkes Clinic in Victoria, B.C. at age 4. This was a center for multi-disabled children. Parents of deaf and hard of hearing children had worked diligently to secure a room at the center's teaching facility. Parents sold raffle tickets and ran a souvenir shop in Victoria to pay for the cost of a teacher who could focus on the needs of their deaf and hard of hearing children. At the time of her admittance in the Clinic, Miriam was the only girl in the deaf and hard of hearing classroom. and was often the ringleader behind mischievous pranks that she pulled on her teachers, particularly substitute teachers.

One day, while at the Pearkes Clinic, Miriam had a substitute teacher for the day. Miriam felt that the teacher was not doing a good job, and she was bored. After observing some of her classmates with epilepsy, she decided to act out having a seizure to liven up the day. What Miriam did not realize was that seizures usually lasted a few minutes. Her performance went on for at least 30 minutes.

> *"One day the school frantically called me and told me that Miriam was having convulsions, and to come as quickly as I could. I replied "What, she has never had convulsions in her life!" Anyway, I had about a 30 minute drive to the school and got there as quickly as I could. Apparently, she was writhing on the floor and foaming at the mouth. When I walked into the room, Miriam took one look at me and jumped to her feet and waved at me with a big grin. I said "What's wrong with her now?" Then the staff realized they had been*

taken in by the whole situation. The doctors warned me when she was 2 years old that I will have a lot of trouble because this is an extremely intelligent girl. Apparently, she saw how much attention these actions got for some of the other children who had legitimate problems and thought she would try it. It worked— she got a lot of attention that day."
(Marjorie Richards, January 2007)

When Miriam was five, it was decided that she would attend the Jericho Hill School (JHS) in Vancouver, B.C. This was not an easy decision for her parents. The residential school was almost four hours away. During one of those short 30 minute flights, Miriam had to use the restroom. She remembers unbuckling her seatbelt and figuring out how to open the narrow accordion-style bathroom door. When she was ready to return to her seat, she could not open the door. She pounded frantically and pulled at the handle, crying as she tried desperately to free herself. The flight attendant heard the pounding and attempted to open the door but could not. She summoned the pilot who used a bobby pin to undo the lock and landed the plane just in time. When her Mum saw her exit the plane with a red face, she could see that her daughter had been crying and asked, *"What happened to my daughter?"*

Such a long trip to a residential school was not unusual for families with deaf children in North America. While some of these schools offered day classes to children who lived locally, most of the time children would stay in the dormitories all week, and then go home on the weekends. During Miriam's first year at JHS, she was able to take a thirty minute plane ride to the school on Sundays and return home on Fridays. Parents in Victoria paid the fare for 6 months and did not realize that they could apply for help from the government. In later years, however, the almost four hour trip would cut severely into Miriam's family time. She would arrive on Friday evening at 9 pm, only to have to leave on Sunday at 1 pm to get to the school before curfew.

Miriam remembers having to wear a bulky Radio-Ear hearing device with hard button plugs in her ears during her first year. The contraption, which fitted over the ears, ended with a wire to a small box that acted as a microphone. A body harness held it in place. The boxed hearing aid set was often uncomfortable, and especially hindering to someone as active as Miriam was. It was commonly worn by deaf and hard of hearing people in the 1970's. She recalls hating the device—often hiding it or "losing it". Instead of helping her hear, the device only transmitted noise that was incomprehensible to her. This noise would frequently cause dizzy spells and headaches.

After a year at JHS, Miriam's parents decided to enroll her at Frank Hobbs Elementary School, which had a room set aside for mainstreamed deaf students. During this time, the trend was to teach Cued Speech in the classroom. Simply defined, Cued Speech is a visual communications system that combines mouth movements with "cues" or hand shapes that distinguish consonants, with four locations near the mouth to distinguish vowels. The purpose of Cued Speech is to help the deaf or hard of hearing individual improve their lip reading and speech capabilities with teachers and family members.

Miriam felt that she did not thrive in this environment, despite the best intentions of the school. She quickly found herself getting bored again, creating distractions to entertain herself and others. Miriam's mother remembers this also as a time when Miriam started becoming more interested in the outdoors and in physical activities.

> *"I would send Miriam to school in a dress and try to make her look the part of a young girl. The teacher called and asked if I would dress Miriam in long pants. Apparently, she was leading the boys in climbing trees at recess. Perhaps this was the beginning of her climbing days."*
> *(Marjorie Richards, January 2007)*

Miriam, an avid camper, would spend hours fishing with her father from age 5 and on. These experiences in the outdoor honed her desire to be in a natural environment. Spending time in the classroom was often torture for her—she preferred to be outside and expend the store of energy and curiosity she always seemed to have. With a sparkle in her eye, Miriam recounts:

> *"I remember being bored in the classroom so I would often make the other boys carry out pranks. I remember one time I made one boy pull a fire alarm. I just walked around with a big grin on my face watching all the action of the fire trucks. Getting out of the classroom for a few hours was a pleasure. I sat in the sun and watched the boy being led off to the principal's office.*
>
> *When I was about 8 years old, it was recess when I thought the boys would have fun if they had an adventure in the woods. So I told them to follow me as we all marched off the playground into the forest adjoining the school. None of the teachers took notice. I showed the 5 boys how to climb trees and applauded their tree climbing abilities and pretended we were in the wild surviving. I acted as their army sergeant training the boys. They obeyed me for about two hours and had a great time. I was satisfied, then I felt it was time to return to school. One teacher stood with her arms folded giving me a stern look knowing who planned this event. I knew I was in a lot of trouble, but it was worth it!"*
> *(Miriam Richards, March 2006)*

After two years at the Frank Hobbs Elementary School, Miriam's parents decided that Miriam was not benefiting from the educational program. Marjorie knew first hand why her daughter was not progressing when she volunteered to help in the classroom so the teacher would have more time to help individual students.

When the other children were still learning to count, Miriam was expected to work independently out of a workbook since she already knew how to count. So Marjorie and Hugh decided to try Jericho Hill School for the Deaf once more. While they knew they would miss Miriam at home, they wanted the best education possible for their intelligent, outgoing child. Once more, she began the trek from Victoria to Vancouver, staying at the school until the end of her high school years.

Miriam remembers her arrival at JHS and her pride with her Cued Speech skills. But students who rejected her Cued Speech as worthless abruptly dethroned her. Worse, she was allowed to stay in the dorms at JHS but because classes were full, she was transported by public transportation street car (bus) for mainstreaming at Henry Hudson School. After a year, Miriam attended classes at JHS.

The history of residential schools for the deaf in British Columbia is interesting. Prior to the establishment of JHS in Vancouver, the first school for children with hearing or vision loss in British Columbia was a privately-run "School for Deaf-Mutes and the Blind" which opened in Victoria in September 1888. The school's founder, John Ashcroft, tried to secure funding from the provincial government. When his request was declined, the school was closed one year later. The government also declined to fund a second school that opened in Victoria in 1900 despite representations made by Victoria City Council and the British Columbia Benevolent Society.

In 1901, the government provided grants for British Columbia children attending approved schools for the deaf and the blind outside the province. Most of the children were sent to the Manitoba School for the Deaf in Winnipeg. In 1915 the Vancouver School Board established a class for deaf children at Mount Pleasant School. Enrollment quickly increased and new classes were established. In 1920, the Department of Education took over the school and renamed it The Provincial Oral School, operating in several locations before moving the school to Jericho Beach in

Vancouver. Soon afterwards, the school assumed responsibility for educating students with visual impairments and renamed the school the British Columbia School for the Deaf and the Blind. It was renamed Jericho Hill School in 1955.

It appears that for many years, Jericho Hill School enjoyed a good reputation, locally and nationally, and was regarded with pride by Education Department officials. But in the late 1970s and early 1980s, stories began circulating about instances of abuse at the school. A number of reforms were initiated at the school to protect students from abusers. In 1991, stories printed in newspapers about continued abuse caused a public outcry. As a result of the publicity, the lack of students and funding, the provincial government closed the school in 1992. While Miriam declines to specify whether she was abused during her years at JHS, she does cite instances of oppression and discrimination during her high school years. These incidents only increased her determination to do well and succeed.

When Miriam went back to JHS at age 10, she was fortunate that her grandparents lived near JHS and would often stop by to give her care packages of food and toys. Miriam instinctively knew that she was lucky to receive family attention while she was at the school, and generously shared her goodies with her dorm mates. The 30-minute plane ride was no longer an option, from now on the ferry was the method of transportation. Her grandparents picked her up from the school a few times on Fridays and dropped her off at the ferry, picking her up again on Sundays to take her back to the school. This lasted for two years, until her grandfather became sick and eventually passed away from cancer, and her grandmother was unable to drive. Fortunately, a husband and wife volunteered to do the transporting to and from the ferry most weekends.

Miriam became interested in competitive sports when she re-entered JHS, often winning awards for being a great team player. When she was eleven years old, she was asked to join the swimming team. After a few practices, she began feeling ill and stopped by the nurse's office. The nurse promptly decided she needed to go to the doctor for a thorough examination. Miriam recounts both the humorous, and serious, aspects of this experience:

> *"I remember taking a taxi to the doctor's office. I was feeling so sick! We pulled up outside the doctor's office and the nurse told me to stay in the taxi while she got a wheelchair for me. While she was gone, I was overcome with nausea. Unable to control myself, I vomited all over myself and the inside of the taxi. Boy, was the taxi driver mad! The doctor examined me and said that I needed to go to the hospital. The nurse had to call for a taxi again, and sure enough—it was the same taxi that I had just vomited in! The taxi driver gave me a stern look and told me not to throw up again! Then he drove as fast as he could to the hospital to get rid of me! When I went to the hospital, the doctor took one look at me and said I needed to have my appendix removed. I was scared about going into the hospital and having surgery, but at eleven years old, I didn't know any better and trusted him. I found out later that I didn't really have appendicitis. The doctor just wanted the money for doing the surgery! Instead, it was likely I was experiencing vertigo combined with swimming and hearing loss."*
> *(Miriam Richards, January 2007)*

Miriam spent a week in the hospital, and then was informed that she would not be able to play basketball for the two month season. The news was hard for her to take—she had looked forward to playing basketball all year. But what she remembers the most about the incident is that she was given the Best Basketball Player of the year award despite the fact she did not play that year. The message behind this gesture, while given with good intentions, would cause her to later question the authenticity of future awards, especially academic awards.

Miriam, as a teenager, pictured with many of her medals from athletic competitions

Teen Years: An Athlete Emerges

Miriam was 13 years old when she began playing tennis, hitting balls against the wall under the dorm at Jericho Hill School for the Deaf on her own just to keep herself busy. She had purchased a cheap wooden tennis racquet near her home in Victoria and took it to her school. After classes were over for the day, the hours could drag until dinner time, unless there was something exciting happening. Always energetic, when there was an hour to kill time, she would go outdoors before the sun went down and find something to do. When many students were chatting in the dorm, Miriam could be seen hitting a tennis ball against the wall under the dorm. A dorm counselor happened to see her practicing and complimented her on her skills and asked if she was interested in signing up for the British Columbia Deaf Sports Federation (BCDSF). Miriam's interest was kindled. She was determined to practice harder to beat the wall.

Miriam continued playing tennis against the wall with her sights on becoming a competitor. She had never played tennis on a real court against a real person. In September 1979, when she was 14 years old, Miriam showed up at registration day for a BCDSF tennis competition and walked up to the chairman of the event. This experience really stayed with her in the years to come:

> *"The Chairman of the BCDSF tennis competition looked me over and asked me what I was doing there. I told him that I came to play tennis and handed him the money for registration. He seemed impressed with my forthrightness, but said that this competition, aimed at the adult population, was open to the entire Province of British Columbia. This wasn't for kids but a minimum age had not been established. As a result, he had no choice but to take my money and let me register."*
> *(Miriam Richards, June 2007)*

Miriam played singles in the B.C. Open Tennis Championship for the Deaf. She lost the first game, but it was not bad for her first time on a tennis court. She knew she had a chance to win now that she was beginning to get the feel of a court rather than the wall under the girls' dorm. Indeed, the wall was more predictable than the human player.

Miriam won the second game and moved up to triumph over every player in the winners' bracket! The crowd was awestruck. At the age of 14, after beating 4 players, Miriam had become the Women's Open Singles Champion and the youngest winner in the history of the BCDSF. Her competition was in their 20's, 30's and older.

When she was given her trophy and plaque in the presentation ceremony, the BCDSF chairman gave a speech recalling the day that Miriam showed up with her registration money to join. He said that he had had misgivings about her age, abilities and experience and could not believe what this brazen 14-year-old child had just accomplished.

Miriam competed again in 1980 and 1981, still reigning as women's champion. In 1982, Miriam made it all the way to the final championship match of the competition. A breakdown in communication caused Miriam to show up at the wrong time for the final match.

> *"I showed up, and found that I was misinformed about the time. The judges told me that the other competitor was given the trophy by default since I did not show up at the scheduled time. I felt very devastated at missing this chance for competition."*
> *(Miriam Richards, June 2007)*

When Miriam tried out for the National Lawn Tennis Trials, she was not informed that she was to play on red clay. It was an entirely different surface than the concrete where she taught herself against the wall and the hard courts where she won the BCDSF

Championship. Miriam did not have ample warm up time to get used to the new surface and the ball behaved differently than on concrete. Because Miriam is not a quitter, she put in her best effort. Unfortunately, she was unable to overcome her inexperience on a clay court. As a result, Miriam was not among those selected to represent Canada to compete in the Deaflympic Games that would be held in Germany on clay.

Miriam was a member of both the 1985 and 1989 Canadian Deaf Tennis Teams competing in Los Angeles, California and New Zealand.

A versatile athlete, Miriam did not concentrate on just her tennis skills. She was also the captain of her high school volleyball team, although she was the shortest member. Her team often played against other adult teams. Miriam encouraged other players, especially when the score was down. When her peers became nervous and felt they did not have a chance, Miriam said, *"We can do it!"* and her team went on to victory.

Miriam received many more awards for team and individual sports. She was a well-rounded athlete and enjoyed all competitive opportunities. Sports Day was an annual tradition at JHS that Miriam looked forward to every year. Miriam still holds records for the girl's shot-put and farthest distance throwing a ball at JHS. Her softball team was called the Bad Bears. They lost every year against the hearing leagues until Miriam's senior year, when at last they made their way to the championship and won.

The British Columbia Summer Games for all people, whether they are deaf or hearing, was another favorite event for Miriam. She has many medals from the two years she competed in that annual event. Miriam competed in cross-country skiing with the BC Winter Games one year.

Miriam lived in the school dorms occasionally on weekends. She loved finding outdoor recreation opportunities. She went camping with friends from her classes. Sometimes, the entire dorm would go camping for the weekend and Miriam thrived on the experience.

One year, she took a leadership training course at a Victoria YMCA that would prepare her to work as a Youth Counselor. They asked her to come back the next year and assigned her to an all-boys group. She took them on a camping retreat. When she woke up one morning, she thought perhaps she slept funny and that was why her back hurt. With a disgusted look on her face, Miriam recalls:

> *"When I got home, I asked Mum to check my back to see if she noticed something wrong like a bruise. Mum had a look and when she saw a tick, her arms flew back and she called my dad to help. He got a match and tried to burn off the tick. It was holding on too deep in the skin and could not be pulled out. My parents took me to the hospital. The physician assured me that the tick was dead, but when he cut it out, he noticed its legs were still moving."*
> *(Miriam Richards, June 2007)*

Miriam excelled in academics, however, she looks back on her classroom experience and feels that some academic honors were given to students with good behavior, misleading them. This made Miriam even more determined to pursue a good education.

When Miriam was seventeen years old, the students in her class and local mainstreamed deaf students were given a Gallaudet entrance exam. One teacher heard that all mainstreamed students passed the exam while none of the JHS students passed. The teacher felt that this could not be possible and went to the principal's office, asking if he could see the letter with the entrance exam results. When the teacher did not get a straight answer from the principal, he decided to call Gallaudet University himself to inquire about the test results. He was told that both Miriam and another student had passed. The teacher encouraged Miriam to go ahead and go straight to Gallaudet. Miriam made the decision to attend Gallaudet that August 1982, rather than finish one more year at JHS. She marched with the 1982 JHS graduating class but was denied a high school diploma.

Miriam playing one of her favorite sports--field hockey

Gallaudet Years

After leaving JHS, Miriam moved to Washington D.C. to pursue her bachelor's degree at Gallaudet University. It was a culture shock for her to be alone among so many thousands of students. Miriam had always been the leader in every school and athletic program she entered. She was only 5'1", 17 years old, in a country unfamiliar to her. Gallaudet has many older students. It was hard for Miriam to make new friends the first semester. Miriam's friendly smile was not enough for busy students to take the time to get to know her. She went through a terrible depression, struggling to not give up and head back to Canada.

Miriam also struggled with the loss of one friend from Canada who died while at Gallaudet during a motor vehicle accident. With one week off during winter term, Miriam's dorm had a snowball party for the prep class. Miriam was enjoying the event while two classmates on the same floor of her dorm drove to an ice skating rink. On their way, they were broadsided by another car. Her friend died upon the impact into the passenger door. There was a memorial service for her at Gallaudet, but her body was returned to Canada.

Anita Marchitelli, Miriam's advisor, was very supportive of Miriam and treated her with respect. She encouraged her and gave her hope that there was a light at the end of the tunnel. Miriam clearly remembers her saying, "*Do not give up, Miriam.*"

Gallaudet University, or simply called "Gallaudet" among students, faculty and alumni, is currently the world's only university in which all programs and services are specifically designed to accommodate deaf and hard of hearing students. It was founded in 1864 by an Act of Congress, and its charter was signed by President Abraham Lincoln.

Gallaudet is truly a Mecca for the Deaf Community. For those unfamiliar with Deaf Culture, one can simply do an Internet search to find a wealth of information about this small, but close-knit community, which is bound together by many components that make up a culture. Often the "D" in deaf is capitalized, and most Deaf people view hearing loss and deafness not as a disability, but as part of socio-linguistic community.

A key element of this community is American Sign Language (ASL), a complete, complex language that employs signs made with the hands and other movements, including facial expressions and postures of the body. ASL is considered the first language of many deaf North Americans, is often said to be the fourth most commonly used language in the United States.

Miriam met many international deaf students who brought different perspectives about being deaf from different countries. It was an exciting, but difficult transition to go from a small school for the deaf in Canada to a University of over 3,000 students from all over North America and many other countries.

At the time Miriam attended Gallaudet, most students had to take the first year as a "prep" year before moving on to freshman status. Miriam was surprised at her inability to pass English class requirements until her last year at Gallaudet. As Miriam described earlier, she received many awards for English while at Jericho Hill School for the Deaf, but she now suspects that those awards were given for having good behavior. Her struggle with English impacted her self-esteem, but as always, she persisted until she reached her goal of passing the class.

> "*I was shocked to go into Gallaudet and find that my English was not as good as I had thought. I believe the awards I received gave me false hope when it comes to the English language. In fact, my English is not good at all! It makes sense, since ASL is my first language, that I would have difficulty with English as a second language. After four years of failing English classes, I had to pass*

> *in order to graduate. If I failed the final test, I would be kicked out of Gallaudet University. I struggled and memorized whole passages, without a tutor to help me. After taking the difficult English exam, I had to wait until the grades were posted. I could not get the test off my mind. That afternoon, I played tennis at Trinity College. My coach Robbie was puzzled by my expressions as I played a strong singles match. She knew that my mind was somewhere else as I was playing. She was right, all I could think about was the English exam. Then I saw out of the corner of my eyes, my friend, Kelly pulled up in my car and signed to me from a distance, "PASSED!" I was relieved when I finally passed!"*
> *(Miriam Richards, May 2006)*

In addition to struggling with her English courses, Miriam had a difficult time adjusting to being away from her beloved Canada. Miriam felt particularly bad that she was away from her parents, knowing that they were concerned about her well-being in a large city, thousands of miles from home, at such a young age. Miriam felt she needed to do well at Gallaudet in order to alleviate her parents concerns. Kelly Butterworth, her college roommate, remembers the first year being especially hard on Miriam.

> *Miriam was quiet and a bit shy that first year. I spent a lot of time encouraging her to keep going, despite some of her struggles with school.*
> *(Kelly Butterworth, February 2007)*

Anita Marchitelli and Jean Berube also noted Miriam's difficulties adjusting during her first year at Gallaudet, but they were impressed with her ability to overcome obstacles.

> *"Miriam received her B.S. from Gallaudet University majoring in physical education. She came to Gallaudet with so much desire and thirst for knowledge. She knew that she had to study hard to get her degree. Miriam hardly had any support, as she was far from home, so she learned how to be a survivor. Miriam was creative, had a positive sense of humor, and was a pleasure to have as a student. She always loved adventure and challenges so she fit perfectly into our discovery program. It was in this program that she learned how to rock climb, thus developing into the mountain climber she is today. Tenacity and courage has directed her life, overcoming obstacles along the way. The seemingly impossible has become the possible for her."*
> *(Anita Marchitelli and Jean Berube, July 2007)*

Fortunately, Kelly Butterworth befriended Miriam and invited her to socialize with her family. At last, Miriam felt included. She was invited to spend Christmas with Kelly's family and ride in their sailboat in the Virgin Islands. In time, Miriam regained her self-confidence and will to carry on and eventually majored in PE.

Miriam soon found her niche within Gallaudet by joining several sports teams. The most notable was her participation on the Gallaudet Women's Tennis team in 1986. She recalls some historical moments during this time.

> *"At the time I joined the Gallaudet Women's Tennis team, this team had never won first,*

second or third place. Our team, however, had some great players, many of them from different countries including a woman from Belgium, one woman from Sweden, five American and one Canadian player. We also had an excellent coach! We signed up for a tournament with seven of the best surrounding university teams, including Trinity. I played single sets as well as doubles with Sheila Farcy from Minnesota.

During the tournament, I surprised myself by winning so many sets, and I saw the board with all of the players' names narrowing down. I just kept playing the whole weekend and I remembered feeling so exhausted by the last game. I won the first set, then the second set and at that point was so exhausted but not ready to give up until the third set. Kelly Butterworth was there encouraging me every step of the way and kept saying "Don't give up! You can do it!" I won the third set and became the Champion for singles out of all seven universities! Three other girls on our team also won the Champion title. I will never forget Sheila pushing herself with me during the doubles games. Her final serve won us the Champion title for doubles! This was the first time in history for the Gallaudet Women's Tennis team. I was so proud of us!"

Miriam credits a great team, and a great coach for making the tennis team experience so memorable for her. Miriam's tennis coach, Robbie Carmichael, was a deaf Olympic tennis player and someone Miriam admired for her skill on the tennis court. Robbie also had great respect for the way Miriam played.

> *"Miriam was a top-ranked tennis player for Gallaudet University. She played both singles and doubles. She also represented Canada at Deaflympics and the Meare Cup (World Tennis Championships for Women). She would never give up, even when she was down. She would come back from losing the first set 0-6 and win the match. She kept hitting the ball back again and again. She had control of the game most of the time. Her secret weapon was the BIG serve. Miriam would get fired up on every point. She looked at tennis as one of the challenges in her life. She took her training seriously, as she put in long hours of practice time in the morning and afternoon. Miriam had enough energy to play for hours."*
> *(Robbie Carmichael, July 2007)*

In addition to playing tennis, Miriam was also on the field hockey team. She excelled at this sport. According to both Anita Marchitelli and Robbie Carmichael, Miriam was a feisty and aggressive attacker and the top scorer in her team. Often she would injure herself, but continue to play, ignoring the pain until the end of the game.

One of her most memorable injuries from field hockey was just before the Home Coming Ball (HC Ball). Miriam had never experienced attending a prom during her high school years, and she was excited about going to the HC Ball with another Canadian student at Gallaudet. As luck would have it, she sustained a painful and obvious injury during a game that occurred on the same day as the HC Ball.

> *"I think we were playing Mary University—and I believe we won that game. During the game, I was blocking the ball with my stick. The game*

rules are that you are not supposed to swing up past waist level. A member of the other team swung up and the stick hit me in the eye, which bled all over the place! The field hockey coach ran over, took one look at me, and told me I had to go to the hospital. I really wanted to go to my first-ever formal ball. I thought maybe the boy who asked me to go with him would have to go to the ball without me. I had to have twelve stitches by my eye six inside and six on the outer skin. By the time I got out of the hospital, it was 7 PM and I thought it was too late to go. To my surprise, when I arrived back at Gallaudet my date was standing there waiting for me. I changed my clothes really fast, and did not put on any make up because of my eye. I went outside and there was a long car in front of me. I didn't know what a limo was at the time, but I was impressed with the fancy long black car. It was my first time going to a ball, and the first time riding in a limo. Unfortunately, I could only handle about one hour of the ball and needed to go back home because of pain and fatigue. My date was nice enough to let me go home in the limo alone. I never had the opportunity to go on another date with him, though."

(Miriam Richards, May 2006)

While sports was a major part of her Gallaudet years, she also spent time with her family, whom she missed dearly.

During the summer of 1983, when Miriam was 18 years old, she planned a surprise for her parents' 25th Wedding Anniversary. She took her dad fishing while her mother went shopping. Miriam and Hugh drove their green van pulling their wooden boat in the trailer. They entered a Native American Reservation close to Sooke near

Victoria, B.C., and put the boat into the Sumas River. Miriam cast her line into the water first with a soft green squid lure and then Hugh cast his with a piece of herring for bait. It was quiet on the Sumas River that day. Miriam and her dad enjoyed many years fishing this way together.

Miriam did not expect to see and feel her rod dropping all of a sudden into the water. She jerked quickly on the line and began to reel in the heavy fish. Hugh did all he could to keep the boat steady as he assisted Miriam in her long ordeal with the fish. As soon as her eyes caught sight of the fish flaying above water, she could not believe the size of it! Miriam was afraid her line might break if she fought the fish too quickly. She was so excited she could hardly believe it! The 10 pound weight on Miriam's line was hardly enough to make much of a difference. Miriam will never forget what it was like seeing the silvery fish lash at the surface, then disappear downwards fighting unseen. As she gradually pulled the fish closer and closer to the side of the boat, Miriam's dad reached for his net. They were glad they had a big net although they had never caught anything anywhere near this large.

It was a challenge for Hugh to capture such a fast moving target. He timed it just right and scooped the net under the fish but could not lift the heavy fish. Miriam carefully set down her pole as Hugh held onto the net and it took both of them to lift the fish into their boat. It took up a lot of space on the floor of the boat. Both stood there aghast. Neither could believe their eyes. It was a white spring salmon weighing 47 ½ pounds!

Miriam and her dad arrived home and showed the fish to Marjorie. She was amazed. They cut the fish into many sections and put it into the freezer. It would provide many delicious dinners for some time. That was one of Miriam's most treasured memories of her life.

Miriam asked her dad to put on a nice tie. She instructed her "Mum" to wear a nice dress to go out. Miriam drove them to Dairy Queen for their 25th Wedding Anniversary dinner. Miriam put on a nice dress too. Hugh and Marjorie's reaction to Miriam's choice of venue was shock. *"We cannot go in there dressed like this!"* they appealed. Miriam was just teasing them. They were relieved when she started up the old Bobcat car again and headed for downtown Victoria. They ate at a luxury restaurant. It was a very fancy expensive meal. The cook came to light a torch to make a brandy drink with hot banana for her parents. They had cause to celebrate and thoroughly enjoyed the evening.

Miriam was also proud to be involved in one of the most historical moments of Gallaudet called the "Deaf President Now" (DPN) protest. In 1987, then Gallaudet University president Jerry C. Lee announced his resignation and leaders in the national deaf community as well as Gallaudet alumni, students, faculty, staff and friends, urged the Gallaudet University Board of Trustees to select a deaf person as the University's next president. On March 6, 1988, the Board of Trustees announced the appointment of Elizabeth Zinser as Gallaudet's next president. Zinser admittedly had little or no ASL or deaf culture knowledge. Students and their supporters refused to accept the board's decision and instead, launched the historic DPN movement that resulted in a week-long protest that captured worldwide attention and created great awareness of deaf people, and their language and culture. Two days after being appointed the new president, and under pressure from DPN, Zinser resigned. Gallaudet's eighth—and first deaf—president, I. King Jordan was selected.

Miriam was an active participant in the protest. Miriam joined in the March on Washington protest. While she was not one of the leaders of this movement, she was, as always, a great team player. She made signs, stood for hours blocking the entrance to Gallaudet, and encouraged others to not give up. She continues to be proud of her contribution to that movement, almost 20 years later.

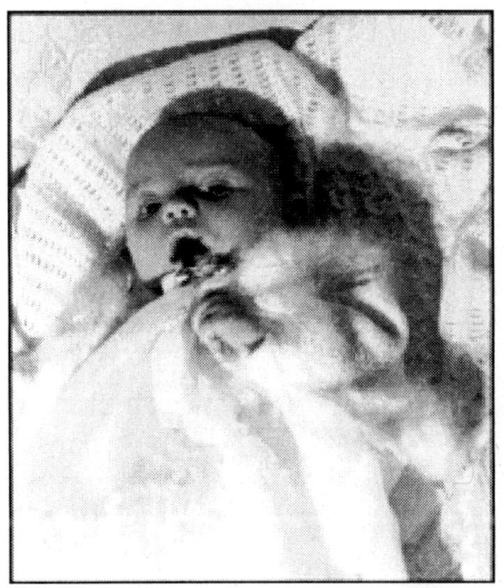

Miriam--a newborn

Miriam holds her favorite toddler toy--a duckie

Miriam and her "Mum" on the front steps of their home in Victoria.

Proud father, Hugh Richards, holds Miriam at age 3 weeks.

Miriam during her first year at Uplands Mainstreaming school (second from the left, front row) wearing her Radio-Ear box

Miriam as an adolescent Girl Scout.....

...and as Charlie Chaplin

14 year old Tennis champion...

...and junior high school swimming medalist

One of the many fish Miriam caught during fishing trips with her family

High school photo of Miriam

Miriam with the Gallaudet University Tennis Team (front row, far right)

Miriam (far right) and her sorority sisters at Gallaudet University

Miriam laughing during an outdoor pledging as a DE sister while at Gallaudet

Miriam receives her diploma from the first Deaf President of Gallaudet University, I.King Jordan

Miriam, pictured with a sign language interpreter, on graduation day at Oregon State University. She received her Master's in Forestry, Political Science and Sociology, in 1998

Miriam, getting ready for a climb along the Potomac River in 1989

Post Gallaudet: Miriam's New Goals

Miriam was fortunate to receive both a green card and social security number that allowed her to work a variety of jobs at Gallaudet University. Upon her graduation, she decided to stay and work in Maryland instead of going back to Canada. She was pleased to be offered a full time job with Family Service Foundation. They accepted her with her green card, permitting her to stay and work in the United States, working as a group home counselor for developmentally disabled clients who were deaf, blind and multi-disabled.

The group home where Miriam worked was a new building set up especially to receive clients. Miriam was among the first counselors at the new facility. A large institution located elsewhere in Maryland was notorious for housing over 600 people with developmental disabilities, with only a limited number of staff. When Miriam's supervisor assigned her staff to visit the large facility in order to select six new deaf or deafblind clients for their small group home, Miriam was shocked to see the horrible conditions. She knew the few staff were considerably outnumbered by far too many residents and the staff had no choice but to put most of the residents in diapers.

After looking around the first large room, Miriam noticed a deafblind woman sitting in the corner on the floor with her legs bent. Miriam inquired about this particular resident and learned that the lady had to keep her legs bent in ready position to kick off others who hit her. In an interview, Miriam recalls her impression of the woman:

> *"She had been at the facility all her life, for approximately 30 years. I knew that because she was deaf, she could not hear people approach. Because the floor was linoleum over concrete, she could not detect others approaching. She*

> *was blind. All she could do was sit in the corner and defend herself— she did not stand or walk." (Miriam Richards, June 2007)*

Miriam carefully walked toward the woman so as not to startle her, gently touched her and signed slowly into her hand. Although the woman did not understand sign language, Miriam knew she was not developmentally disabled, just deprived of proper upbringing, education, care and love. Miriam chose this woman, while Miriam's co-workers selected five others. They revisited the residents one more time before all the paper work was completed.

Once Miriam's new client was sitting in the van with the others, Miriam saw that the lady's legs bent upwards even in the vehicle's seat. Miriam's strong determination led her and the other staff to break the fear this woman had been living with. It took a lot of care and patience, but eventually the woman learned to stand up and walk. It took time but she eventually learned to sit without having to bend her knees upwards for protection. She learned some basic signs. She no longer had to wear diapers. Miriam will never forget the time she made the lady smile and laugh. At last she would live in a safe environment.

Miriam did not want the group home clients to have to spend all their time at the home; she planned for retreats and cabin camping in the Maryland woods. She drove them to the beach. They thrived on exposure to a variety of environments.

One time Miriam planned a winter retreat. She worked hard to organize the trip. Four days into the retreat, she became dizzy and had to be hospitalized. She had been so excited about the winter retreat and was disappointed to have to leave. As Christmas neared, Miriam was surprised when all the clients walked into her hospital room to visit her. Although many did not understand what was happening to their beloved counselor, Miriam was pleased with the surprise visit. Now as Miriam looks back on that moment in her life, she realizes it may have been a precursor of Multiple Sclerosis.

Miriam worked 60-80 hours per week. Her job was challenging, both physically and mentally. She had to help cover for other staff members when they were ill. Over time, the stress may have weakened her defenses when she was exposed to mononucleosis or Epstein-Barr virus, and she could not fight off the disease.

Miriam was off work for two months, feeling extremely weak and lethargic. Her condition deteriorated to the point where her mother flew from Canada to Maryland to help her. Miriam slept for most of the two months she was off until her blood test results cleared her to return to work. By that time Miriam had worked enough hours so that her workmen's comprehensive covered her missed hours. She was able to pay her rent.

While she worked long hours at the group home facility, Miriam continued to indulge in outdoor adventures. She joined her friends from Maryland for numerous ski trips. She went to France for skiing and had a wonderful time exploring the country. She water-skied and rode an inner tube behind a boat. Miriam, Lindy, Debbie, Ken, Bill and Jeannie went for a 184-mile bicycling trip around Maryland. That was Miriam's first experience with long-distance bicycle riding. They rode from Cumberland, Maryland to Washington, D.C. along the Chesapeake and Ohio Canals.

After three years working at the group home, Miriam was given a special commendation award. She became resident supervisor. She fought for employees to receive double pay for Christmas and Thanksgiving and after a long battle, her wishes were granted. By her fifth year, Miriam was worn out and ready to move on to something else. She dreamed of majoring in Forestry.

Miriam came to Corvallis, Oregon with the intention of obtaining her MA degree in Forestry at Oregon State University. Her goal was to become a National Park Ranger. She came west following Kelly Butterworth, her former room-mate during their years at Gallaudet University in Washington D.C. where they were both active on the Women's Field Hockey team. Both Gallaudet graduates continued their involvement in sports activities in Oregon.

Miriam was impressed with the beauty of Oregon, and the reputation of the Oregon State University forestry program. She was a little nervous about making it through the Master's program, given her struggle with English courses, but her belief in herself and the support of family and friends, helped her prevail. She received her Master's in Forestry, Political Science and Sociology in 1998.

Miriam did not realize at the time that her biggest obstacle would be after she received her MA. She struggled for years to obtain a job as a forest ranger. For four years, she persisted in applying for forestry related positions. After repeatedly being turned down for interviews and jobs, she decided to fly to the National Interior Headquarters in Washington, D.C.

Miriam obtained an appointment with the human resource department. She was informed that she was among the best qualified candidates for the position, but that they were required to hire veterans first and that applicants with disabilities were moved further down the list of potential interviewees.

This was devastating for Miriam. She felt that she did all of the things she needed to do in order to secure her dream by obtaining a specialized degree, combined with her love and knowledge of the outdoors. Miriam continued to apply for a while after her discussion with the Washington, D.C. headquarters, but eventually gave up her dream. In need of a job, she was able to find part-time work at Western Oregon University as an American Sign Language instructor.

Despite her disappointment in not obtaining her dream job, she continued to explore her passion for the outdoors. Perhaps her need for a new goal led her to one of her most challenging, yet rewarding, new sport--highpointing.

Miriam signing “PAH!” after she finally reached the high point of Mt. Hood in Oregon.

Mt. Hood, Oregon: The Fall and the Recovery

In 1994, less than a year after moving to Oregon from back east, Miriam began her first attempt to climb Mt. Hood. It is one of the most popular mountains climbed in the world and as a result, the Search and Rescue Teams, all volunteers, are often called upon to help those who get into trouble from unexpected changes in weather or injuries.

After learning about Mt. Hood from a fellow mountain climber, Leslie Beilstein, Miriam became interested in climbing the majestic peak. Leslie explained that anyone can do it, a permit was not needed, and it could be climbed in one day. Of course that meant leaving at 2-3:00 AM from the trailhead. Leslie and her husband George led Miriam on her first climb. George was an experienced mountain climber and a mountaineering ranger on both Mt Rainier and Denali in Alaska. He has performed numerous rescues of victims both dead and alive.

Miriam was thrilled to have the opportunity to learn about high altitude mountaineering. Having grown up at schools in Vancouver B.C., and Washington D.C., she had not encountered such high mountains. This new sports experience appealed to her. She learned how to put sharp crampons on her climbing boots, how to self arrest with her ice ax in case of a fall, how to use climbing ropes, a harness, and a helmet with one of the more experienced mountaineers in the state.

Unlike her former college roommate, Kelly Butterworth, Leslie was hearing and she did not know sign language. She enrolled in ASL I, a non-credit course at the local Community College. Her instructor was Hilary White. Hilary remembers Leslie as one of her students who soaked up the language and learned very quickly. In addition, Leslie was interested in learning more about interacting with deaf blind individuals and eventually became involved in DeafBlind retreats. Needless to say, Miriam was pleased that her friend was so enthusiastic about learning to communicate in her language.

Climbing a mountain is not a place to write notes back and forth. One's hands are needed to hold trekking poles or ice axe. The beginning of the climb is done in the dark. With the strap of the ice axe wrapped around the wrist, sign language can be done with the free hand.

The climbers continued as far as 9,000 feet where it levels off. At that point, they were faced with a white-out, a common occurrence on Mt Hood, so they turned back. Although they could not summit that day, Miriam's flame was kindled and she knew she wanted to try again.

Miriam hired Timberline Mountain Guides to take her on a climb up Mt Hood. The day before she was to leave, she and Hilary played several sets of tennis at the club where Hilary played and competed. Miriam had not been playing tennis daily, but she was very strong. Singles tennis involves more running than doubles so Miriam had a pretty good workout before her Mt. Hood climb.

It is interesting how Hilary and Miriam became friends. They had briefly met at a DeafBind Snow Retreat at a Mt. Hood camp February, 1994, but did not remember seeing each other during that time. Both were volunteer SSPs (Support Service People) who guided deafblind campers in their enjoyment of winter activities in the snow and in the lodges. During these retreats, the focus is on ensuring that each deafblind individual is able to fully participate in the activities.

It was not until after the annual DeafBlind Spring retreat in May 1994 at Lincoln City that the two friends actually spoke to each other. On the last day as people were leaving the retreat, Hilary spoke with another SSP who happened to be her daughter's tennis coach the previous summer for high school students. As they chatted about tennis, the coach told her that Miriam had been looking for someone to play tennis. Hilary did not know who Miriam was. The coach told her she had been at the retreat all week-end and had just left to head back to Corvallis. Hilary took her phone number and called her on the TTY to invite her to play tennis at her tennis club. Since then, the two of them have been close friends.

Second Attempt Climbing Mt Hood Excerpts from Miriam Richards' Journal:

The day before the scheduled climb, I was awakened about 4 AM by a crawling movement. Something was on my bed. I am very sensitive to movement because I am deaf. I lay stiff, but opened my eyes to see a black apparition with two white glowing eyes moving from my right across my waist, its touch created a tingling sensation through me.

I was transfixed as it continued to move across me to my left, its eyes still on mine. At the left of me, the figure stopped, moved its arm across my body, fingering its hand up my right arm, up beside my eye. Terrified, knowing this was not a dream, I quickly reached with my left hand to turn on the light, and the apparition vanished. I glanced up at my clock; it was 4:00 AM. I immediately got up. I felt like I never wanted to go back to sleep again, I turned on more lights and paced around my living room thinking, should I go on this climb or not? I decided to put this aside and go ahead with my climb.

The next day, February 26, 1995, I was excited as I collected my ice axe, crampons, and helmet. My desire to reach the top had been strong ever since my previous climb when I didn't go all the way to the summit. I met my guide, Peter Keane, who had climbed Mt. Hood's summit for 7 years. We rode a snow cat machine up to about the 5,000 foot level. I became more relaxed as I viewed the city of Portland from the snowcat. Although I communicate in ASL and Peter did not know ASL, we found it adequate conversing in gestures. An interpreter had been available for the practice session I passed prior to our climb.

We started to climb from 8,500 to 11,352 feet, all ice. The weather was perfect for the climb as we proceeded at a slow pace. I was entranced by the beauty of Mt. Hood. We stopped now and then for short rests. Suddenly the most spectacular sunrise reflected the peak's silhouette onto the snow in a lovely shadow below us. I took pictures as I ascended with my guide. Everything went smoothly. We couldn't have asked for a more perfect day.

We arrived at 10 AM at the Hogsback, 10,600 feet level, for our final rest before we were to reach the summit. I smelled the strong sulfur odor that reminded me that this is a volcano, still very much alive down under this Devil's Kitchen area, and venting off steam. Putting our ropes on and leaving our backpacks, we climbed a very steep vertical precipice, then caught sight of three climbers who had surmounted the summit and were returning around a crevasse. My guide and I had to climb through another deep passage. I was feeling a little exhausted so I signed to Peter to find a place to sit and rest for a short time. But Peter motioned to keep going a little bit.

I remember taking one step, looked up, then all of a sudden ice was breaking in front of us. What happened next was erased from my memory.

Later I learned the details. As I was nearing the summit, only 100 feet from the top, the ice I had planted my ice axe in had been melting as a result of the hot sun that unusually warm day in February. A large area of ice gave way, sending me down the mountain with it, only to be stopped by the quick hand of Peter Keane who immediately dug his ice axe into the mountain. Initially he was able to hold onto me. However, the powerful impact of my plunging down was enough to dislodge Peter's axe. As Peter was pulled downwards, he plunged his ice axe back into the ice. He was so trained and experienced.

My unconscious body, still on his rope, swung into the mountain where the sharp ice cut into my face, breaking some bones in my chin. Again, the swinging jerking motion dislodged Peter's ice axe. As he fell, for a third time, Peter plunged his axe into the mountain and held on as long as he could, however his hold gave way and he plunged after me for the remaining portion of my fall. An onlooker from another climbing team described my last free fall as cart-wheeling down with my legs bending in positions not normal for the human body. My helmet protected my brain even though the total fall was 1,000 feet into Devil's Punchbowl.

I remember waking three times but was unaware of what had happened. My eyes opened first, the way a camera shutter opens and closes, seeing angels standing all around me in a blur. I didn't feel pain, but my body felt a warm rush after the angels touched me. The second time I remember opening my eyes and seeing a man with ski goggles and a long moustache talking to me. Then I woke to feeling a strong stinging wind against my face and at the same time the jarring of the helicopter I was in. I realized someone had put a covering over me. My face hurt, but the rest of my body was numb.

In the days afterwards, I was told that the time between my fall and rescue was six hours of exposure to ice, snow, and wind. Although the weather was perfect for my climb, it quickly changed as winds moved in. Rescuers, at first not knowing if I was alive or dead, wrapped a sleeping bag around me. Peter had an injured back from his fall.

Attempts were made at first to get us off the mountain immediately with the helicopter from Timberline Lodge, but it had some mechanical difficulties, so the Life Flight helicopter from Emanuel Hospital was called. Winds were much too strong for the light helicopter, so a heavier military helicopter was finally called to the scene. Rescuers realized both Peter and I needed to be lifted out at once, but the military helicopter could not take all the weight, so all unnecessary equipment had to be removed at Timberline Lodge before returning to the mountain to pick both of us up at the same time. We were transferred at Timberline Lodge from the military helicopter to Life Flight for transport to Emanuel Hospital.

My friend Hilary had been called via TTY (Teletypewriter for the Deaf) with news of my fall. She was the first person summoned to hospital. She was given a bag of my clothes that had been cut off my body upon my arrival at the trauma unit. She thought she was being handed my clothes because I would no longer be needing them. Her assumptions were confirmed when she saw my body being wheeled out on a gurney, looking like a cadaver, beat up and bloody, my jaw turned grotesquely out of position, broken in three places, bleeding from mouth and face, with my eyes swollen shut with yellow pus. She thought they expected her to identify my body, and recognized me by my foot about the same time the person standing next to the gurney signed, *"alive."* The next sign she saw was "*on the fence*" meaning that I could live or die and would need surgery.

The doctors said I was lucky to have survived. My injuries included torn ligaments, broken elbow, jaw, ankle, but the most life-threatening injury that could lead to brain damage from internal bleeding was the blood clot near my right eye, the same place the ghostly apparition from the night before had placed its hand.

People keep telling me that it is a miracle I am alive, and I look back to the night prior to my climb, and realize that a spirit was trying to warn me. I had never expected to ever confront a spirit in my life. I have heard of others claiming they had encounters of one type or another, but this is the first time it happened to me. Perhaps I will be better prepared should I be given a message or warning of spiritual guidance again.

I do not blame anyone for what happened. The unusually warm sun just happened to melt the top of Mt. Hood that day. The recommended season to climb Mt. Hood is May through July. Normally the ice remains hard in February.

When my parents were informed of my fall off Mt. Hood, they were astounded and in disbelief because they were totally unaware of my involvement in climbing. They immediately grabbed up their belongings and drove straight to the ferry from Victoria to Vancouver British Columbia. Just as they were pulling up to the ferry, it was leaving. They just missed it. It was very difficult for them to wait until the next morning before making the trip to see their daughter in hospital.

Hilary told me that once she realized I was still hanging onto my life, she could see my left hand begin to move in spite of the rest of my still body. I am right-handed so it came as a surprise to her that I would fingerspell with my left hand. My right elbow was fractured and swollen. I lacked the energy to lift my arm or wrist so all my letters were formed downwards into the bedding.

Hilary remembered me telling her three things: 1. Cancel tennis Monday 2. Cancel our snowshoe trip around Crater Lake 3. Call Lindy Deane TTY (I gave the telephone number from memory). Hilary was relieved that although my body was destroyed, my helmet protected my brain case and that was what was most important, that is, if my body could survive! But when I indicated "*Maybe cancel Crater Lake snowshoe trip,*" she realized that I was unaware of the extent of my injuries and, afraid I might give up my fight to live, asked that I not be shown my face in a mirror.

Hilary waited outside the door to the surgical room while I was having my jaw returned to its original position. As she walked beside me while I was wheeled back to my room, she tells me that she was pleased to see that the blood and yellow ooze was cleaned off my face during the surgery. My parents had just arrived and were led to my empty room. As I was pushed into my room, Mum told them, "*This is NOT my daughter.*" However, my dad took time to scrutinize me and remarked that it really was my nose.

I remained at Emanuel Hospital for another month and a half, eventually moving to their physical therapy wing where they worked hard to teach me to walk again. In the next two years, I had up to 12 surgeries related to my fall, my jaw was wired shut, and it was not until two years later that the fracture in my ankle was discovered.

Hilary reminded me of the time she asked me to help her by putting postage on her envelopes. At the time, they had not yet issued the self-adhesive stamps. She asked me why I was taking so long and said, "*Hurry up!*" I could not figure out how to lick the stamps with my jaw wired shut. All my food had to be taken in through a straw. I had to endure painful TMJ surgery two more times after leaving the hospital. The nurse gave me a pair of scissors to keep in my pocket just in case I felt claustrophobic and needed to cut the wires in an emergency situation such as choking.

Third Attempt Climbing Mt Hood
Hilary's perspective

Two years later, in 1997, I was willing to climb with Miriam on Mt Hood once she had finally gotten her body back into shape by backpacking, hiking, and climbing mountains. She and her father climbed Guadalupe Peak, Texas. She joined my tennis club and played regularly. Miriam led me on many backpacking and climbing trips in the Cascades. We were both in good shape.

We stayed overnight at a house on the Columbia River so it would be a close drive to meet the guides very early the next morning on Mt Hood. We spent the next day practicing self-arrest methods. We were tested by the two guides who would be taking us up the mountain early the next morning--a man and a woman. We had to plunge ourselves backwards down an icy slope at a good speed and use the techniques they taught us to force our ice ax into the slope to stop ourselves. We were instructed how to put on our harnesses and rope ourselves in and we practiced with the four of us traversing a slope with our crampons on our boots. Then we were told to go to bed in the late afternoon and drink as much water as possible even if it meant losing sleep. We were to meet again around 2:30 AM.

We drove back down to the house on the Columbia River and slept as well as we could before driving back up to meet at Mt Hood's Timberline Lodge. Sleeping at sea level preparatory to a high altitude climb the following day is not recommended, however we had a half-day of training on the mountain the day before our climb. Other groups were preparing to climb, some with guides, some without. We met our guides who inspected our equipment and met the snowcat that would take us to the drop off point at the top of the ski lift. The snowcat was filled with no other seats to spare. This ride would save us precious time.

Our climb began in the dark with our headlamps providing some light. At the beginning, our heavy plastic mountaineering boots were sufficient. After a time, the guides instructed us to put our crampons on our boots as we were approaching more ice on the slope. The guides matched our speed, our steps became methodical. It was the middle of the night and felt like a dream. The lights from headlamps of climbers ascending the mountain ahead of us looked almost like a candle procession, a lovely sight. Watching the sunrise made us realize how high we had climbed as we looked down on the landscape below. Miriam loves to see the pyramid shape that results from the shadow of Crater Rock. She was pleased to see it again and point it out to me. All those who have climbed this south approach of Mt. Hood would see this remarkable image upon sunrise unless they were in a white out.

The Hogsback looks exactly like its name. It appears as a very clear line where two slopes meet, showing the backbone or hair down the middle of the hog's back. We straddled the Hogsback as we discussed what was next. Miriam, although in excellent physical shape, felt excruciating pain in her right ankle. Although she had come this far and had the highest hopes to conquer this stubborn mountain, she admitted that she simply could not continue with her painful foot and ankle.

There was still time to climb to the top before the hot sun would shine on the summit. The guide, Peter, would escort Miriam down the mountain while his assistant would take me on up to the summit. By this time we could clearly see other climbers ascending the steep slope above. I did not want to betray Miriam by continuing to climb, so we descended together as a team. She and the mountain were much the same; both stubbornly wanted to conquer the other. The mountain won again. By the time we reached the lodge, her ankle was badly swollen and an ice pack would be a temporary solution. Later, an x-ray would reveal that there was an old fracture in her ankle resulting from her fall off Mt. Hood two years ago. I remembered Miriam's difficulty learning to stand on that foot when the physical therapist at Emanuel kept urging her to put her weight on her right foot. She could not. She had been walking on a fractured ankle for two years!

After our climb, Miriam was sent to surgery to repair the old fracture and ended up with a bulky cast. Once her ankle healed, she could not flex her foot upwards so another surgery was necessary, this time cutting the hamstring in a Z cut to loosen it. Hiking uphill had been coming along without any problem, but the Z cut was necessary to allow her foot to take her downhill.

I remember Miriam becoming so proficient with her crutches during this time. She zoomed around quickly and up and down stairs. I drove Miriam to places around Oregon she wanted badly to see. She attended her class reunion in Canada. She guided deafblind campers on horseback with her leg still in the cast. Soon after her second surgery, however, Miriam asked me to take her fishing. I remembered the spot she saw from a bridge on our drive back from the coast. Her leg was supposed to remain elevated so I told her "*No*."

But Miriam went ahead and asked her friend Leslie to take her fishing. When she was not content casting her line from the bridge, she went down the cliff in order to get a better spot and slipped down the embankment into the water, soaking the cast inside and out. She had to go back to her surgeon to have the cast cut off since the moisture caused it to swell and her toes were blue. As he put on a new cast, the surgeon was shaking his head as he told Miriam to keep it elevated and no more fishing. Miriam would have to learn how to sit still.

Fourth Attempt Climbing Mt Hood
Miriam and Hilary's perspective

We thought we would try climbing Mt Hood this time without a guide. We had more experience climbing, backpacking and hiking. This time we felt it would be a good idea to sleep at high elevation rather than driving up from sea level as we did with the previous climb when we were on the Columbia River. We drove up the day before and walked around, then as soon as it was dark, slept in a van near the trailhead.

We left the van at 11 PM, earlier than before, since we would not be riding the snowcat. The moon was full and the stars put on an incredible show. Hilary's fear was that with the quiet of the snow she might not hear the snowcat approaching. She kept looking back, afraid that it would suddenly appear over a ridge and run over us. Although the snowcat route is easy to follow, we tried to stay to the right of it as we ascended. We moved quickly, all was well until Hilary's headlamp started to flicker and dim. We had spare batteries but her cheap headlamp eventually went out altogether so we were left with only Miriam's headlamp. The full moon illuminated the snow enough so we could continue for several more hours fully confident we could succeed this time until Miriam's headlamp began to flicker and dim as well. Miriam let out a scream of frustration. *"I cannot believe this! Why is this happening to me! Why can't this foreboding mountain let me climb it?"*

We sat out the next hours under a space blanket shielded from the wind by the massive Crater Rock and dejectedly returned to the van parked below at sunrise.

Fifth Attempt Climbing Mt Hood
Miriam's perspective

After so much physical training getting my body ready for climbing Mt. Hood, I was willing to spend the money I had saved from odd jobs to join a 3-day climb I saw advertised by Timberline Mountain Guides. I had been working out at an athletic club all winter using the stair climber and treadmill. This was bound to be successful since I would have a night sleeping in a tent at 8,500 feet prior to climbing the second half of the mountain. I was not the only client this time, there were five men going with me in addition to the two male guides.

I carried my sleeping bag in a backpack up to the 8,500 foot level farther up than the highest point of the ski lift drop off area. We had our training session near our tents. The weather was perfect. I had been through this routine before and had more experience on this mountain than the other clients. As the only female, it was rather awkward for me to sleep in a tent with them. It was difficult to find privacy when I had to go to the bathroom. My stubborn determination to climb Mt. Hood helped me endure the inconveniences.

The stars that night were incredibly beautiful as we begun climbing around 3 AM. The sunrise was so lovely and seeing the pyramid-shaped shadow from Crater Rock gave me a good feeling. However, I noticed all the men in rapid conversation with one another and with the guides. Although I had been here before, I felt some nervousness, perhaps due to stress, perhaps due to the fact that the men were all very strong and I felt pressured to keep up with them. In the past, I did not attempt this mountain with a group, only with private guides. Perhaps my nervousness was due to the spell the mountain seemed to put on me. I wanted to break the jinx.

The guides were fully aware of my past experience on this mountain. They gave me their full support and chose me to lead off. When I was in front, I kept my mind focused ahead, not looking back. We crossed around a crevasse and headed up through The Pearly Gates, a gully with rocks arched overhead. It became very steep and icy and I was concentrationing so fully, it was almost like a trance. Then as I stepped out of The Pearly Gates, only the summit remained. I thought, "*This is it?*" I could hardly believe it! There was the summit! There were about 100 people on the top.

My guides approached me to hug me. I cried. It was hard to believe I was really on the summit of Mt. Hood, 11,239 feet at last! This was May 22,1999, a date I will never forget. This was indeed a triumph for me. The view from the top was surely the icing on the cake. I could see Mt. Adams, Mt. St. Helens, Mt. Rainier, Mt. Jefferson, the Three Sisters and 360 degrees in all directions. My dream had come true.

One of my guides spoke through a special radio system to inform Roy, the owner of TMG that Miriam was on the summit of Mt Hood at last, after all she had endured to get here. The other clients in our group gave me their full support and congratulations. However, the hardest part was ahead.

Descending is more difficult than ascending because the snow tends to become softer, particularly as the ice has broken up from the heavy traffic, but also because you are looking down and it is a long way down. Nervousness sets in. All climbers are roped together. If one slips, it is the responsibility of the whole group to use their ice axe to stop the fall. Slowly but surely, the sharp crampons turn to the side of the slope and find firm ice to hold as they move with duck-like steps, being ever so careful not to catch a crampon blade onto the side of one's pant leg. The adrenalin is working overtime; the tension is in the air.

It wasn't until I reached the Hogsback and began the descent from there that I knew I was over the hardest part and could now claim my victory. I took my time and the others got ahead of me at this point. We no longer needed our ropes and harnesses. I was the last person in my group to arrive back at the lodge. I went into the shop and purchased a Mt. Hood hat and champagne to celebrate. I did it!

Hugh Richards rests at the top of Guadalupe Peak, Texas. It was Miriam's first successful summit after her Mt Hood fall.

Guadalupe Peak: Father and Daughter Bonding

Prior to Miriam's successful ascent to Mt Hood, she needed to climb a smaller and safer summit to gain the confidence necessary to move forward with her highpointing goals. She asked her father to accompany her to Texas in July 1997. This chapter shares both father and daughter's accounts of this summit.

Guadalupe Peak: Hugh Richards' Perspective

The purpose of this trip was to discover how many of the National Parks we visited had access for deaf visitors. Miriam's Masters Degree at Oregon State University would not be completed until she had obtained more information on services currently available. Miriam's goal was to have accessibility to educate the deaf as to how to identify trees, flowers and other plants unique to each National Park as well as geological features. Her dream was to become a ranger for the National Park system.

Our first stop was Yosemite. All the camping spaces were booked. We were given a disabled parking spot because they had not had a physically disabled person request that spot all year. The next day we went to the Visitor Center so Miriam could see what services were available to her. We were informed that one of the rangers was fluent in ASL but she was occupied elsewhere at the time. We contacted her later that day, revisiting the Visitor Center with the guide, walking with her while she and Miriam discussed accessibility in ASL.

We made an appointment to meet the ranger at Glacier Point where she explained that during the last ice age, everything below was covered except El Capitan and Half Dome.

It was helpful having the ranger use ASL to communicate the present and past of this National Park. Miriam's dreams were to be able to do the same as a guide for deaf visitors. This would be a first.

Next to the visitor center was an Indian Cultural Center and museum depicting the history of the Miwok and Paiute people. Yosemite Valley is so remote that the coastal Indians did not know it existed. The Miwok lived in this valley for 1,000 years before white people came and took it over. The deciduous trees on the valley floor are black oak. The Native Americans gathered acorns for food after crushing and soaking them in water for three days to remove the tannic acid. A type of porridge was the end result. Holes in the rocks can be seen where they crushed the acorns into meal. We read the signage in order to obtain this valuable information.

There were no other means available for deaf people to obtain the information available to the hearing world. Miriam saw so much more that she wished she could learn about from the nature talks that she saw rangers giving as well as the uncaptioned films. There were only titles or subject names visible. There was no elaboration on subject matter. A deaf person would be completely unaware of the explanations I could hear. In ASL, the sign "*good enough*" translates to mean more like the bare minimum rather than adequate. Miriam knows many other deaf individuals who have a hungry desire to learn more than what is currently offered for education of the deaf.

The next day we visited Petrified Forest National Park. A ranger gave a talk. Miriam was told she could purchase a book to read. There were no handouts for her to look through. Their most important message was to let Miriam know not to pick up samples of Petrified Wood to take home as if she were an uneducated visitor. Their efforts to write notes were only to talk down to Miriam. This only made Miriam more determined to fulfill her goal of becoming a forest ranger to serve the deaf population with the respect they deserve. Still the large logs of petrified wood were very impressive and worth seeing.

The next day we set out for Carlsbad Cavern National Park. On our way, we passed through Roswell, New Mexico, where they were in the middle of a celebration of the coming of aliens. Police guided us through detours via roads of black dirt, however we could see the carnival that was taking place in the middle of town as we passed by.

Miriam had hoped to learn about the Caverns at the National Park but here again, they had nothing for deaf visitors, not even a printed version of the talk the guides give. They connected Miriam to a young woman selling tickets who could sign only marginally.

Part of Miriam's MA program involved taking statistics. Records of deaf visitors to National Parks are inadequate due to the fact that the deaf have an invisible disability. One cannot look at a single deaf individual and pick her out from a crowd as being deaf. Miriam does not wear hearing aids. Hard of hearing visitors such as Hilary White may have their hearing aids hidden by their hair or cap.

The caverns were large and well lit with many stalagmites and stalactites. Miriam loved the visual show of the bats as they emerged and began circling inside the cave in the shape of a hurricane twister before flying out of the cave entrance. A ranger explained how important bats are to a local farmer. Bats from this area numbering 100,000 with each bat eating two ounces of bugs per night reduce the insects to a tolerable level so humans and animals can exist.

Guadalupe Peak: Miriam Richards' Perspective

When I lived in Maryland, I had no knowledge of "high points." I decided to move to Oregon and the first time I saw Mt. Hood, I was amazed. I asked if anyone had climbed Mt. Hood. I was told that it was possible, and I thought *"Why not me?"* Still, I had no idea of what a "high point" might mean.

That was in 1994. So, I tried to climb Mt. Hood two times. The first time, I was stopped by the weather. The second, I was stopped by a horrible fall, the third time, I almost made it to the top with my friend Hilary, but ankle problems forced me to turn back (I was unaware that I had been climbing on a fractured ankle). Hilary and I attempted one more time (the fourth time) but her headlamp died and we could not make it in the dark. Finally, on the fifth attempt, I summited, after three years of trying!

After my fall on Mt. Hood, someone asked me if I was aware of the "high points" in all of the states. I really had heard nothing about that, and I was intrigued. So, the summer of 1997, as I was conducting research for my Master's degree, I traveled to several national parks.

My father and I drove together, pulling an RV behind us, as we toured the national parks in the Southwest. One of the high points was located in a national park that we visited, and my journey began. My first summit was Guadalupe Peak, Texas.

When I arrived at Guadalupe National Park, I decided to camp in Pine Springs, a campground. I had purchased a book listing the state high points, and noticed that Guadalupe Peak was listed. I asked my father if he would like to try and climb the peak. He was 65 years old and had never tried such a thing in all of his life! But his response was *"Let's try."*

We had been warned that the weather could be very hot, and sudden lightning storms could materialize. We decided to leave at 6 AM the next morning to minimize our risk.

In the early morning light, the brilliant orange striated cliffs rising suddenly from the desert floor was an inspiring sight. Palm trees and cactus added their unique beauty to the landscape. The trail was in good shape and the climb was gradual. The hike totaled 8.4 miles from camp to the summit and back. As we climbed, I was so impressed with my father, and noticed that, in spite of his age, he was in good physical shape. I followed behind him on the trail. The sight of a cactus fully covered by ladybugs amazed us. Later that morning, a mild breeze began to blow, which helped to cool us in the desert heat. The view from the summit was magnificent with the desert perspective a treat for an artist's eyes.

I looked across mountains and canyons. The pines at a distance looked like an unshaved face. This was an exciting moment for me, because of my two failed attempts at climbing Mt. Hood. Finally, I had mastered a high point! We were greeted by a silver pyramid with gold plaques honoring the founding of American Airlines through the efforts of stage drivers and airmen who pioneered the mail services.

While I was celebrating my success, my father found an old ammunition box with a registration book inside. I signed and wrote that it was nice to have reached the top of Guadalupe Peak, 8,749 feet as a father and daughter experience. I felt as if I were a bride, and my father was "giving me away" to the climbing adventures that awaited me. But this, in Texas, was my first, and my father was there to share it with me. I had 49 more state highpoints to go and was thrilled for the unknown adventures.

Gualalupe Park: Hugh Richards' Perspective

When we returned to our RV trailer after having successfully summited our 1st State Summit Highpoint, I soaked my feet in cold water and Miriam went to sleep.

Our next stop was Big Bend National Park in Texas. After having driven 250 miles, we arrived late in the afternoon while the temperature was still as high as 110 degrees. The place was nearly deserted. Visitor season was over and the Ranger station was closed. We left early the next morning due to the extreme heat.

We crossed two time zones and stopped 25 miles west of Tucson at Saguaro National Park. We were fascinated with the variety of cacti growing in the park and we were lucky to happen to have visited when most of them were in bloom. A family of wild pigs lived around the ranger center. There were no services available for deaf visitors. We drove around the loop photographing cactus and very tall saguaro. The cactus looked like people standing at attention.

Joshua Tree National Park in California had no access for deaf visitors. The ranger's speech focused on the park's coyotes and rabbits. The Joshua Trees had tall trunks with branches spreading out 7-8 feet providing needed shade in this desert habitat. There were large formations of huge smooth boulders all around.

Traveling north to Sequoia and Kings Canyon National Parks, we asked what preparations they had available for deaf visitors. They were non-existent. We continued north to Mount Lassen Volcanic National Park and stopped to camp. We woke early to climb the trail up Mt Lassen. As the trail neared the top, snow was about 3 feet deep with lots of bare sharp rocks pointing through. We could see other snow capped peaks to the north and south. The visitor center showed films that were not captioned, however a TTY was available for use in the small town of Mineral at the southern entrance to the Mount Lassen Volcanic National Park.

Miriam and friends on top of Mt. Whitney, California

Mount Whitney: A White Family Outing

Miriam and Hilary planned a family outing to climb Mt. Whitney in California. They were joined by Hilary's husband, her son and his wife. This chapter is Hilary's account of the third summit Miriam climbed on her list of high point goals.

Hilary's Perspective

On July 27, 2000, Robert and I flew to San Luis Obispo, California to meet our son Nathan and his wife Stacey prior to our climb of Mt. Whitney. Nathan and Stacey paid the climbing fee in February and submitted two dates for a required new lottery drawing to climb Whitney. If we were lucky enough to have one of our dates drawn, we would receive a permit to go. At the time, unsure how many would climb in our family, they submitted for a group of five. When Robert and I purchased our airline tickets, we did not know that Miriam would be the fifth climber. Once Miriam decided to join us, her airline ticket had to be purchased separately. She would meet us later.

Nathan, Stacey, Robert and I did last minute inventory of our climbing equipment while packing. I forgot my sleeping pad so I emailed Miriam to bring it.

We left at 5:45 AM on July 28th for the climb. Stacey and Nathan rented a van that would fit our 4 loaded backpacks and paid $10 per day extra for insurance since there was a strong possibility of a bear trying to break into the van. We drove Hwy 58 over the Tehachapee Pass. We were on a time crunch to get to the Whitney Portal and set up our tents before dark. As we were driving along highway 14 way out there in the middle of nowhere, we saw a coyote in daylight standing beside the road. Nathan said that he was Wile E. Coyote waiting for his ACME order. Nathan looked for the road-runner--he knew that he must be somewhere around. Those cartoons are his favorite. The only problem is that you can never get him to stop laughing when he sees them.

Nathan parked the van facing a cliff in the overflow parking area since he thought it would be more difficult for a bear to get a good foothold before ripping out a windshield. We rented 3 bear-proof canisters and had to dispose of some food that wouldn't fit into them. We ate as much food as we could for lunch. The best treat was smoked salmon from the Stirlings in Alaska. It was delicious on cornbread crackers and bagels. We were at 8,420 feet. now, the Whitney Portal.

We began our ascent at 1:50 PM after leaving a message for Miriam. She was flying from Portland to Reno, renting a car to drive to Mt. Whitney. Nathan and Stacey, both triathletes, raced ahead. We crossed some nice streams as we went in and out of shade. The trail was very steep. Our packs were heavily loaded with food for four days. Empty, the bear canisters weigh 2.7 pounds each.

We arrived at Outpost Camp about 5:30 PM. Nathan set up 3 bearproof counterbalanced bags hanging from trees. As he was using his best baseball form to fling the rock with an attached rope onto the end of a high branch, other campers watched in awe. After a while, they heard some chuckling coming from some onlooking campers at the far end of the camp, knowing that the entry board had warned that Whitney's black bears know how to pull down tree bags.

I knew there was no reason to worry about Miriam hiking alone. She is an experienced mountaineer, but as the sun began to go down, we were a little concerned. When she arrived just after dark with a full pack, she told us how much she enjoyed the view of the big rock canyon among tall trees. She especially loved looking back down to all the open space in the distance. She did not bring a bear-proof canister since her arrival was after the Whitney Portal closed. Nathan had to find another branch to throw her M&Ms, crackers, & trail mix up in a tree since all three bear-proof canisters were full of food, trash, soaps, chapstick, and toothpaste.

After dinner, Nathan started to get a headache. We went to bed about 9:30 PM when the sun went down. The sugar coated pain pills were in the trees, so Nathan wasn't about to pull them down.

Around 10:30 PM, lights shining from nearby camps were aimed in our direction, waking us. I put my hearing aid on to hear scratching sounds coming from close by where Nathan and Stacey were in their tent. Then Stacey asked us if we could see the bear in the tree right next to our tent. Robert and I had zipped our tent and rain fly closed and we weren't about to open them now. Nathan and Stacey had theirs open since the message board said that if the bear wants to inspect your tent, it may rip it open. If you leave it unzipped, the bear will do its inspection and leave you alone when it finds no food in your tent.

Nathan and Stacey had a clear view of the bear in the tree about 4 feet in front of them. They said it was SO big, trying to get Miriam's stuff bag that had M & Ms among other things. It was up that tree for quite a while swatting at the stuff bag as if it were trying to play tether ball, but it could not reach it.

The bear brushed against my side of the tent. Through the nylon, I could see the black fur, so I moved way over to Robert's side. I was worried about Miriam but had no way of informing her. She did not have her Blackberry pager at that time. One camper had a big maglight shining on the bear. The campers who laughed after Nathan had thrown the bags in the trees had the bear visit their spot, too. The father had only his sleeping bag, no tent, so he watched the whole show. His daughter had some strong smelling lotion or perfume that attracted the bear to smell her where she was sharing a tent with her sister. That terrified the father to watch from his sleeping bag. Then the black bear picked up a back pack and started off with it. A group of Boy Scouts shouted to scare it off.

The bear-proof canisters had been inspected by the bear and left untampered. Nathan had been sick all night, but finally got some sleep so we all slept in until around 7 AM. I had to go to the bathroom so bad, but was afraid after the bear encounter, so fate had it that Nathan was looking around with a flashlight for some Ibuprofen and was throwing up. I got up to look in Robert's unzipped back-pack and there was some Advil in his little first aid kit. That gave me a chance to go to the bathroom. Nathan got sick from dehydration. He had taken Diamox, a preventive altitude sickness pill, but that acts a bit like a diuretic, so he got sick from having it without enough water. He and Stacey had gained altitude too quickly on the trail, too. Rapid ascents can cause altitude sickness.

Miriam, sleeping for the first time in her one person bivy tent, was unaware of any bear visitation even though lights were shining in our direction as if a movie were being filmed. Her tent is a very low, elongated triangle shape with little clearance. She was next to our tent. How she missed getting stepped on by the bear, we will never know. She could have been crushed. Nathan's boot had a deep impression of a bear paw print. He photographed it.

Stacey cooked a good pancake breakfast adding my dried blueberries. Yum! As we rearranged our packs to go from Outpost Camp to Trail Camp, Miriam ended up carrying a full bear canister. I'd carried about 50 lbs the first day, so this was much easier for me. The trails are so nicely kept and the rock formations are stunning.

Miriam recalled her attempted climb of Whitney back in October with her deaf friend Heidi when the trails were covered with snow. Miriam had mistakenly taken along her summer sleeping bag and shivered all night. The following day, another climber told them they could not climb Mt. Whitney due to the deep snow so Miriam and Heidi gave up and turned back. Another time, she took along her friend Leslie's dog Tilly Jane. A ranger told Miriam the trail was closed due to dangerous snow conditions. She changed her plans and visited Bristle Cone National Park where she enjoyed seeing very old trees that had been growing on earth over 2,000 years ago.

There are many lakes that look pristine, although we were told there is giardia and viruses in the water, so we used Nathan's super filter/purifier and iodine. When I got pretty warm, I bent over to cool off my head in a stream. Mirror Lake and Consultation Lake were spectacular. The last tree that we saw as we climbed above treeline is a landmark white bark stump around 4,000 years old, an old Yellow Fir. Nathan liked the trailside meadow; he said it was so nicely landscaped as to be almost surreal.

Stacey liked seeing the marmots with their babies on the boulders. Robert was enjoying the chance to back-pack again with his old 1970's REI pack, a classic! It was two and a half miles from 10,360 feet Outpost Camp to 12,000 feet Trail Camp. After setting up camp, cooking freeze-dried pasta and filtering lake water from the bear canisters into our 15 water bottles, Nathan hung the trash from the boulders marmot-proof style. Our tents were placed in a spot where we could look up and see the trail zigzagging all 97 switchbacks, watching people go up and down. We could view the summit of Mt. Whitney, watch the marmots, and check out all those passing us on the trail. We saw joggers run by and others limp past.

Miriam was thrilled to see the beautiful lake at Trail Camp that had been covered with snow on her previous attempts. She set up her bivy tent near the lake. She had a perfect view of the top of Mt. Whitney, but that night she felt uncomfortable with the cramped quarters of her one person tent.

The next day was July 30th. On this date the previous year, Robert, Miriam and I climbed Mt. St. Helens. Like today, the weather and trail conditions were in our favor for a successful summit bid. It was decided that Miriam and I would leave at 5 AM to get an early start. Nathan, Stacey and Robert would begin their climb an hour later. The stars were bright and it was warm enough for shorts, but we had long sleeved fleece. I'd neglected to pack my headlamp, but strapped a small flashlight to my waist pack. The trail was excellent, we were traversing 97 switchbacks up a sheer cliff. Some switchbacks were very close to those before and after.

Imagine walking up Lombard Street in San Francisco with 97 hairpin turns. Ice covered rock, and we were concerned we might slip. I shone my flashlight in the direction of our three tents way down at Trail Camp below and Robert just happened to be looking up the mountain at that moment. I thought I saw him shine a light and he confirmed it later when they caught up.

There were only a few men ascending at the time we were climbing prior to sunrise. From where we watched the orange-red sunrise, we could see Mt. Whitney north of us, looking much taller than it did from our camp. There were patches of ice on all sides of the trail in spots. Streams ran under our trail or across the rocks and drained through them when we descended in the afternoon; the hot sun melted the ice, causing the streams to flow much heavier than they did in the early morning hours. But our thick-soled hiking boots kept our feet dry as we searched for the higher rocks to step across. The water ran clear, the lakes were like mirrors, everything appeared clean and fresh.

The morning sun made long shadows of the people waking at Trail Camp, enlarging them for us to spot from above. Now I know why hawks hunt at dawn and dusk.

Miriam and I lost about 40 minutes when we reached an ice patch covering such a large area of the mountain-cliff that we couldn't see over it well enough to determine which direction the trail exited the snow field. Since there were few climbers at this time, we had to figure this out ourselves. Miriam headed straight through the ice. I bouldered around the snowfield looking for a distant trail. After fretting about the waste of time, we piled rocks to mark the trail for Nathan, Stacey, and Robert. Afterwards, they thanked us for the rock cairns, preventing an interruption in their upward momentum.

We encountered some pretty hairy drop-offs. I was glad that most of the trail was not slippery or icy, though we are used to mossy rocks in Oregon. Where the trail narrowed near steep cliffs or rounded a hairpin turn at a high ridgeline, I felt for Stacey. I'd promised her this trail would be safe and she wouldn't fall off and die. *"I like my life,"* she would say. She'll have Robert and Nathan with her. She runs marathons and defends a round black and white sphere with 11 people charging at her with spiked feet; she's tougher than me.

At last Miriam and I reached Trail Crest. Whew, a dizzying blast to the eyes of 3-D scenery, as Miriam calls it. This was totally unexpected after rounding the last bend in the trail. A large sign announced Sequoia National Forest and sure enough, if you were able to see down far enough, there were some trees like thick green moss growing way down below. The spiked rock formation like those in Bryce Canyon towered above the lakes and earth below. I would have been awed to see this out of an airplane window. The view of the Sequoia side to the west from your toes down was remarkably different than the view from your heels down the East where you'd just been. I was relieved there wasn't a strong wind to send me forward or back as my eyes were feeling as if they were in a virtual reality mask not sure where to focus. My boots were glued to their spot, but I was afraid to move my head forward or back for fear of losing my balance.

Those cresting this spot from the Sequoia side, or John Muir Trail, were equally as astonished at the view of our panorama encompassing our camp, the valley, Lone Pine Lake, and many ridgelines way down to the trees.

I wasn't surprised to learn later that this is where Stacey decided to turn back. This was a summit, all 13,700 feet. She's worked hard to become an architect and has her MBA as well. Why risk it? If you thought about your situation here long enough, you would be wise to get out of here quickly. Only a few steps further on this trail you will see the sign warning of Extreme Lightning danger. After scanning the list of warning signs such as ozone odor, hair standing on end, a bluish halo surrounding boulders, and tingly fingers, you wouldn't want to pause here for a picnic lunch.

Now we had to go north and pass four pinnacles to reach Whitney, the fifth. From past experience, I've learned to ignore what I'm afraid of by not looking in the direction of blood or steep drop offs. With age, as the eyes are slower to focus, why bother them to make the radical adjustment from 2 feet to 60 miles? Just shut up, stay in the middle of the trail and look only at where your boots are to step and plant your poles firmly. Wait until you're able to pull off the trail at a level enough spot away from the precipice before drinking from your water bottles.

We all wondered how these trails were made, who had to chisel, dynamite or place stones for a rock wall to help us feel some protection. In contrast, the giant spires above and below us seemed as if they had been arranged by the Gods playing a game of Jenga. Here, the forbidden word is earthquake. Don't even think it, equally as frightening as lightning. We'd already survived the bears. Last night, when nature called, I unzipped the tent and depended on the brightness of the stars to find my way to a place to squat. My new Marmot long underwear made specifically for women allowed me the discreteness of just opening them from underneath rather than having to pull them down to my knees.

My romantic section of the brain told me to look at the stars and hold the precious moment forever in the photographic memory portion of my brain. My instinctual self-preservation section of the brain told me to get my eyes off the sky and look around for a large black mass and run back to the tent ASAP!

The squat was a comfortable position from which the sore quad muscles in my legs were reluctant to lift to a standing position. No lights were on me. But as soon as I re-entered the tent, lights shone at our camp almost as a re-run of last night's bear in the tree fiasco. I was to learn later of reports of a bear in our camp last night. I laughed and said it was only me in black long underwear. Nathan said, "*But maybe it was only you AND a bear.*" Miriam took pictures. We kept moving, expecting Nathan, Stacey, and Robert to catch up soon. Before long we could see the cabin on Whitney's summit, built in 1909. Amazing! How did they get there? We have lightweight fleece and polyester. They had wool and heavy canvas. We have to filter our water, they didn't. We have aluminum poles, they used wooden sticks.

At this time, Nathan, Robert and Stacey arrived at Trail Crest. They were there for about 20 minutes discussing Stacey's plan to return alone to our tents. They were surprised to see a man avoiding all the trails, just running up the straight ridge slope of scree with his two poles jabbing into the rocks. He was breathing hard as he approached them, looked at his watch and said, *"Two hours, just like yesterday, great!"* He looked at them and advised them to avoid all the trails, it would go much faster. Stacey, a marathon runner, listened in awe. As she sat at the top where climbers from both sides meet in Sequoia National Forest prior to heading up the summit trail, she didn't tell him she was deathly afraid of a sheer drop off a cliff.

There was an ultramarathon being run and filmed while we were there. From our tent area, Stacey and Robert would hear, *"I made the 60 hour cutoff by 12 minutes, so now I'll summit."* These are people who began the race from the lowest spot in California to the highest, from minus sea level in Badwater, Death Valley to the highest 14,494 feet. These were some of the world's top athletes.

The trek from Trail Crest was taking about 2 hours moving steadily, only pausing briefly for water and GU for oxygen and energy. If you moved too fast, you'd notice less oxygen, around 1/3 less than sea level, but Miriam and I were used to high altitude. The heat was not bothering Miriam at all. We summited Mt. Kilimanjaro in February of this year, only 5 months ago. If these amazing athletes could acclimatize in one day climbing Whitney, surely we could do it in three and a half days.

I concentrated my thoughts on the three people behind us, wondering where they were, hoping that if I thought hard enough, I could wish them to me. I closed my eyes, resting on a boulder. I opened my eyes to see a young man smoothly slithering along the trail as if it were a people mover escalator carrying a small flag from Greece. He made eye contact with me as he floated closer, "*Your husband Robert and son Nathan asked me to tell you they are coming,*" he said.

I was pleasantly surprised. Even better, he told me he was from Corvallis, Oregon, too, a student at OSU! Small world. Mike had come from Badwater, Death Valley, to do this summit so he couldn't stay any longer to talk. We saw him later napping at the summit. I'm always amazed at the strength and endurance of Olympic athletes. Now we have the privilege of performing alongside them. As the Africans say about Mt. Kilimanjaro, Mt. Whitney is also "no joke." Mike is from the country where the first Olympics began. I'm overcoming the same mountain he's winning the prize of ascending. I thanked him, realizing his pause caused him to lose some time from his race. He smiled as he gracefully drifted up the last slope. There was one more snowfield for us to move around. This would be a piece of cake since we could clearly see the way to the summit. I saw Miriam behind me delightedly greeting Nathan and Robert, but where was Stacey?

The last steps toward the summit were not at all scary. It was a wide surface of big granite rocks easy to step over, like walking out on a jetty. I sat down to look at the moonscape as Robert and Nathan caught up to me. Robert was very concerned about lightning--it was 11:10 AM. Everything we'd read about this mountain warned about sudden changes in weather, particularly around noon into the afternoon. Someone at the summit felt a drop of rain. I wasn't sure what to do with my aluminum trekking poles as we hastily posed for pictures, took pictures of other summiters and a fellow who wanted to have Mt. Russell in his background since he'd just climbed it yesterday! Wow, what an honor to take his picture and have him take the four of us with the Palisades in our background at his recommendation.

I quickly clicked some pictures of Miriam at Robert's urging to hurry down. She was brimming over with pleasure, lying on the plaque indicating the location and elevation. Then she stepped out as far as she safely could to peer down several thousand feet to our camp below. I was glad that Nathan and Robert summited their record high point on earth, and so pleased that Miriam accomplished another of her major summit goals. We were on the highest mountain in any state except for Alaska. With Nathan's 6 feet added to 14,494 feet, he figured the top of his head was at exactly 14,500 feet.

As I mentioned before, I wasn't going to look down. We were being reminded of the clouds above. Smoke from a major forest fire near Kern County obliterated a clear view. We signed the log book at the old shelter built in 1909. Nathan, as any engineer would, inspected the strong stone structure. He said there was a wall inside dividing it in half. The building appeared empty. A sign outside the building indicated it wouldn't provide protection from lightning. We saw it had lightning rods on all sides, another reminder for us to descend immediately. Mike from Greece was napping in his white running shirt at the south side of the building. He did not have a tent among his scant cross country racing provisions. He had been awake many hours. Robert urged us off the summit due to the lightning threat. As we headed down, many others were finding their way through the boulders towards the summit.

Nathan hurried on ahead to get back to Stacey at camp in a fast two hours. The threatening clouds hovering at the summit when we were there had moved on. We felt a few more raindrops. Miriam expressed disappointment about not having taken more time to savor her summit experience. It rained lightly on Stacey at the camp. Miriam told me to go ahead without her. She wanted to take her time exploring the amazing landscape and was the last to arrive back at our tents. Once we passed the Trail Crest Junction we were fairly confident lightning would not hit us. It was fun going DOWN the 97 switchbacks, following all the people going downwards as if we were in a modern dance routine, zig-zagging in and out as marching bands perform, except there weren't as many of us. If I'd had a movie camera, I would have filmed this moving art form. The shiny pink feldspar and quartz shone in the sunlight.

Nathan and Stacey left a message drawn in the sand near their tent that they'd left to bathe at Consultation Lake back down the trail about 1/3 mile. Stacey told us that while we were up near the summit, it had rained slightly at our camp.

We ate lots of food and rested. Miriam said goodnight and entered her one person tent at 6:30 PM. As she entered her claustrophobic enclosure, she thought about a runner she spotted sleeping inside the summit hut, wondering what it would be like to bed down in the open air without a tent. I felt as if I'd sleep straight through tonight after the long summit climb.

I was wrong. Again, I had to get up since I drink lots of water for oxygen at high elevation. After getting back in the tent, perhaps an hour to half hour later, Robert heard and I smelled a bear by our kitchen area two steps from our tent, one step from Nathan and Stacey's tent. This bear was breathing very hard like a hugely overweight man who'd been running, but it was also making sniffing smelling noises. Robert listened long enough to know it was a bear, then he made so much noise groping for a flashlight that the bear was probably scared off. By the time Robert opened the zipper and shone the flashlight, it was gone.

Our camp odors must have been attractive to the bear to come all the way above tree line to visit us. But Nathan always made sure our food and scented items were stashed well enough away. Our camp, with a granite ledge, made a nice shelf with a straight wall rising above it and a trashbag hanging out of reach of chipmunks and marmots. There was a slash in the double black garbage bag from the bear's swat.

Whenever Stacey took a break from all the meal preparations, she would sit on the rock ledge in her dark fleece looking like a marmot scanning its territory. We were situated at a straight span of the trail where the limpers, joggers, or spirited rhythmic walking stick trekkers would look to us as if we were the race officials, seeking some sort of acknowlegement. All the mountain people were friendly, a large percentage were foreigners. Robert is good at getting people to tell him something about themselves or their progress. He would grimace at those descending late when he saw they didn't have overnight gear. Stacey offered them food. Those who passed our tents going up felt a need to report to us going down without losing a beat to their steps. Some had skinned legs, knee braces, bandanas hanging out under their hats, zinc oxide on their noses, water bottles clearly visible from waist packs, day packs, or overflowing back packs, or no packs. Is this anything like soldiers returning from battle?

Back at the trailhead the first day, we read that it's best to leave zippers open on your backpacks and tents so the bears can sniff inside to make sure you didn't leave anything in them. We heard of people leaving windows open in their cars while they're camping so the bears may have a look inside. We left our pack zippers open, but not our tent. Nathan and Stacey's was unzipped, but slept through this bear visit. The next morning, after cooking freeze dried scrambled eggs, we hiked all the way out to the cars. Miriam purchased a shirt at the portal store "Mt. Whitney 14,494 ft."

We said good-bye to Miriam as she left for the Reno airport. She had a difficult time staying awake, nodding off a few times. It was 104 degrees as we drove through the Mojave desert in our air conditioned rented van heading back to San Luis Obispo.

Miriam and Hilary on top of Borah Peak in Idaho

Borah Peak: The True Meaning of Exposure

Miriam had the patience to wait until Hilary completed her last day teaching summer term before taking her to climb Idaho's highest mountain, Borah Peak in August, 2000. However, Miriam did not want to waste a minute more. Miriam's car was packed with backpacking equipment prior to Hilary's last class of summer term. Miriam napped in her car in the college parking lot. As soon as Hilary was finished at 10 PM, she shook the car to awaken Miriam and they headed off to find Highway 84 leading to Idaho.

They drove all night, taking turns sleeping and driving. There were many trucks on the road. They stopped only for gas, and coffee for Hilary, at small truck stops. After many long hours driving highways in the dark, they selected the Sawtooth Scenic Byway to get them to the vicinity of the remote trailhead. The map did not do justice to the amount of bends and hairpin turns on that windy road with views of lovely white pine trees through the pristine river valley. Although they drove this road after sunrise, they remembered encountering only one other vehicle and it was going in the opposite direction.

At last they pulled up to a gas station in the small town of Challis where they encountered a very strange sight: a long line of men waiting for the restroom while there was not a soul waiting for the women's rest room. The men were all wearing bright yellow. As they approached, Miriam and Hilary realized they were firemen. They came to fight the Salmon River area fire and had been dispatched from many states as summer crews. They looked very hot in their heavy suits and helmets, awaiting transport. Miriam and Hilary joked with them as they exited the restroom and Miriam gestured for them to use the women's restroom. They all had big happy smiles. Hilary remembers being concerned that smoke from the forest fire may drift to Borah Peak.

Miriam always has a good sense of where the highest peak is located. She thought she spotted it in the distance. They passed many miles of open land with sagebrush and grazing land, but they were surprised to see a change in scenery when they drove past Craters of the Moon National Monument. It really did look like moonscape. After so many hours of driving without sleep the imagination may play tricks with you.

Hilary had written Lost River Ranger District to ask about the best time of year to climb and equipment needed. She had been told that the mountain was fine except for exposure. Hilary had always known the term "exposure" meant dangerous weather such as thunder and lightning, heavy winds, unexpected changes in temperatures involving extreme heat and cold such as snow and sleet. Both climbers had extensive experience backpacking together. They climbed Mt. Shasta with a guide on a day that happened to be more icy than usual. Their helmets helped protect them from falling rocks, cameras and water bottles from climbers above them. They snowshoed a trail leading in to Mt. St. Helens during a heavy snow year when the roads were impassable. They set up their tent on ice. They trekked through the heat of Africa. They knew about exposure. However, neither of them knew the true climbers meaning of the term "exposure." They were to find out.

Driving down the long dusty gravel road, they hoped they were on the approach side of the mountain. Miriam looked up at the massive volcano and said she thought it looked easy. As with many other trailheads, it was remote and the approach not obvious. It was afternoon and getting hot, they were tired, but the adrenalin started to kick in as if they were getting close to lost treasure. They drove back where the gravel road had forked and had another look. Miriam, remembering there had been a recent earthquake in the area in 1983 noticed a long strip that appeared to be a fault. At last, they saw a few trees and as they came closer to the mountain, Miriam spotted a sign that read "Borah Peak Trailhead." They saw one other vehicle parked here. Although both were extremely tired, they did not want to sleep under the hot sun at the trailhead.

As they loaded their backpacks, they knew they would spend one or two nights on this mountain. It was the end of summer, so that meant no water on the mountain. Miriam had packed a large water jug. The trail showed no mercy. It was steep at the start with no switchbacks. As they climbed higher and higher, there was some shade from trees. Miriam's style is to keep going at an even pace and not break the rhythm. She fares well in extreme heat, while Hilary does best in the cold. Hilary stops to remove or add layers and take a sip from her water bottle. She must move like a rabbit to catch up for her stops. This 2,760 foot altitude gain is described as "hill from hell" in a book entitled Highpoint Adventures by Charlie and Diane Winger.

After several hours, they could see ahead where the tree line stopped. With lightning in the area, they decided to camp at the top edge of the tree line. However, there was no place in sight that was level below the tree line. Both dropped their packs and searched desperately for an area that could be flat enough for a 2-man tent to rest. All they could do was set up the tent where a fallen log would prevent the tent from falling down the hill as they slept.

Sometime during the night, they unzipped the door of the tent to see a beautiful spectacle. The wildfire, although at a distance, was extensive enough to provide a great light show for Miriam and Hilary. This was bittersweet as they knew the awe-inspiring sight of flames and glowing hot coal came at a great cost to the flora and fauna of the area. Smoke from the fire made the full moon glow orange. Both were spellbound by the scene.

The next morning, the two travel weary climbers woke at sunrise to begin their climb from the treeline. Their breakfast was small snacks they had packed in their pockets and day packs. They left the tent in its place trusting it would still be there upon their return from the summit. As soon as they began their climb they saw rock faces ahead and high sharp rocky ridges. Other climbers were ahead and behind them. Several came back down toward them indicating they were turning around due to extreme danger.

Ahead was "Chicken Out Ridge" 10,200 feet elevation. They had read about this place. It was very sharp and steep. They trod gingerly trying to be sure-footed like goats. Miriam could feel her heart beating with memories of her fall off Mt. Hood. She surely did not want it to happen again. Falling into snow and ice off Mt. Hood was different from this climb. All that lay below were rocks straight down. There was nothing to break a fall. Others have died in this very spot. There are no crosses to mark where others have fallen as they alert us along roadsides. On Chicken Out Ridge, one fall and you are dead. The mood here was solemn and slow. They began to realize the true meaning of the climber's term, "exposure."

Their day packs were not heavy enough to hamper climbing but they contained rain gear, emergency First Aid, plenty of water and snacks and a space blanket. They were prepared for what they had thought "exposure" meant. However they did not have ropes or harnesses. They could have really used them at that point. They had read all the information they could locate from two highpointer books and written communication from Lost River Ranger District. However, the ranger had never climbed the mountain. Borah Peak would have been easier to climb during snow season. Some climbing books have rating systems. These may be misleading during off-season attempts. Neither Miriam nor Hilary wanted to take risks. Both took extreme caution although they were determined not to chicken out. They saw a boy about 15 years old talking to some other climbers, apparently discussing whether or not to turn around.

As they made their way around the high ridge, they came upon some men navigating the treacherous traverse. Aside from the parking area signage indicating Borah Peak's trailhead, there were no more signs such as rock cairns or markers showing the route. These people had been here analyzing the best route and surely from what Miriam and Hilary had scouted out, this was the route. A man reached out his arm to assist his friend across an area where there was no foothold. A very tall person could probably reach with a giant step. Hilary was close to him. Her jaw dropped.

Before she knew it, the man's arm was extended toward her. She had no time to hesitate. As she looked back, Miriam signed, *"grab it!"* The opportunity was at hand. Hilary realized this was her only opportunity and she grabbed it. As soon as she landed on solid footing and thanked the gentleman she started wondering how she would get back across this place on the return trip.

Miriam was next and she landed with a smile of confidence. Ahead was a place where climbers needed bouldering skills. However, they had to drop down before meeting the trail leading to the summit. Bouldering is usually easier going up than going down. Miriam is shorter than Hilary. She opted to work her way down another way that was not as steep. However, as Miriam made her way back up toward the trail, she encountered scree. This loose rounded rolling volcanic rock is like popcorn. Sand on a dune is easier to traverse. Climbing scree can slide you down more than you gain. It can come out from underneath like an avalanche. Miriam wished she had brought along some rope. Another climber above her said that Miriam's route is easy with snow on the ground. This was the right trail at the wrong time of year. A boy scout tossed a rope down toward Miriam assisting her up the scree slope. At last they were back on a trail with some earth underneath heading in the direction of the summit. It was getting very hot and their work-out and anxious moments added to their sweat.

As they gained more altitude, the thinning air began to slow them down. Less than two days ago they were in Corvallis, Oregon, not much higher than sea level. They knew that afternoons bring winds and sometimes lightning to high mountain peaks. So far, they were not breathing smoke from the forest fire. Acclimatizing takes time and should not be rushed. The air started to cool. They watched others descending from the summit. They knew they would eventually reach the summit, there were no more obstacles in their way, however they could not rest on their laurels because their tent was a long way below.

The summit was very windy and they may have been the last to summit that day. They took pictures of each other and Miriam set up her camera to take a picture of them together. After admiring the view and signing the summit register, they lost no more time at the 12,662 foot summit before heading back down. Miriam remembers wondering, *"Who will be there to help us get across the risky traverse on the return trip?"*

Once they reached the notch, they were again having to make the decision as to which route would be safest to go back up and over skirting Chicken Out Ridge. They thought they were alone, but happened to notice a couple just heading back over the top and down. Just as they disappeared from their view, Miriam saw the man beckoning them in his direction. This type of climb is referred to as scrambling. Those with longer legs have more options for foot holds. It is basic rock climbing without ropes or harnesses. After struggling, the two tired climbers made it up the rock face and their last major obstacle was the exposed traverse. For reasons they cannot figure out, a man was there to assist them, as if he appeared out of nowhere. How did he know they would need him? What caused him to be right there for them at that moment? They will never know, but they showed him their relief and appreciation before he headed down immediately after his kind deed. They never saw him again.

Now they were in view of the treeline. Miriam and Hilary hoped the tent would be as they'd left it early that morning. They triumphantly eased their way back down from the ridge and came upon a sunburned man showing them a photo of his son and a note asking if they had seen him. They remembered seeing this boy on their way over Chicken Out Ridge. The father asked if they saw him coming back. No, they hadn't. The man was very distressed particularly because Miriam and Hilary, those two ladies using sign language, were the last people off the ridge. As it turned out, the son wanted so badly to summit, he told his father to wait for him and went on over Chicken Out Ridge alone. His father and other family members had been waiting most of the day.

That night, as Hilary and Miriam slept in the tent, unbeknownst to them there were helicopters, search and rescue teams, and rescue hounds looking for the lost boy. They had logically assumed the helicopters were part of the Forest Fire management. As Miriam and Hilary awoke and packed, they saw people coming up the trail searching for the boy. Again they were asked if they had seen the boy. It wasn't until they reached the bottom that they saw the boy's sunburnt father with the good news that his son had been found. He pointed out the long route his son had taken from the summit way down the gully through the brush avoiding Chicken-Out Ridge. It had taken the boy most of the night to work his way down the mountain aided by the full moon through a route without any trails until the search party found him.

Upon return to Miriam's Toyota Tercel sedan, they loaded up and hurried off to their next state summit. In four days, Miriam would have to drop Hilary off at the Salt Lake City airport so she could return to attend the annual Seabeck DeafBlind retreat in Washington.

Miriam on top of Mt. Elbert, Colorado, holding a climb register (log book). She signed her name in log books on each summit that provided them

Three State High Points
Excerpts from Miriam Richards' Journal

After dropping Hilary off at the Salt Lake City airport, I made my way to her brother Brian's house in Loveland, Colorado. On the way, I stopped at Dinosaur National Monument to learn the history of the area. We stayed with Brian's family several years ago in order for me to acclimatize prior to my Aconcagua, South America climb. At that time, we went to Estes Park to snowshoe and cross country ski, remaining at high elevation in order to increase my red blood cells. This would carry oxygenated blood to my brain and muscles and decrease the possibility of contracting altitude sicknesses: HAPE or HACE: High Altitude Pulmonary Edema and High Altitude Cerebral Edema.

I am grateful to my friends and friends of friends and relatives of friends for opening their homes to me. People wonder how I keep down my expenses with all the traveling I do. Hilary's nephew calls me "Aunt Miriam" and I feel that I have a wealth of relatives through her extended family.

I had three more states to touch on this trip: Kansas, Nebraska and Colorado. I discussed my plans with Brian's family. The kids were in school and Brian had to work. His wife Ellen was the only one available to ride along with me to Kansas. She had never thought of driving to Kansas just to touch the highest point. *"Will it be a long hike?"* she asked. I explained that it would be a "drive-up" since Kansas is so flat. It was a good thing that Mt. Sunflower is on the far west border next to Colorado so we would not have to drive far into the state. Ellen smiled and agreed to go.

Mt. Sunflower, Kansas

We left on August 26, 2000 for Mt. Sunflower. It took about six hours round trip. Just after crossing the border into Kansas, Ellen and I were greeted with millions of sunflowers showing us their happy faces. Our route was to go down a gravel road, but a sign told us "CLOSED due to Flooding." Everything appeared dry and this may have been an old sign so we went ahead until we reached a tall monument in the shape of a sunflower.

It was the most beautiful artistic design that I had seen on any of the state highpoints. A barbed wire fence surrounded the monument to protect it. A carved stone indicated this had once been an old homestead. Ellen walked the 50 or so steps with me and asked, "*That's all? We drove all the way here for this?*" I said, *"Yes, congratulations, Kansas is your very first state highpoint, 4,039 feet on August 26, 2000!"* As I prepared to take her picture, she proudly posed for her photograph in her dress at her first state summit with her hands holding the registry book. The book was available to us from a mail box hanging on our side of the fence. It appears that Kansasans are proud of their high point by the way they take care of it. The fact they call this "Mt. Sunflower" was amusing. Ellen told me she would love to go with me to Nebraska the next day. She seemed addicted already. Ellen drove my car part way back so I could rest.

I offered to cook a trout dinner for the family in exchange for their hospitality. All of them knew some sign language which made me feel even more comfortable in their household. Ellen spoke so jubilantly of her highpoint adventure, helping me convince the family to come with us the next day, Saturday. Back when Brian was in his early 20's he moved to Colorado specifically for rock-climbing, bouldering, bicycling and ice climbing. He has a sailboat in his shed that he has been building for over a decade. He offered to take Hilary and me up Longs Peak some day, but I am focusing on my highpoints first. My "nephew" Peter and "niece" Anna have also summited Longs Peak, one of the Colorado 14'rs. But none of them had ever topped a state highpoint.

Nebraska's Mt. Constable or Panorama Point

The next day, on August 27, 2000, we all piled into Brian and Ellen's car and headed off to attempt to conquer Nebraska's highest point. Brian and Peter brought along their ice axes as a lark. We headed north and stopped at the Tri-State Marker. None of them had ever been to this point where they touched three states all at once right where the borders of Colorado, Nebraska and Wyoming intersect. The monument was a fun place to photograph.

Our next destination, Mt. Constable was not far. It is also known as Panorama Point, boasting 5,424 feet, slightly higher than one mile (5,280 feet). Our expedition began by making our way through a grassy field. I headed onward at my usual speed, and then when I turned around, Brian reminded me that their family walked slowly. Ellen had a parasol to keep out the summer heat. I slowed while they caught up with me. Peter was carrying Brian's old wooden ice axe, pretending to look around for the big mountain. The monument was just high enough to see it above the field of grass. When we reached it, Anna held the ice axe over her head in triumph as Peter and Brian stood alongside. Ellen and Brian posed happily with them on Ellen's second state highpoint within two days!

Colorado's Mt. Elbert

After a nice week-end with Brian's family, they went back to their usual routine, so none of them could join me for my climb of their state's highest point, Mt. Elbert. I drove to Half Moon Campground just outside the town of Leadville in the southwest part of the state. Oddly enough, the highest mountain in the state of Colorado is not in the Rocky Mountains. The area was desolate. Colorado has 53 peaks higher than 14,000 feet. I felt cold with the black clouds looming overhead. I could not see the mountain.

I spent the night in my tent, which I put in my trunk and at 6 AM, I had to walk into the trailhead because I did not have a 4-wheel drive, just my Toyota sedan. The bumps and holes in the dirt road were deep with large tree roots to step over for a mile. The quaking aspens are lovely with their pale green leaves and white boulders amongst them. I made my way in and around the obstructions in this so-called "road" realizing it would have been impossible to drive it with my car. My trip so far had been warm but today, August 30, 2000, it was almost fall. The cold weather was moving in quickly.

I would have to go eleven miles in one day, half of it uphill. I arrived at the trailhead, 10,100 feet, and knew I would have to climb more than 3,500 feet to high altitude. I had acclimatized with the Borah Peak summit 12,662 feet 11 days ago, up to 10,800 feet in Utah and remained above mile-high Denver elevation ever since, so I felt confident in my physical ability to pocket this summit.

From the trailhead sign, I crossed a brook and from there the trail meandered uphill in and out of the lovely aspen forest. I looked up to see the clouds coming from the east. Eventually, the trail widened and I would have taken more time to appreciate the view if this were a two-day trip and if the clouds were not so heavy and dark. My physical stamina was at its best so I kept up a pretty quick pace with my daypack. I was about half way up the mountain when I encountered four climbers coming downhill toward me gesturing for me to go back down due to lightning strikes. I could see the huge thunderheads but hadn't seen the lightning until they mentioned it because my eyes had been focused on the trail ahead of me. I was on a mission to reach this summit and did not want to turn back.

I stepped up my pace passing the tree line and followed the rocky trail through the alpine meadow gaining on two older men barreling up the grade. As they crossed the switchbacks, they signaled to me below the direction to take. I waved that I knew. They waved me up the trail. Eventually I caught up to them. Lightning struck and we all turned our heads to look. I shrugged as if to question whether or not to turn back as the men beckoned me to join them pointing up the mountain, *"Come on!"* I was not going to turn down their offer. The men were in great shape for their age so I imagine they do quite a bit of climbing or long distance trekking. The lightning struck on and off but they continued as if it were not a problem. When the three of us reached the top, quite miraculously the clouds opened up all around us and allowed 15 minutes of sunshine to announce our victory. We were lit up on the highest stage in the state of Colorado, 14,433 feet! I was thankful for the sunshine to provide good photographs of me with the valley below.

I was astonished when a group of drilling soldiers rounded the summit coming from the other direction. I located the registry tube and pulled out the book to sign. The older men and military personnel were surprised; they told me they did not know there was such a thing. I pointed out the benchmark as well. I noticed the rocks in the area were all blackened, quite different from the lighter colored rocks down below. I realized these rocks had been struck by lightning on numerous occasions. I remembered reading about that anomaly when I climbed Mt. Theilsen with Hilary in Southern Oregon. Mt. Theilsen, with its iron-rich boulders, is nicknamed "the lightning rod." There was no snow on Mt. Elbert at this time although there would be soon with fall approaching. I enjoyed looking 360 degrees with such a clear view. I knew I had to start down before sundown, so I went ahead alone as the men took more time to take in the sights.

After passing the tree line and rounding another hill, I came upon four girls hiking up toward me, a little breathless. I could see they did not have packs so I asked them if I could catch a ride with them from the trailhead back to my car. They watched my sign language and puzzled, answered, *"No."* I realized they had no idea what I was asking. So I continued downhill. The girls gave up their plan to climb to the summit and turned around heading downhill. I stayed close enough to meet them at their 4-wheel vehicle parked at the trailhead. As they began to pull out, they waved to me to hop in. It was a very uncomfortable bumpy ride, but as it was getting dark I was relieved not to have to walk back on the horrendous "road."

The long drive back to Oregon was arduous. I was pleased with the four summits gained out of my five attempts. The weather changed frequently, the most frightening being the lightning strikes as I drove out in the open. I was anxious to return to find out from Hilary how she enjoyed her week-long DeafBlind retreat at Seabeck, Washington. I wanted to ask her lots of questions and to share my experiences.

Miriam outside of the Mt. Driskell Marker in Louisiana. She summited 12 state high points in just over two weeks

High Point Marathon—12 states!

In the fall of 2000, Miriam received exciting news from SCA (Student Conservation Association) that her application to work as a forestry volunteer in Florida was accepted. Earlier (around Spring 2000), she applied to work on a forest trail crew that provides free room and board in exchange for labor to clean up forests, repair hiking trails, build bridges and provide volunteer support during natural disasters. Miriam believed that this volunteer experience would fulfill several goals. She would enhance her outdoors and forestry skills, do something good for the environment and best of all, visit 12 high points in Florida and surrounding states without considerable expense. Excited, she agreed to spend at least three months volunteering in Tallahassee, Florida.

Miriam worked for SCA in the Tetons in the past before her senior year at Gallaudet. She enjoyed the good teamwork that summer. Although it was extremely tough work building horse bridges, she thoroughly enjoyed the leadership, camaraderie and experience. She hoped this would bring her closer to her goal of working as a ranger for the National Parks. That happened to be the same year of the horrible 80,000 + acre forest fire that struck the Grand Tetons National Park that July.

Perhaps it was an omen, or a sign of things to come, but the Amtrak trip from Albany, Oregon to Tallahassee, Florida was disastrous. She left September 11th at 5:15 PM and did not arrive in Florida until September 15th at 3 AM, a full day later than originally planned. Changing trains in Los Angeles, delays that lasted between 4 and 15 hours due to mechanical or schedule difficulties left Miriam with little opportunity for a full night's sleep. In addition, because she could not hear the conductor announcements, she had to stay alert and read people's faces. Each time the train stopped for a length of time, and she saw that people were visibly angry, she would ask them to write down the reason for the delay, hoping to piece together an approximate time of arrival in Florida.

Throughout the trip, she tried to keep her spirits up. She took notes on the beauty of the changing countryside she viewed through the window, and reported seeing deer, pelicans and coyotes. She especially loved the sunsets. On the second day, she met another deaf woman and her mother who were on the way to San Antonio, Texas, for her daughter's Air Force graduation. Miriam felt especially bad for this woman, because a four hour delay in El Paso almost caused the woman to miss her daughter's ceremony.

By the time she arrived in Florida, physically exhausted and irritable, she received another shock. Instead of a reasonably clean trail crew boss, she was greeted by an older man she described as having "longish dirty, uncombed hair, scruffy beard and wearing dirty clothes." Despite this first impression, she appreciated his his attempts to learn some of her signs. Soon after arriving at the camp, she went straight to bed and slept through the next morning.

Over the next few days, Miriam met with the rest of the volunteers and was surprised to find that they were all between 18 and 24 years of age, younger than Miriam by at least 10 years. She also spent some time trying to adjust to her small living quarters and the environment, which was vastly different from Oregon. She described the trees as "much skinnier than Oregon trees, varying between longleaf pine, cypress and magnolia." Being a true explorer, Miriam noted the type of insects and animals outside of her quarters, including banana spiders, four inch grasshoppers, love bugs, Lyme ticks, chiggers, alligators, a variety of snakes, and creatures that she had never seen.

Miriam's first day at work was September 20. Her crew was fortunate that Hurricane Gordon, which ripped through much of Florida, missed her area completely. Her journal reflected her feelings on her first day of work:

> *"Sept 20. First day at work. We hiked and built a bridge for 9 hours. I told the crew the importance of teamwork, taking turns and*

> *good cooperation. I took pictures of the bridge progress! Mosquitoes were in the way—I hate that! Very humid! My clothes were easily wet from all the heavy sweat. I drank lots of water. We dug, installed wood, hammered nails. Long day! My body is not used to working 9 hours straight."*
> *(Miriam Richards' journal, Sept 20, 2000)*

Within a week, Miriam had experienced a great deal of nature, including the insects! A tropical depression hit the Tallahassee River and she saw floods, tornados, and power outages all in one day. Later that week, the crew stepped into a large beehive and was stung so badly that three of the crew members had to go to the hospital for injections.

Miriam experienced deep cuts in her hands from cutting wood, and at the end of each day, she was covered with mosquito and chigger bites. The hours were long, the work was hard, and the heat was almost unbearable. The worst thing that Miriam had to deal with was her phobia of snakes. She had not realized that wading in flooded rivers, she would come in frequent contact with snakes. Once, she had a dangerous encounter. She wrote about this in her journal.

> *"I was in the river clearing some of the brush with the crew when all of a sudden, I bent down and there was a copperhead snake that reared up its head close to me. Luckily, it lost interest in me and went away, but I had a really hard time calming down after that."*
> *(Miriam Richards' journal, September 24, 2000)*

Despite these discomforts, Miriam strove to be positive. By the end of the second week, however, she began to experience increasing isolation. Part of this isolation was due to the fact that she was the only deaf person in her crew. Communication was difficult, especially since it was not always feasible for her to bring paper and pen while working outdoors. On more than one occasion, the crew forgot completely that Miriam was deaf. Several times, she did not hear the crew's warnings when heavy logs slid her way and almost broke her arm once when a log hit her. Most of the crew had never been exposed to another deaf person and had many misconceptions. Miriam found herself educating her co-workers and boss about the most basic myths, including the myth that deaf people cannot drive. She had to prove that she was able to drive the truck to haul equipment and remove debris from fallen trees and plants. Initially, some of the crew learned basic signs, but gradually lost interest as time passed.

Another reason for Miriam's isolation within the crew was the fact that her value system was very different from theirs. With the exception of the crew boss, Miriam was older than the other volunteers by at least 10 years, so her perspective was different by at least a generation. Once, during a weekend, the crew decided to go out and drink. Due to her moral beliefs, Miriam did not agree with excessive alcohol consumption. The crew pressured her into being the designated driver. It was uncomfortable for Miriam to see people intoxicated and acting in a way that she felt was immature. She was concerned that after the incident, the crew perceived her differently for not drinking with the rest of them. Several times, she smelled alcohol on her crew boss during working hours, and felt that as the supervisor, he should have modeled better behavior.

Miriam's work ethic also set her apart from the crew. A hard worker, who believed in working as a team to balance out some of the harder tasks, she felt that she was given the majority of the difficult tasks because the crew boss knew she was dependable. Miriam thought some of the crew slacked off during work—several of them quit and were replaced during the time she volunteered.

By the end of September, Miriam decided to venture out of Florida for a few days and visit the first half of the high points on her list. Because of the expense of renting a car, and the limited amount of time she could take time off from her volunteer job, she crammed six state high points from Georgia to Tennessee in just three days. She set out on October 1, 2000.

Throughout the three day trip, Miriam had to sleep in her car to save on expenses. It was a little frightening for her to be on her own, sleeping in unfamiliar areas, but she was determined to make her goals on a tight budget. The first night, she slept in a parking lot next to a church. At 4 AM, a van drove up, and stopped for a while. Nervous, Miriam was ready to leave when the van left. She decided to find a safer place to sleep after this.

Brasstown Bald, Georgia

The first high point she visited was Brasstown Bald in Georgia near the Chattahoochee National Forest, approximately 16 miles from the state line of Tennessee. Brasstown Bald stands 4,784 feet and indeed resembles a rounded bald head. Miriam pulled up at 6 AM in her fancy little red rental car and had the place to herself. It took approximately one hour for a round trip hike to view this summit and she enjoyed the solitude moving through the dramatic early morning mist. The leaves were turning into a beautiful fall color, and the backdrop of a mountain made Miriam homesick for Oregon.

Sassafras Mountain, South Carolina

Miriam struggled trying to locate the trailhead to Sassafras Mountain in South Carolina. She drove back and forth in attempts to locate the entrance but street signs were non-existent. The area was trashy and she could see this was a “red neck” area. Her determination to complete the high point and get out of there kept her focused on her goal and not let her vulnerability prevent her from going on. She really did not want to have to come back here ever again. Sassafras Mountain was a quick walk because the starting point for hiking the high point was only 50 feet with a highpoint of 3,560 feet. Miriam accomplished this in ten minutes.

Mount Mitchell, North Carolina

Next was Mount Mitchell, in the lovely Blue Ridge Mountains in North Carolina. The highway passage to this mountain was gorgeous. Appalachian trail hikers and tourists are drawn to the beauty of this popular area, so much that she had trouble finding a place to park. This was a strong contrast to the ugly vandalized area of the previous highpoint in South Carolina. Mount Mitchell's summit of 6,684 feet is the highest point east of the Mississippi River. Mount Mitchell was named after Elisha Mitchell (b. 1793, d. 1857). Mitchell was a scientist and a professor at the University of North Carolina—Chapel Hill who first suggested that Mount Mitchell was the highest point in Eastern United States. Apparently, during one of his many exploratory trips to the summit, he passed away at a waterfall. Mitchell's grave is placed at the summit. After hiking back down hill, Miriam had a delicious lunch and purchased a nice hat to help her remember this lovely place before driving away.

Mount Rogers, Virginia

Miriam drove to Virginia where she stayed overnight in Grayson's State Park in Virginia. She felt safe there in the beautiful park with a clean pleasant campground. The next morning, she woke early and climbed Mount Rogers, which uses a portion of the famous Appalachian Trail to reach Virginia's high point of 5,729 feet. The round trip hike for climbing Mount Rogers is 8 miles and takes approximately 4 to 6 hours. The high point happened to be on a boulder so the benchmark was embedded into the hard rock, not on land.

Miriam felt at peace while viewing the surroundings of Mount Rogers. Her journal reflected her inner thoughts as she took in the views around her.

> *"I like hiking Mt. Rogers because of the beautiful cliff shape, wild ponies and the colorful leaves. It took four hours for a round trip hike. Nice weather! Very quiet and*

peaceful, especially because there are no dangerous insects or animals. I feel so peaceful and relaxed. After a deep breath, I felt that everything will be alright."
(Miriam Richards' journal, October 2, 2000)

Black Mountain, Kentucky

The next highpoint Miriam visited was Black Mountain, located in Southeastern Kentucky, near the Virginia border. The road getting into the trail was curvy with lots of ups and downs so Miriam had to estimate where the summit was located by her common sense navigation skills. She turned back and tried again to find the summit after realizing she was driving more downhill than uphill.

At the time, there were no GPS pointers in any of her highpoint guidebooks. Some of the adventure, intrigue and mystery will be replaced by clearer signage or the highpoints will become more popular in the future, thus easier to find. When Miriam came to the small town of Lynch, Kentucky, she waved to some people and gestured *"Up,up, where?"* and the people pointed her back in the direction she came. It took a while, but eventually Miriam found a well-hidden sign.

Many high points are very tricky to spot and this was certainly one of them. In addition, Miriam did not realize she needed to write ahead to the Penn Virginia Coal Company in advance to receive a waiver to cross the property. As she entered the road, she spotted a spinning aviation control radar beacon. Unaware of the need to obtain a waiver, Miriam later learned she could have been fined $500. There was not much of a view at Black Mountain, just weeds and a tower that people are not permitted to climb at Kentucky's 4,145 feet high point. After a few minutes at the site, she drove on to the Great Smoky Mountain National Park to visit her last highpoint in Tennessee.

Clingman's Dome, Tennessee

It was dark when Miriam arrived at the trailhead. Although not a designated rest stop, Miriam parked overnight. Strong winds shook her car all night, she was only able to cat nap. By dawn, she saw the area was a barren place. She was unimpressed with the forest, finding it bereft of the color she saw at the other mountains. It was very cold hiking to Clingman's Dome at 7:00 that morning. She was surprised to learn that Tennessee's highpoint was a concrete bridge structure. Clingman's Dome is located in the Great Smoky Mountains at a height of 6,643 feet. Miriam easily made the one hour round trip hike to visit the site, wrote her name in the log and then drove nine hours back to Florida to prepare for work the next day.

For the next two weeks, Miriam found her volunteer job to be increasingly physically and emotionally challenging. Originally, the shifts were supposed to be four days a week, ten hours a day. Because some of the crew quit suddenly, she had to work five days a week until their replacements came. In addition, because she was so dependable and hard working, her crew boss placed more demands on her. This increased the number of times she got hurt during work. Several times throughout the week, she had to carry heavy tools for one mile in the humidity. Miriam resented this because she saw that the male crew members took their time building bridges, taking many breaks. She slipped several times in the mud and hurt her knees, cut her thumb deeply and continued to battle the bugs that seemed to enjoy feasting on her skin.

One of the worst moments she recalled was seeing her boss displaying anger and rude behavior towards her. When she tried to communicate with him, he often turned his back on her without answering her questions. When one of the department heads complained that a bridge was built without appropriate safety features, the crew boss blew up at all of the crew members. He threw all of the dishes into a trash can because he was not happy with the way the crew cleaned. In reality, Miriam always cleaned up during her shift, and it was the other crew members who did not do a good job. Yet Miriam seemed to get the majority of the blame for the lack of cleanliness displayed by her crew. Miriam was ready to quit when the crew boss finally acknowledged that the other crew members were responsible for the mess, not her. This apology came too late for Miriam and she was counting the days when she would go home again.

On October 14-16, 2000, Miriam rented a car again to take in the remaining six states on her highpoint marathon list. The drive from Miriam's crew compound to Louisiana's high point was due west crossing three states horizontally. Although the highway passes along the Gulf Coast, Miriam could not see any water. Instead, the drive was a dizzying hypnotic blurr of small trees. Without companion or ability to hear a radio, she could practically tie down the steering wheel and sleep the long dull hours she zoomed along highway 12.

Driskell Mountain, Louisiana

Miriam's first summit during this trip was at Driskill Mountain in Louisiana, way at the top of the "L" shape of the state on the far western side, taking her 14 hours of driving time to get there. Louisiana is quite flat, so the high point is a low 535 feet of elevation. Miriam thought *"It's a wonder they called it a mountain at all?"* When she arrived, there was a church with a cemetery. Miriam followed the gravel path and was waylayed in the wrong direction, adding extra time to her tight schedule. The actual hiking distance from the starting point to the high point is two miles. The interesting thing to note about Driskill Mountain is that part of the hike is on private property. Visitors are asked to help maintain the trail by picking up trash or cans that are found along the way and closing any gates that are found open. Miriam reached this summit at 8:55 AM and found another hiker at the top who took a picture of her.

Magazine Mountain, Arkansas

Her next stop was Magazine Mountain of Arkansas. Miriam headed north from Louisiana, however the various highways and remote roads she had to navigate were much like climbing through a spider web. There are no direct easy routes to and from all these remote high points. None of them are near any major cities. The high point of Arkansas would have been much easier to get to as the crow flies. Instead, Miriam had to only wish she had time to stop at Hot Springs National Park where Arkansas's famous mineral baths are located. When she saw the sign, she could only dream of taking a bath after the long hurried solitary drive. The high point of Arkansas is named Signal Hill, 2,753 feet elevation in the Ozarks. Miriam had an adventure there while trying to sign the registration book at the high point. A large wasp seemed to take interest in her and chased her around for a while before finally flying away.

Taum Sauk Mountain, Missouri

From Arkansas, Miriam continued north to Missouri before heading diagonally across Missouri trying her best to stay awake. She had to remain alert for the frequent changes to different highways, on the road for hours upon hours in such remote areas that she never saw another car. After 20 hours of hard driving through lightning and the dizzying monotony of her windshield wiper, she finally saw the sign for Taum Sauk State Park where she stayed overnight. These are not the large state parks Miriam is accustomed to on the west coast with all the amenities; it was October in Missouri and Miriam was the only car in the entire state park! The next morning it was raining hard. Miriam was thankful that she slept in the car instead of a tent or she would have been soaked. She set out for the Taum Sauk Mountain high point that morning. Taum Sauk Mountain is 1,772 feet in elevation. This was Miriam's favorite stop and she felt her spirit refreshed by the climb. The picture Miriam took of herself reveals the rain drops on her camera lens.

> *"Lovely rain with fall colored leaves. I love that! [At the summit]I jumped on the big rock and reached my arms to the sky. I felt happy!" (Miriam Richards' journal, October 16, 2000)*

Woodall Mountain, Mississippi

The next stop was at Woodall Mountain in northern Mississippi. The weather along the way changed from rainy to sunny. Woodall Mountain is 806 feet in elevation. The site is a drive up since the starting point and the high point are at the same level. Miriam was very disappointed to see the litter around the elevation plaque. In fact, several high point books and magazines state that this high point is the most unkempt. She made the summit at 2:30 PM, took a picture of herself and then rushed to get to Alabama before it was dark.

Cheaha Mountain, Alabama

Miriam continued east to Alabama, then south arriving in the late afternoon, reaching the Cheaha Mountain high point at 6:30 PM, just in time for the sunset. Some of the websites and guidebooks state that Cheaha is an American Indian word meaning "high." Some of the literature goes as far as to say the word comes from the Creek language. Cheaha Mountain high point, 2,407 feet was also a drive up. Fortunately, the high point was easy to get to, however Miriam did not realize until she got there that winter hours meant the campground gate would close at 7:00 PM and she had just enough time to take a picture of the sign, her self portrait, and get out of there. She really wanted to stay overnight at the Alabama Upper Top Campground, but she had to drop off the rental car by noon the next day so she hurried back to Florida to reach the last highpoint. Along the way, she passed a sign "Helen Keller's Birthplace and School for the Deaf" and was very disappointed she could not stop by as she admired Helen Keller.

Lakewood Park (also Britton Hill), Florida

At 11:30 PM, in the dark, she reached the final high point of her figure eight-12 highpoint marathon—Lakewood Park (also known as Britton Hill). Britton Hill is the smallest high point, ranking 50th at 345 feet. Miriam had to use her headlights to see the spot, knowing the area was ripe with poisonous snakes and nocturnal creatures. She used the flash on her camera at this high point so close to midnight. Exhausted after driving through four states in one day, she stopped at a Walmart parking lot and slept there overnight.

Two days after she reached her last summit in Florida, she went back to work. The peace and quiet she felt during her drive to the high points was replaced by anger. Another crew member quit and as a result, the crew boss held a meeting with the crew. During the meeting, the crew boss informed the crew that there was only one person he could depend on (one of the male members of the crew). Angry, Miriam wrote a letter to her crew boss sharing how she felt about his announcement.

> *"I already wrote the note for the next meeting. I wrote 'I disagree that you depend on [name withheld] for bridge tasks while me,[names withheld] carry wood and tools and clean up all of the time. You tend to work yourself. How can we get the benefit of your experience before we get home? Your role as a leader is to teach, observe and improve the crew's skills. I want to be prepared to see an interviewer in Oregon and if I want to apply to become a Trail Coordinator, I want to be ready with new skills taught by the leader of the crew..."*
> *(Miriam' Richards' journal October 20, 2000)*

Miriam did not feel that her situation improved. She was thankful that she had letters from her family and her friends, especially Hilary White, to help her get through the times she felt isolated and frustrated. She fought with the SCA to get an airplane ticket home, instead of taking the train again. She had faithfully done all she was expected to do. After a period of time she had begun to feel trapped by the fences around the dorm compound with an electric gate that only the boss was allowed to open.

On the airplane, she was so emotionally distraught from her experience that she became physically ill, vomiting throughout the trip home. Fortunately, a nurse happened to be sitting across from Miriam and helped her through the trip. When Hilary and her husband Robert were eagerly awaiting Miriam's arrival from her plane, the nurse somehow guessed they were waiting for Miriam, so she told them that Miriam had been very sick on her flight and would be disembarking soon.

Looking back, Miriam realizes that she was given an opportunity to see 12 summits. She felt that sacrifices she made were worth the experience, although she may never again volunteer for a trail crew so far from home. While she experienced what she felt was terrible leadership, she also thought about the qualities that would make a good leader and has applied them to her daily interactions with other people. Overall, it was a different experience, if not a great one, and it made her appreciate her home, and the people in her community, that much more.

Hilary White on top of Mauna Kea, Hawaii

Mauna Kea: Through Hilary White's Eyes

Miriam searched for low cost airfare on the internet through Travelocity and found two round trip seats on a Canadian Airline from Vancouver,B.C. to Kona Hawaii for $120 (U.S. dollars) each. The airport charges and other fees brought the price a little higher. The highest mountain in Hawaii is Mauna Kea located on the big island named Hawaii. Miriam and I drove from Oregon to Vancouver, B.C. on January 26, 2001 to visit Miriam's friend, Sharon Lee, who is deaf. We left Miriam's car at Sharon's, promising to see them the following Sunday at the Deaf Church, and took a bus for $2 (Canadian dollars) to the airport.

We needed our U.S. passports since we were leaving Canada to enter the U.S. in Hawaii. Royal Aviation provided great meals and topped it off with Irish Cream. The plane stopped briefly in Kaua'i for fueling. We stayed in Kona with my relative, Arlita who told us to get to bed early because we would go snorkeling immediately after breakfast.

The best snorkeling spot in Hawaii must be the one where Arlita goes almost every morning. We saw a huge green sea turtle sunning itself on the rocks. It looked dead at first, but we soon saw that it was alive. Arlita told us there was a $500 fine for touching these turtles because they are endangered. When we saw the turtles swimming, they had such grace that Miriam went so far to say they swam like angels, a great difference from their clutsy movements on land. The fish are incredibly colorful and cartoon-like. Eels hide low in little caves with only their heads showing. This was January in Kona but felt like summer in Oregon.

After Arlita pulled into her driveway, we stepped out of the car and saw a yellow jacket or bee that she'd just run over being quickly devoured by other bugs that left as quickly as they'd come. I had seen this on nature programs of rain forests but never witnessed it so close. There were geckos crawling on trees. Arlita said they were in the house as well. She had unscreened windows left open.

Rather than fight off the creatures, she relaxed and adopted the philosophy that the house is set in their domain so if anyone is invading someone's territory it is us invading theirs. The zig-zag spider rested easily on its web, knowing that Arlita was not going to swat it down. The brown cane spider is extremely large. Miriam saw one out on the lanai (Hawaiian word for porch). Arlita just said, *"Oh, that one is from the sugar cane."* We never ate a meal indoors while we were there. Every morning, Arlita poured seed into a feeder made of bamboo on her lanai. Miriam was particularly taken by the beauty of saffron finches and Brazilian cardinals. She noticed that the birds all arrived at once and within five minutes were gone.

The next day Miriam and I prepared for our trip to Mauna Kea. She rented a four-wheel drive vehicle as required to drive the road to the mountain. Along Highway 11 that circles the island, there are many messages left on lava written in lettering made by placing white coral "rocks" against the dark lava. These can easily be seen beside the road. Flowers are placed by some of the names. Arlita calls that "island graffiti." It does not have to be whitewashed to clear it, the coral may be rearranged.

We drove out Saddle Road to 9,300 foot Mauna Kea State Park Visitors Center in time for the opening at 7 PM. We saw a captioned film about the observatories. Volunteers outside set powerful telescopes for us to view Saturn which looked like a white plastic toy tilted sideways. Miriam was excited to see the Andromeda Galaxy. It was fitting to learn about the mountain prior to our night climb.

Miriam ate a banana, then folded down the back seat so we could doze off for a few hours in the back of the vehicle to acclimatize prior to our climb. Miriam felt she was having digestive difficulty that occurs sometimes after having eaten a banana. She told me that she had some reservations about climbing with her stomach bothering her. High altitude can add to such a problem. I knew that Miriam would be disappointed to have come all this way and have to turn around. We filled out the climbing permit and deposited it in the box and woke at midnight to begin our climb. There were no other climbers on the mountain the entire day or night. We could not find the trail as described by rangers so we ended up going the whole way by dirt road, four miles longer. We climbed under clear skies for 9 hours straight. It's kind of like going up a very steep wheelchair ramp. I think it leveled off briefly only one time for a few yards. There were some switchbacks, but no let up from the monotony of the steep grade. When you see the road signs with a triangle under a truck warning of a steep downgrade 7%, that is what this entire road is like. There are warning signs everywhere to set the gears low or you'll burn out your brakes and it cannot be done without a 4 X 4. We saw the same lovely sky we'd seen in Africa exactly a year ago in February. We saw so many stars without interference of city lights. There were many shooting stars that night. This time we were without the company of a group or any landmarks to measure our progress, just up, up and up.

The night was very cold with a mild wind. We wondered what the baggage inspectors may have thought looking through our clothing bound for Hawaii. We wore long polypropelene underwear, fleece pants and windproof pants over those two layers. We had thick wool socks over silk liners and heavy trekking boots. Four layers of shirts of succeeding thickness were under a water-proof jacket. Two hats were worn under the jacket hood with a headlamp strapped over them. Our hands remained inside two layers of gloves. We stopped only briefly to discuss anything that came up. It is a little complicated to watch someone sign because their headlamp shines in your face. It is almost as difficult to move your hands in sign language while wearing thick gloves. Of course mittens would have been worse, keeping four fingers pressed together with only the thumb free to move independently. But Miriam and I have known one another long enough to understand each other in spite of the cumbersome gloves.

Our visibility was limited to seeing the road immediately in front of us. Rock cairns that mark the trail on the sides would have been very difficult to see at night. We did not notice them until we were on the way back down after sunrise. It was just as well that we were adding the four extra miles by road as it would have been easy to get lost in the dark. My night vision is very poor and Miriam's is quite good, so she had me wear the headlamp. I think it was annoying for her when I turned to walk backwards since my headlamp shone back at her. But my legs were so sore from the drudgery of walking up that "ramp" that I had to switch to a back-pedaling step. It's like those "moon-walk" type machines at the exercise clubs, it is a relief to go backwards after going 20 minutes forward. As we approached two miles of the summit, the dirt road changed to pavement and there was a white line I could follow backwards with my head lamp off. I developed a good rhythm in this backwards motion and it wasn't so bad. I think you can go on forever like that. When you are tired and it is dark, you sort of forget where you are and just sleep on your feet.

Of course we had to remember to keep drinking lots and lots of water to keep acclimatized because water gets the oxygen to your brain. There is only half as much oxygen at the summit as there is at sea level where we were snorkeling yesterday. Miriam had one problem with some diarrhea, most likely due to the banana. I had brought along GU, the same product I ate in Africa that is easily digestible protein. We had read that many people get altitude sickness on Mauna Kea. The film about building observatories spoke of many workers who succumbed to the sickness, some of the brightest scientists in the world. One scientist kept cutting a piece of metal again and again because it wasn't big enough to fit the area he wanted it to cover. There were no houses on the way up Mauna Kea so the scientists drove up from near sea level, contributing to their chances for altitude illness.

When we were around 11,000 feet elevation, I saw some strange stars shooting off my headlamp and realized it was a light mist. My body was so well covered with warm clothing that I saw the mist before feeling it on my face. The mist did not hamper our trek and it may have helped settle the dust on the road. Only about four off-road vehicles with observatory scientists passed us going up and down. In the daytime we could see the insignia of the country they represented: Japan, France, Canada, or the University of Hawaii. We had been told that you would not want to walk the road in daytime with all the dust and smell of burning brakes from the four-wheel drive vehicles.

This has got to be about the ugliest mountain I have ever climbed so it is just as well that we did it in the dark. I think it is a good choice for an observatory location as you might as well be trekking on a moonscape. We could see pretty Mauna Loa in the distance. There hadn't been any creatures along the way of any kind, not even a bug. There were no plants. The most lovely view of the stars visible along our journey made up for the lack of foliage. The moon was crescent shaped, not large enough to light our path. Now we were looking forward to sunrise, hoping it would show us that we were almost to our goal.

Eventually we rounded more crossbacks and started to see various summits. We were looking for the rounded observatories but they were not visible from the approach side. There were summits of sorts along the way and we would get hopeful that we were almost there, then as we got higher than those "summits," realized they were like illusions and we looked for another candidate. Mauna Kea is not one rounded top, it is a series of many rounded tops. Later from the true summit, we would see into the craters of those hills on top of the massive mountain.

When a vehicle heading for an observatory drove past us, I tried to follow its route to determine which way or how much further the summit would be. The vehicle disappeared then the lights reappeared up higher, and judging by the time it took to reappear, we knew the switchbacks would be very long.

From this high altitude, the sunrise beginning so far below was spectacular and serene. The ocean appeared massive compared to the island as it did from the airplane. Mauna Kea, 13,796 feet measures 32,000 feet from the sea floor making it the world's highest mountain from bottom to top. As the day brightened, we were able to see some observatories, but not all on the same hill.

The eight domed buildings are spread over several hills at the top. From the University of Hawaii and Japanese observatories sitting next to each other we could see an altar made of bamboo and rushes with a path leading to it. So we headed downwards across the lava and then up toward the true summit. The wind was exceptionally strong as we neared it. We put our ski hats into our daypacks. I replaced mine with an expedition hat to shade my face and neck from the strong Hawaiian sun. There is a clip in the back of my hat to hold it onto my jacket. With the strong winds, I was not sure the clip would hold. So I held onto my hat with one hand on my head.

Miriam and I like to make a practice of summiting at the same time so we adjusted our steps to match as we arrived at Hawaii's highest point. We saw fresh fruit and coins on the Hawaiian structure at the summit. Miriam's camera was not working. I photographed the bench mark and we took turns photographing one another. No one was anywhere around to photograph us together. With the wind blowing so hard, we could not remain on the summit much longer.

There is a special excitement to summiting when you have worked so hard for it on your own two feet. It is important to take a few moments to breathe in the fresh air and just be self-righteous! Miriam described her amazement at seeing the ocean, earth and blue sky all in 3-D. In ASL, the sign meaning *"been there"* is *"touch-finish."* The English term *"been there"* is so vague, it could mean that you simply rode past the place. The sign *"touch-finish"* is more concrete and its true meaning melded with our hands on the bench mark. This was the moment for us to take pride in ourselves. I felt grateful to Miriam for bringing me to this place. I took a picture of her with an observatory in the background and the camera was slow to react. This is the same thing that happened to my camera on the summit of Mt. Kilimanjaro. My pack was not insulated enough to protect my camera from the extreme cold during our climb on both mountains.

Once we started back down Mauna Kea, we removed many layers of our winter clothing since the morning sun was warming us sooner than expected. A Hawaiian man and his grand-daughter offered us a ride down and we accepted. Miriam's knee was beginning to bother her and she thought she may need to have additional surgery. Now we got to see the route we'd walked and it was very steep. The driver told us that he does not see many mountain climbers on Mauna Kea, most people get 4 X 4s and drive up. He congratulated us on our feat. We were dropped off at the 9,300 foot level where Miriam had parked at the Mauna Kea Visitor Center. Miriam felt obliged to purchase a paper weight replica of the summit benchmark. We were tired.

Miriam wanted to circle the entire island. She turned in the 4-wheel-drive vehicle and traded it for a cheaper sedan. We visited Hawaii Volcanoes National Park and swam at one of the few white sand beaches at the north end of the Island. The waves were quite large. Miriam wanted to warm up on the beach first so I went ahead and body surfed for a while. Miriam went in the water after I had finished. Miriam had never experienced such strong currents with the waves that toss the swimmers to where you feel like you're in a washing machine, not knowing which way is up and which is down. She did not realize the current had pulled her farther out and that she had become trapped by another wave and another in rapid succession. She cart-wheeled in the water and could not breathe as she struggled to get out. The lifeguard was in ready position to rescue her but she managed to get out on her own. She was scared to death. This happened on her birthday, February 2, 2001.

We returned to Arlita's place. For her birthday celebration, Miriam treated us to a Luau on a beach where a pig was roasting underground. By chance there was an interpreter visiting with her husband from Canada. Arlita loved seeing the grace of the interpreter's signing. Watching an interpreter was different from seeing Miriam and me converse in ASL. Hawaiian dancers performed on an outdoor stage. The "King and Queen" arrived by boat carrying torches. Miriam purchased a special flower vase decorated with three green sea turtle sculptures as a special memory of having swum with them.

The last day on the island, after one last snorkeling adventure, Miriam drove to a hardware store in Hilo and purchased the necessary parts to repair Arlita's carport cupboards. Miriam worked her best to balance the louvred doors. Our flight back to Canada on Royal Aviation was slated for a near midnight departure. After Arlita dropped us off at Kona airport, we were told that our plane would not leave until tomorrow. The delay was due to a flat tire which happened when the plane was in Mexico. The Cozmul airport did not have any spare tires to fit the plane. So Royal Aviation shuttled us to the most plush hotel in Kona for one night before shuttling us back to the airport for 8 AM departure. We realized we would miss the Deaf Church service in Canada and we'd have to drive straight back to Oregon since both of us had to work the next day. At least there was no traffic that night, just an easy 8 hour drive back home. We arrived in Corvallis at 3:00 AM.

Miriam on top of Charles Mound, Illinois

Hilary and Miriam Summit Five Mid-Western States

Hilary White's Perspective

Miriam and I flew into Chicago 10:52 PM on June 12, 2001, rented a small car and headed north on toll roads, stopping briefly to throw our exact change of 40 cents into the plastic collection baskets as we passed toll points. The price was worth it because cars were not entering the highway from the sides, so there was no need to change lanes. We were heading towards Wisconsin for our first of five mid-western state summits.

Timm Hill, Wisconsin

The drive to Wisconsin was relatively uneventful. Nothing was out there except trees and fields alongside the roads. The front passenger seat folded all the way down flush with the back seat so I just slept through most of the night until Miriam stopped for a turtle as large as a raccoon crossing the road. She asked me to get out and give it a push to hurry it along, but as I looked at it, it's long tail and legs spun itself around quickly and gave me a look as if to say *"You'd better not touch me, I'm a snapping turtle."* This one was not slow and friendly like a tortoise or the lovely sea turtles we snorkeled with in Hawaii.

The lakeside trees in this North Woods area of Wisconsin were lovely ash, birch and white cedar. It was 5:30 AM when we pulled up to the gated entrance to Timm's Hill. We decided to wait several hours for lightning to pass. Miriam pulled over alongside the road and we dozed for a few hours before the car started shaking and we woke to see that a man was trying to get our attention. By luck, we were sleeping in front of the house of the man who had the special tool to open the gate for us! He had to clear the fallen trees and repair power lines from the tornado that came through two days ago and was reluctant to open the road to the public. We explained we'd come all the way from Oregon to reach Timm's

Hill, Wisconsin's highest point. Fortunately he let us in. He pointed out fallen live power lines to avoid.

We headed up the trail as soon as the heavy rain and lightning passed and climbed the wooden tower on the summit. From 1,951 feet we could scan the view of the large lake below and the lush vegetation of beautiful Wisconsin, in the freshness of the early morning sunshine after a night's heavy rain. Because of the lightning scare, we did not delay. The caretaker of the park told me that there's only a one in a million chance of getting hit by the lightning. We took summit pictures as proof for Miriam's high point record. This summit was my fourth high point after Mt. Whitney, Borah Peak (Idaho) and Mauna Kea. This was Miriam's 21st state summit.

Mount Arvon, Michigan

Miriam hadn't had any sleep yet, since we'd pulled an all-nighter so now it was my turn to drive and Miriam's to sleep. I drove to the little section of Michigan that is separated from the rest of Michigan by Lake Superior, not that far from Wisconsin, so close to Canada. The Northwoods are lovely! The little towns are nice, some of them have a Scandinavian flavor. Land O'Lakes is a small town that is unincorporated, almost on the border as we were leaving Wisconsin. The directions took us to remote gravel roads way out in the boonies: 6.1 mile this way, then right at the fork and 17.7 miles that way, and so on, and so on, until we reached a gravel pit. We were a little confused by a sign at this point so backtracked, got out and searched. Finally a gravel truck driver came by and pointed in the direction of Mt. Arvon. *"I don't think you'd really want to go that far, though,"* he said, "*It's really way out there on a treacherous road more than six miles."*

We waited until the man drove off before proceeding through the gravel pit onward until we got to the bridge mentioned in the directions. It was questionable whether a car could make it safely across this narrow wooden bridge with boards falling away; it didn't appear to be more than a foot bridge. Our Chevrolet Metro was small and light and Miriam said, *"Just go fast!"* You know we made it or you wouldn't be reading our story. We went as far as the car could go, then got out and walked. I'd read that AAA wouldn't be able to tow us out of here and it was a long way back to civilization. The L'Anse Indian Reservation was out there somewhere. The top of Mt. Arvon was in deep woods; we found the sign and the register book at 1,979 feet. Someone had written of the ticks in these woods so we didn't plan to camp here. We headed west along Lake Superior where 10% of the world's fresh water is. Previously, when I thought of Michigan, I envisioned Detroit where they produce cars, now that image has changed considerably. Northern Michigan is spacious.

Eagle Mountain, Minnesota

The next day, Thursday, June 14, we continued across northern Wisconsin again to get around Lake Superior and head north along the coast of Minnesota towards Grand Marais, nearly to Canada. The shoreline reminded me of our trip along the bottom of the big Island Hawaii that Miriam and I took in February this year. There have been some rough storms along this road so the Native Americans named the rocky shoreline area "Savage Castle." Signs warning of moose were everywhere but we never saw one here. I'd had too close an encounter with a moose while backpacking in Denali Wilderness.

We needed to obtain a permit to enter the Boundary Waters Canoe Area Wilderness. No motorized vehicles were allowed, so we knew we'd be again entering some pretty wild country. When we'd checked ahead about camping, we learned there were bears, timber wolves, and moose along this trail, *"But no one camps there in tents because of the swarms of black flies,"* we were forewarned, *"You should get mosquito netting for your head."*

We headed up Gun Flint trail past Caribou trail, turning this way and that for this and that many miles, until at last we ended up at the trailhead for Eagle Mountain, Minnesota. We dropped our trail permit into a box. There was only one other car way out here. We didn't have to wait to find out if the mosquito netting was really needed, swarms of little mosquitos began biting as soon as we opened the car door. The weather was warm but we kept our long sleeves, long pants and boots on. The trail was rocky with roots woven throughout, we had to complete this trail in daylight or we'd trip over every step. This would not be a trail for someone to need to hike on to get help for a twisted ankle. We did not take trekking poles on the airplane so we'd have to be cautious.

I had a Minnesota Northwoods Wildflower book with me. The bunchberry flower was everywhere along the forest floor, a white flower in the middle of corduroy leaves, no berries yet. The black bears will be back for those after we've left. We crossed some wooden boards spanning the swampy ponds, knowing this would be a favorite haunt for moose among the tiny wild callas. Farther on I spotted bluebead lily. It's a yellow flower atop a tall thin stalk that will produce inedible blue berries after we've gone. Little papers were along the path, fallen from the paper birch trees or messages left by Hansel and Gretel.

Miriam's knee was holding out after her recent surgery so we moved along pretty quickly. We vowed to stop at least every half hour to drink water. It isn't easy getting a sip of water with mosquito netting over your head. You must either sip the water through the netting or let in a handful of mosquitoes. The worst bites I received were on my neck from some angry mosquitoes probably trying to get back out. Oh well, those were my souvenirs, proof that I really climbed these mountains way out in the middle of nowhere. We don't exactly travel like tourists, but we do have adventures. I had gotten ahead of Miriam, distracted by flowers, when I heard a strange loud noise very close to me. The trail was socked in between thickets of growth so I could not see very far into the greenery. It's like looking in a hedge for a moose, the most likely candidate for that odd sound. I slowly pulled off my mosquito netting to get a closer look since Miriam was behind me and I did not want her in danger either. The noise sounded again, perhaps a warning for us to get out of its territory. So we proceeded quickly, stealing glances behind us as we moved up the trail.

We soon arrived at the false summit and watched closely for signs of the true summit. We had to backtrack when we missed some rock cairns off the trail. Following a series of well placed cairns, we left the trail until we finally reached the large plaque cemented to a boulder telling the story of Eagle Mountain and that this igneous rock is over a billion years old. What we could see far below was carved by ancient glaciers. Ulysses S. Grant II mistakenly named another summit the high point when he surveyed parts of Minnesota. Eagle Mountain was located years later by air surveyors at 2,301 feet. We took each other's pictures and enjoyed reading the amazing accounts people wrote in the register book. This was my 6th state summit and Miriam's 23rd. Miriam indicated that she is deaf, I wrote that we'd summited one continent high point, Mt. Kilimanjaro.

We stopped back at the false summit to admire the view, seeing nothing in the miles and miles except wilderness. It was breathtaking, greener than green and lakes upon lakes. We headed down hill. It was not far before I heard that strange sound again in the same vicinity we'd passed climbing up. I remember hearing people talking about special moose calls, but don't recall what they sounded like. This did sound as if it could get angry. Miriam told me to raise my hand when I heard the sound but to just keep going. So we whizzed by stealthily. My heart was pounding and I kept checking back. In Alaska, they told me that an angry moose can be worse than a grizzly bear, they can kick and stomp you to death. There aren't any pointers for defending yourself against them. Standing up tall and looking tough doesn't quite cut it with a moose. Rolling over and pretending you're dead doesn't impress them either.

Hawkeye Point, Iowa

Miriam and I stayed overnight near Minneapolis with Miriam's sorority sister, Sheila Farcy from Gallaudet University. As tennis partners at Gallaudet they were champions as well as Delta Epsilon sisters. Sheila introduced us to her deafblind friend who knew many of our deafblind friends in Oregon and Washington, small world. Her husband is a chef and we had the privilege of tasting his incredible dishes.

It was a lovely drive to Iowa. Minnesota is so lush and green, even greener than Oregon at this time of the year, perhaps because of all the rain showers and lightning storms. I saw three jackrabbits that had died at the sides of the roads; they have very long legs and looked like small kangaroos. We saw a huge herd of elk from the highway. There were wide expanses of flat green fields, each with a farmhouse and silo encircled by leafy trees. We just barely went over the border into Iowa since the state high point is so far to the northwest corner of the state.

We had already written from Oregon to notify the Sterlers that we would be coming. We had to go right through the middle of their farm to get Merrill Sterler's attention since he was driving a tractor. We did not want to startle him. He said he'd been expecting us. He led us to the high point at the end of the cattle trough. The ledger book was full of fascinating stories from people from all over. Mr. Sterler told us to get key chains from the register box showing the high point and elevation 1,670 feet on a map of Iowa. Donna Sterler rode out on a tractor waving to us with a camera. She asked if she could take our pictures and took another using Miriam's camera. She told us that she grew up on the farm, used to have cattle. She said that her father told her that he knew they were living at a high point because the trains going by would be really chugging as they neared their farm, stopping to leave a few cars and returning to pick them up after having dropped some off further up the line.

It was not until 1972 that Iowa was surveyed topographically and the high point was found to be at this farm. It was originally thought to be at a grain elevator Donna pointed out to us 10 miles in the distance. She said they waited up until 4 AM to greet a group of motorcycling highpointers who ended up mailing them the book they'd written about the lower 48 states they'd completed, one of them a high school senior.

Donna pointed out the damage to a shed from a heavy storm just two days before. We were lucky we missed it. All the neighboring farms were also heavily damaged. Donna asked Miriam which state she thought would have the most dangerous highpoint. Miriam guessed Alaska. Donna said, "*Rhode Island is the most dangerous.*" She'd heard that the man living on land accessing the trail to the high point pulled a gun on someone trespassing. There were only four special dates open each year to highpointers visiting Rhode Island. If the man yelled at Miriam to stop she would not be able to hear him and could be shot. In contrast, the Sterlers were the most welcoming summit greeters we'd ever encountered.

We took turns driving back to Zombrota, Minnesota, to visit with Sarah Nygaard, my step-sister and her family. As we entered the town of Zombrota, population 2,400, was having a parade, celebrating their annual Covered Bridge Days. We looked for Sarah at both parks among all the festivities knowing she would be helping with something. We spotted her driving a tractor in the parade, and reunited after 30 years of not having seen one another.

It was wonderful seeing all the excitement with many German and Norwegian families. Once we met up with Sarah and her family, they introduced us to many of their friends and relatives. Sarah explained the tractor "float" was for her daughter Chelsea's Girl Scout troop. We watched the parade with Harlan and their four-year-old daughter Michelle. The whole town lined the streets. This had to be the best parade I've ever seen because it was made up entirely of local people.

We cheered as the huge fire trucks, the marching band and Flower Guild passed by. A mower was popping wheelies and chasing a small tractor. There were very small children and very old townspeople. Harlan knew them all and told us how many years so and so owned the trucking company or which school the marching band was from. It was neat just watching the people on the sidewalks this warm evening in Lake Wobegon. We almost felt we belonged there.

The next day, Father's Day, we bicycled all over Zumbrota guided by Harlan who showed us many century old homes and favorite places he used to play when he was a little boy. Families were watching the baseball game in the park or swimming in the pool. We saw Sugar Loaf Hill the day after having seen a school bus printed with that name in the parade. This surely had to be where Garrison Keeler got his stories. Harlan could not get very far without having someone calling out to him. He told us that Minnesotans always say they are *"Pretty good,"* no matter if they are really not so good or really super good. He told us that Minnesotans say *"You know."*

Our evening was nice sitting out by a bonfire in the backyard watching the lightning off in the distance. The sky lit up with the most fantastic cloud show and light show. Sarah pointed out the opposing movements of groups of clouds swirling around to set up the beginnings of a tornado. From where we sat we could clearly see how it happens. The news was reporting tornado warnings for the night and the next day. Sarah told us that if we could not outrun a tornado with our car then to get out of it and lie down in a ditch because a tornado funnel could lift up the entire car. She showed us her basement hideaway where they hide under the stairs when sirens warn of tornados. Miriam and Harlan played a game of pool in the basement.

The Nygaard family house is more than 100 years old, complete with playroom and two stories. It has a lot of personality. Sarah's grandmother used to come to this house to play with a friend. She showed us the house behind hers that her great grandparents built when they came here from Norway. We know we could enjoy staying for a week but had to head back to Illinois. They had made us feel such a part of their town it was hard to say goodbye.

Charles Mound, Illinois

The drive was lovely back through Wisconsin to northern Illinois. Getting to the highpoint of Illinois, you can visit the "Field of Dreams" movie location near the Iowa/Illinois border not far from Dyersrville. Coming down toward the Mississippi River we could see the bathrub rings the river had carved at flood stage on high cliffs bordering the roadway. It was a really round-about way to get to Charles Mound. As we approached, the lightning was hitting full bore with no let up and the rain was heavy. We waited in the car at the road leading to the Wuebbels farm. Once the lightning moved away from us and the rains weakened, we made a run for it to the high point. I left my glasses in the car, but Miriam had to carry her camera to get the proof she needed for her summit goals. The lightning was striking in the distance. I've read that you watch for your hair to rise on your arms or notice an ozone smell and neither happened. The distant bolts are still scary since they really light up the sky.

One of Miriam's high point books indicates that three states can be viewed from this point, but we found the benchmark, filled out the register quickly, exchanged the camera and left as soon as we could. Charles Mound, 1,235 feet, was our 5th state summit this week-long trip, Miriam's 25th and my 8th state high point.

We had a lovely trip all the way, except in fast paced city of Chicago, and arrived in Portland, Oregon, around midnight. Just before Miriam turned the car into our neighborhood, she slowed to watch two foxes cross the road into the open fields.

Kelly Butterworth and Miriam Richards in front of the Rhode Island high point sign

14 NorthEast States in 9 Days
Excerpts from Miriam Richards' Journal

Miriam decided to take in another high point marathon, this time with various friends she had met during her Gallaudet years. She started out July 21, 2001, ending her high point marathon on July 30, 2001. She summited 14 mountains during that time. Below are excerpts from the journal she kept.

Mount Davis, Pennsylvania

I called Debbie Richards, a friend I had worked with at the Gallaudet University post office, to ask if she would be interested in doing some highpointing with me. She had never heard of such a thing, but we hadn't seen each other for a long time and she was game to go.

It happened to be Debbie's day off work when I arrived on July 21, 2001, so we drove to Mount Davis, Pennsylvania, a 3,213 foot drive-up. I was surprised to find that the high point benchmark was not on the ground, but imbedded in a boulder. If it had been a drive-through like Burger King, we would not have "touched" the state highpoint. This is one of the 21 state high points that may be reached by wheelchair. After approximately 100 steps, Debbie exclaimed, *"That's it!"*

A tower is situated on Pennsylvania's high point, and I felt inclined to climb it. Debbie did not see any sense in climbing the dangerous-looking structure so she waited below as I reached up to the metal bars and climbed all the way to the top. From the very top of "Mount" Davis, I saw lovely rolling fields of Pennsylvania.

Backbone Mountain, Maryland

After Pennsylvania, Debbie and I followed the map, driving on country roads between fields and farms to Maryland. There were no signs to indicate the location of the state high point. A red spray paint zigzag pattern was the only indicator of the trail. It was not a welcoming trail. We hiked uphill two miles round trip, through deep forest. We could reach our hands over the border to West Virginia, but unfortunately it was not anywhere near West Virginia's highest point. Debbie was becoming more intrigued with the state high points venture. We opened the registry box and pulled out certificates to register our accomplishment of having reached Backbone Mountain, 3,360 feet. The total trek took us about an hour.

Spruce Knob, West Virginia

From Maryland to West Virginia we enjoyed the beautiful blue spruce trees in their natural habitat as opposed to the many farm grown Christmas trees in my home state of Oregon. Spruce Knob is located on the east side of West Virginia. We dissected the state driving horizontally across it to another drive up at 4,863 feet. Debbie and I walked to the tower. I explained to her that most state high points also have benchmarks. She searched the area until she found it on the ground and photographed my boot posing with the benchmark. We had just completed three state high points all in one day and it was beginning to get dark so we stopped by a motel for the night. Debbie was worn out due to the intense driving, but eager to do more the next day.

Campbell Hill, Ohio

Back when I was strategizing for this 14 states in 9 days trip, I called ahead to the Vocational Rehabilitation Center (VRC) in Ohio asking for permission to drive on their road as it was private property. They gave their consent to let me drive through on this Saturday, July 22, 2001. I did not realize at the time of my call that they normally close on week-ends, causing me anxiety as we approached Campbell Hill. I noticed a church named "High Point." As we made a sharp right turn toward VRC, the gate was open! I was thrilled! We followed the road up a gentle slope to a mere 1,550 foot high point amongst tall trees towering overhead. A high pole held the American Flag. I was highly excited upon completing Ohio's high point and so grateful that someone left the gate open for me that I drove down the hill faster than I normally would. A police officer had been clocking me and I was ticketed for speeding. I felt foolish.

Hoosier High Point, Indiana

I drove ever so cautiously after having received a speeding ticket. I had called ahead to obtain permission to drive across private farm property in order to locate the Hoosier High Point. Fortunately, Indiana's highest point, 1,257 feet, is just across the border from Ohio, so we did not have to drive very far. The elevation hardly changed. However we viewed miles of cornfields on the Indiana side. We turned onto the dirt road driving past the farmhouse to a stile, wooden steps built for people to cross over the fence to the trees. A cornfield was on the other side of the road. We photographed one another next to the high point marker. We had completed two state high points for the day when we drove back to Maryland. It was Debbie's turn to drive. She sped back to her home state and a policeman pulled her over. Her speeding was waived. I told her, *"Not fair!"*

Ebright Azimuth (Tower Hill), Delaware

Debbie contacted her friend Richard Blake to join us on our mission to find the highest point in the state of Delaware. Richard said, *"What! State high point? I have never heard of that!"* Debbie and Richard followed me in his car. Delaware is a tall narrow state with its highpoint at the high north pointed end of the state. He couldn't believe it when he saw that the high point was right in the middle of the street! We read the sign on the side of the road claiming Ebright Azimuth, Delaware (previously named Tower "Hill") to be 448 feet elevation. It was a busy street. We had to wait for the traffic to clear before running into the center of the road and photographing one another over a blue circle of spray paint on the pavement. Then we had to hurry back to the side of the road just in time before more cars came along.

As we were about to leave, a lady came out of the house where we were standing. Richard interpreted for Debbie and me. The lady explained that her house happened to be located on the border covering both states: Delaware and Pennsylvania. She explained that her bed was in one state while her husband slept in the other, yet their beds were side by side. I asked her which state she must pay her taxes. She told me that was a good question.

That was the last time I saw Richard before he was deployed to Iraq as an MP. I think of him and hope he is alright.

High Point, New Jersey

After saying goodbye and good luck to Richard and Debbie, I drove far north to New Jersey. Again, the state high point was to be found at the very top of the state, almost in New York. New Jersey, the Garden State, is a lovely state, but I was very tired now that I was back to driving alone. I had so enjoyed the company of Debbie and Richard and the opportunity to chat along the way. When I arrived at "High Point" New Jersey, 1,803 feet, I was puzzled to see a monument that was a replica of the tall monument that I had seen in Washington D.C. back when I was a Gallaudet University student. I asked some people nearby if they would be willing to take my picture for me, which they did. Tired from the long drive I looked for a campground but there were none. I could not even find a restaurant so I drove to Salisbury where I found the only hotel in the town for $125 per night. My credit limit was $500 so I had to be careful not to go over that amount on this trip.

Mount Frissell, Connecticut

The next day, July 24, 2001, I set out for the next high point on my list. Connecticut had the most beautiful white oak trees. The trail to Mount Frissell was 2.5 miles round trip, a very easy stroll up a hill and over. However, the trail would be too narrow for a wheelchair. The reason I think of these things is because I am aware that someday in the future, my MS may get to the point where I become wheelchair-bound. I would love to share my joy of highpointing adventures with people who cannot climb high mountains, but would love to get out and about as I do. As I walked on this trail I thought about how this could perhaps be made accessible.

A snake woke me up from my musing. Up and over a roller coaster hill, then up again to Mount Frissell, 2,380 feet, I happened to have walked right past it without realizing it and crossed over into the state of New York. Once I realized I was heading downhill, I turned around and looked back, to find a cairn marking the spot and stopped to take a picture of myself. I found it fascinating that so many state high points happen to be on borders and corners of states as this one was. I suppose the surveyors found these high points convenient when they laid the states out? Part of the rock structure was in New York while the other was in Connecticut. I wished that I could kill two birds with one stone and bag two different state high points in the same location, but no such luck.

Mount Greylock, Massachusetts

I drove Highway 7 heading to Massachusetts where the next high point would also be at the far northwest corner of the state. When I arrived, I saw the Appalachian Trail passed through Mount Greylock. A war memorial was built right over the highest point in the state to memorialize Massachusettans who died in wars. It appeared to be open to visitors around the clock so I went inside to observe the state high point on the floor, at 3,491 feet.

Next to the building was a bunkhouse with a big sign aimed to please hikers passing through via the famous “A.T.” Showers and a small restaurant offered solace to tired hikers. I know the Appalachian Trail is very popular with hikers but I would rather hike the Pacific Crest Trail in the west.

I drove to a nice campground at Adirondak Loj in New York. It was a very small town where I found some pizza before climbing into my tent.

Mount Marcy, New York

Last night, it was nice to sleep in my own single-person tent at Adirondack Loj. I had to get up very early this morning (July 25, 2001) because the trail was 14.8 miles round trip. I expected that I would hike more than 10 hours. Before departure, I had to register my hike at the trailhead. I was so excited and looked forward to another adventure and started hiking through white birch forests. It was important for me to watch for the yellow blazes on trees marking the trail.

After about two miles, I enjoyed walking across a bridge at a dam and watching the clear water flowing. After crossing the bridge, I was lost for a short time because I missed a yellow blaze. The trail split in two and I was not sure which trail I should take. A family appeared surprised to see me and I asked the father to point me in the right direction. I was relieved and immediately the trail changed to a steep upgrade. I was surprised that I hiked slowly. I passed two streams: Phelps Brook and Indian Falls.

I repeatedly stopped for a lot of breaks. My problem was possibly related to my MS. At that time, I had no idea what was wrong with me. However my mind won over my physical limitations. I feel very fortunate that I have a good strong mind and spirit. That is what is unique about me. I stopped and looked up searching for the summit. I said to myself, "*Oh no, the summit is still very far away!*" I consciously forced myself to focus on the Mt. Marcy landscape which offers a variety of flowers, trees and animals.

I saw a wooden sign with arrows indicating the distance to the summit, only 1.5 miles to go! After passing the Hopkins Trail, I came out of the woods to open space. Then I leapt up rocky terrain. All of a sudden I could see several cairns that people had placed, showing me the way. I kept climbing toward the summit and finally made it to 5,344 feet after having walked non-stop for eight hours. The weather was perfect with a very light breeze. I searched for the benchmark as it took priority over my need to rest. I took a picture of myself with my shadow on the Mount Marcy benchmark.

It turned out to be really neat! I sat down and ate my lunch. I was surprised to see Lake Placid in the distance. I thoroughly enjoyed the view.

I had made the mistake of not bringing extra socks. It was very humid and perspiration contributed to bad blisters on both feet. I struggled to climb down in seven hours. Several people who passed me worried about me as I struggled to climb down. They said they wished to help carry me. They offered to have a look at my feet and then put blister pads on them. So sweet of them! At last I returned to the trailhead and signed off in the register. I slept at the same campsite one more night because I was too worn out to do anything else but sleep.

Mount Mansfield, Vermont

I studied my map and noticed that between New York and Vermont I could save time taking a ferry. Otherwise, I would have to drive my rental car around half the state. It was only a short drive from Lake Placid to Burlington by ferry. I saw two big factories that produced Ben & Jerry's Ice Cream and Teddy Bears. I wished I could tour both, but time was very limited.

That morning, July 26, 2001, I drove to Stowe, Vermont where the high point, Mount Mansfield, is located in a ski resort. I remembered having read a book explaining three choices of trails to reach the summit. I chose to ride the ski lift because of my bad blisters and also because I enjoyed riding ski lifts. It gave me a cheerful start to my hike of the day. I got off the ski lift and saw a sign that warned climbers not to climb this trail alone. "*Now they tell me!*" I said. I had come this far alone and had accomplished many feats alone that others thought could not be done, so I took the risk and went ahead alone hoping rangers would not send me back. I would act dumb and claim I had not read the marker.

I did not realize that the Cliff Trail involved Class 2 and 3 rock scrambling. I began to understand the need for someone to push me over the huge boulders. I took a gamble and with all my guts defeated each boulder. I saw several people turn around at this point. They were shocked to see me without a friend or companion. I shrugged to grin and bear it and continued forward. They warned me to please be careful. They told me they did not want to see me getting seriously injured. It was miraculous that I made it all the way to the summit without any mishaps.

When I reached the summit of Mount Mansfield, 4,393 feet, it was gorgeous looking down on the Vermont countryside. I could not believe that I did not bring my water bottle. I saw a ranger who had a water bottle and I politely asked the ranger to give me some water. I was so thirsty since I had worked so hard to be extra cautious. The ranger was happy to offer me water. I took a long rest before going down. Again I made it down past the difficult part and I was happy. I conquered a mountain that was not meant to be conquered alone. The next time I will bring my friend along. From Vermont to New Hampshire it was a longer distance driving the winding roads but I love weaving in and out among white birch trees. I arrived at a little town named Gorham and slept overnight in their only motel. I was worried about my blistered feet because my sores were not healing fast enough before another major climbing adventure in Maine later in the week.

Mount Washington, New Hampshire

Mount Washington, New Hampshire offered several accesses: Auto Road, Cog Railway and trails. I selected Auto Road because time was limited. I set out on July 27, 2007 early in the morning. I arrived at the Toll House and the gate was not yet open. I assumed that I was an early bird. I waited for a few minutes and the gate was opened at 8 AM. I paid the fee and drove eight miles, gaining 4,725 feet in elevation. The gentleman warned me about going down. I must repeatedly brake and drive very slowly because the road was a 12% grade. I drove slowly and saw some deer in the forests. Once I reached the Mt. Washington parking area, it was very windy. I could not stand up without holding on tightly to something firm. I had to balance my body by holding my arms out. I saw a huge plaque saying "The summit of Mt Washington on

April 12, 1934 recorded wind gusts of 231 mph!" My mouth opened in amazement. I approached a marker with a pile of rocks. Oh boy, it was so cold and this was July! I had to wear my jacket and fleece hat. Wind gusts tried to blow me away but I fought against them. At last I reached the top: 6,288 feet. I lay down next to the benchmark and took my picture. Then I entered the Tip Top House, which offered use of a computer, a restaurant, and a souvenir shop. The computer monitored the wind daily and it happened to record 40 mph when I was there. I tried to imagine what it was like for Appalachian Trail trekkers attempting to walk against the strong winds here on Mount Washington. This mountain had quite a history and I decided to buy souvenirs.

Mount Katahdin, Maine

New Hampshire to Mt. Katahdin, Maine was a long drive as it is located toward the north end of the state. I was only about an hour or so from New Brunswick and Quebec. I love the Maine countryside, its unique environment, city style, house style and ocean. Baxter State Park, very popular for the recreation it offers, is the only state park in Maine. I was concerned about camping. I arrived at Baxter State Park campground where the ranger told me he was sorry, but the campsite was full. He told me to turn back and look into one more public campsite. I checked the place but it was full too. I thought, *"Oh no, where can I sleep?"* My plans changed and I chose The Moose Inn, costing me all that I had left on my credit card for two nights. I made the right choice by staying at the Inn because I needed a comfortable sleep. The much needed restaurant food was included in the price. The bathroom had a big old-fashioned tub. My blisters needed the chance to heal. I went to bed early.

The next day, July 28, 2001, I could not figure out how to deal with a strenuous 10.4 mile trip hike toward Mount Katahdin because my blistered feet were not healing. The trailhead parking was full. I gambled by driving over a curb and parking on a dirt slope next to the cars in the lot. I registered and paid my $8.00 entry fee. I followed the Appalachian Trail (A.T.). Toward the beginning where the trail was flat and easy, I approached a huge boulder that blocked the trail access. I tried to figure out how to continue. I saw a handhold and jumped, attempting to get my fingers to grip, but slipped back down to the ground. I tried again, reaching a high edge to get a grip on the boulder. I was frustrated and hoped other hikers would come and help me, but no luck! I got short-tempered enough to get my adrenaline stirred up and jumped my hardest to reach the top. Pah! I made it! But I could not believe that I had ripped my shorts apart. I did not bring a needle and thread or duct tape to patch up the hole. I didn't care whether or not other hikers would see the hole in my pants because I wore long black boxers underneath.

I persisted hiking until I was confronted with another major problem. Once I left the treeline, I came to a cave with two large rocks leaning against each other. I yelled out, angry at the boulder. I knew that I would face the same boulders on the return trip. The iron bar placed for hikers to grab was too high because I am short. I turned around and was surprised to see a group. Wondering how long they had been standing there watching me struggle and yell at the boulder, I grinned like the Grinch. I wrote a note asking them to help me reach the iron bar. One of the men in the group worked at the Maryland School for the Deaf so he happened to know sign language. He lifted me up and I grabbed a single iron bar. It was hard work scrambling on boulders. I signed *"Thank you."*

With wishful thinking, I hoped that I would not encounter more boulder obstacles, but I was wrong. The ridge once called Devil has had its name changed to The Gateway. I was so freaked out and scared crossing it, I thought it should still be called Devil. It was a Class 2 but it looked to me more like a Class 4 technical climb. I had to climb very carefully, maneuvering around the boulder field with my backpack. The scenic view was stunning! I reached a small plateau. Then all that remained was a long gradual slope. I sighed with relief, but two miles remained to reach the summit.

I hiked at a snail's pace because of my painful feet. Many hikers passed me and I fought against the loose rocks. I started to cry before reaching the summit: 5,268 feet. The summit marker explained "A.T. trail from Mt. Katahdin to Georgia 2000 miles." I asked someone to take a picture of me with both the summit marker and benchmark. I cried again because my big question was how I would handle the pain when I descended.

A family saw me cry and they offered to assist me, hiking back down. I walked crippled all the way and faced the same boulder problems but what a blessing that the family was there supporting me! They helped me climb down as far as the iron bar. I told them *"Thank you so much!"* and waved good-bye. I hiked a total of 16 hours and arrived back at my car. I was relieved that it was unscathed in spite of its precarious parking position.

I drove back to the Inn and saw a menu posted "Special dinner 11 pounds of Lobster, $8.99." Wow! I walked straight to a table even though I was dirty and with the hole in my ripped shorts. Other diners were well dressed, but I was hungry and had earned the meal. The waitress brought a handsome lobster plate. My hands were shaking and I politely asked the lady to crack open the lobster body. She said of course, and was happy to do that for me. It was perfectly delicious! I felt I deserved a special reward. After dinner I took a hot bath to relax my painful body and foot. It was a very interesting day.

The next day I drove to Providence, Rhode Island where my former Gallaudet roommate Kelly Butterworth now lives. Kelly saw me wobbling horribly. She lifted my left arm and carried me into her house. Although Kelly and I were so happy to see each other again and would have liked to have headed off to some fun physical activity, we made an agreement to have one day off. I had not seen Kelly for a long time and we chatted non-stop. I recalled many wonderful memories that Kelly and I shared during our Gallaudet years. I always stayed with Kelly's parents for the holidays beginning when I was only 17 years old, 3,000 miles away from my home in Victoria, British Columbia. The best memory was when Kelly's family took me along on a sailboat for two weeks through St Thomas to the British Isles during the Christmas holidays.

Jerimoth Hill, Rhode Island

Kelly had never been to the high point in her own home state, Jerimoth Hill, 812 feet elevation. Of all the state high points, Rhode Island was notorious for being the most dangerous of all due to problems encountered by people crossing private property. One state highpointer reported having had a gun drawn on him for trespassing on private property. I was scared to death because both Kelly and I are deaf and would never be able to hear the warning, *"Get off my property or I will shoot."*

Kelly and I thought our best chances were to start off early in the morning on July 30, 2001. All we wanted to do was reach the high point and take pictures of ourselves. Our hearts were beating and our adrenalin running as we quickly made our way to the summit, perhaps two minutes, and ran back as quickly as possible. I missed Hilary's e-mail telling me that the man living in the house on the private property by Jerimoth Hill had passed away. We had been paranoid for nothing!

Later I learned that too many trespassers had bothered the man over the years, not just highpointers, but because of a variety of other factors such as the proximity to Brown University. He had been nice enough to assign specific dates for highpointers to cross his property rather than have people coming and going all the time. In retrospect, I understand.

All of the fourteen state high points that I had planned to reach were successfully completed in only nine days, some grueling some harrowing, and others easy going. It was fun reuniting with my friends from the east coast and sharing my adventures with them.

Miriam photographed in front of a stunning view at Lake Louise in Banff, Canada

Miriam surveys the vista at Mary's Peak

Miriam in front of the Sunflower structure in Kansas

The Smith family (Brian, Ellen, Peter and Anna) on top of Mt. Constable, Nebraska. Peter is holding an ice axe, which he brought along as a joke

Picture of the structure at Mt. Mitchell, North Carolina

Miriam at the Michigan high point

Picture of Miriam's feet next to the Signal Hill, Arkansas, marker

Hilary next to the Eagle Mountain, Minnesota sign, with her mosquito netting

Mr. Sterler, owner of the property where the Iowa high point is located, gamely poses for a picture with Miriam

Debbie and Miriam outside the High Point marker in Maryland

Miriam at Mt. Frissell, Connecticut

Miriam on top of Mt. Washington, New Hampshire

Structure on Mt. Greylock, Massachusetts

Miriam and friends photograph the Ebright Azimuth, Delaware high point marker--in the middle of a street.

Rare picture of Miriam in action, climbing Granite Peak, Montana

Miriam after ascending the difficult Maine high point

Miriam in Estes Park, Colorado, where she was acclimatizing in preparation for Denali in May 2006

Miriam at Gannett Peak, Wyoming

Miriam at Mt. Rainer, Washington wearing a t-shirt from Balance Bar, one of her sponsors

Miriam with deaf river fishing guide (King of the River) on the Kenai River, after the Denali Climb. She caught a 30 lb King Salmon

Guide Kathy Cosley and Miriam before ascending Denali, Alaska

Miriam at "End of the World" on Denali, Alaska

Good friends, Miriam and Hilary, on one of their many adventures together

Multiple Sclerosis: Miriam's Villain

Miriam had many barriers threatening to obstruct her climbing goals. Another factor slowly sneaking its way into her life to foil her pursuits was an unknown villain whose name she had not yet learned. Odd things began to happen for no rhyme or reason.

When Miriam was attempting to get comfortable in her sleeping bag inside her tent, she was only able to sleep on the right side. If she wanted to roll over and rest her head on the other side, she became extremely dizzy. Sleeping in a tent was second nature to her. Never having heard any forestry creatures lurking such as wild boars scavenging, bullfrogs' mating calls, owls hooting, the twittering-whistle of racoons, bears sniffing tree-cached food, porcupine grunts, and mosquitoes buzzing in her ear, Miriam sleeps peacefully. The forest is her element. Miriam is fully aware that more danger lurks in populated cities than in a tent in the wilderness.

Over the years Hilary began to notice subtle quirks in Miriam's physical abilities that were inconsistent with her strength and agility. She was awed by Miriam's skills at building and repairing fences and gates. She witnessed her speed and strength using a maul and pry bar to unearth old concrete fence posts and her precision with a plumb line while installing sheetrock. She recalls a winter backpacking trip where they hiked several miles in the dark on snowshoes. It was Hilary's birthday, March 25. The Hail-Bopp Comet was clearly visible in the clear night sky that evening back in 1997.

Miriam was carrying more than her share of weight as usual. After about two miles of hiking through the woods, Miriam suddenly slowed. She did not claim illness or offer any explanation for not carrying her usual load. Hilary picked up some of the weight. That night was a particularly rough night for Miriam. She woke to the bright sunshine reflecting on the ice where their tent was set up.

Although she slept in a sleeping bag labeled as –30 F while Hilary slept in a sleeping bag claiming 25 degrees F, Miriam was the worse for wear. This was the first indication Hilary remembers that all was not well with Miriam.

After hiking many miles, climbing many mountains, one learns to recognize a typical walking gait, climbing gait, and fording stream gait. This was one way Hilary detected something wasn't quite the same with the Miriam she knew. One backpacker may help lift a heavy pack onto the back of a fellow backpacker. Backpackers share in the building of a good campfire, cooking meals, caching food, and dismantling the tent. Food and water is carefully shared, rationed if necessary. Tarps, hats, bandaids, moleskin, gloves, propane, ibuprofen, water purifier, flashlights, pocket knives, lip balm, pots or pans and compasses are some of the items that should be carefully inventoried to make sure they are not causing unnecessary weight by duplicating items. There should always be room for flexible give and take between backpackers helping one another with weight. One may carry the tent while the other carries tent poles and stakes.

All the talking in the world may not bring one closer to knowing how the other is feeling. Miriam is a very quiet hiker. She normally has no reason to rush over trails new to her; she wants to see the flora and fauna. She knows how many miles she and Hilary can comfortably backpack in one day and how much weight each is capable of carrying. She can read topo maps and judge timing, distance, the elevation and grade of a trail and factor in temperature, wind, and rain to determine destinations. Miriam has successfully guided treks she has never hiked. According to Hilary, she has an uncanny ability to know which fork to take and which direction to go although she has never been there before. Hilary sometimes refers to Miriam by the name sign *"compass head."* Two hikers communicating solely by ASL happen upon more wildlife than those communicating by voice.

Miriam said that the odd symptom of having one eye jerk was very unsettling during hikes. Having it happen while bicycle riding was worse. Miriam tried to brush it off rather than dwell on the annoying sensation. She never set her sights lower. "*Can't*" was not a word in her vocabulary. Miriam wanted to look forward, never back. Her odd symptoms would subside at times, but her villain would show up to harass her, trying to trip her up. Miriam formed a close bond with Dr Connie Graham, her primary care physician, also a Canadian. Dr Graham marveled at Miriam's physical determination and sighed over her ailments. She was instrumental in helping Miriam cope and referring her to appropriate specialists. Dr. Graham even took an ASL class, enabling her to manage in crisis situations when an interpreter is unable to be reached in time.

As Miriam endured her various infirmities, such as a gallbladder surgery, she viewed them as mere stumbling blocks to her ultimate goals. With each doctor appointment, she mentioned her odd symptoms. It was not easy to describe them, and they would come and go or manifest in varied forms. While recovering from surgery, she had her plans fully scheduled. During breaks between jobs she squeezed in as much life as she could from a week-end as if she only had so much time in her life. However she welcomed every odd job, from cutting down a tree for a widow, dog sitting, dog walking, house painting, building steps and ramps, delivering phone books, mowing, weeding, operating a forklift at a winery and clearing brush.

Miriam's family physician eventually referred her to specialists in an attempt to determine the source of her "jerky eye." An Ear Nose Throat physician (ENT) thought perhaps a crystal in her ear had been dislodged during her fall off Mt. Hood back in 1995. Miriam recalls bouts of dizziness her entire life, but more closely resembling vertigo. It wasn't until her fall off Mt. Hood that Miriam was able to enjoy two years of freedom from her dizziness. But when it resurfaced in 1997, she and her physician took more aggressive steps to get to the root of the problem. Miriam's neck became stiff following a stressful climb. She was unable to obtain relief from chiropractic services or the procedures for the dislodged crystal.

Balance was not an issue for Miriam as it can be for some people who are deaf. So she went to an eye doctor for prescription glasses. Miriam had never had glasses, so this was a possible answer to her "jerky eye" problem. However, as soon as she tried reading through them, she knew immediately that she could see better with her naked eyes.

Miriam was first referred to a neurologist in 2002. She chose a young woman with whom she had played doubles tennis, Dr. Cecilia Keller. Miriam remembers her as a very tough tennis player, but one of those who begged for mercy when Miriam was serving.

It wasn't until May 2004 that Miriam was officially diagnosed with Multiple Sclerosis. At last she had a name for the mysterious villain that had harassed her. Although the label of MS is a life-shattering one, after the initial realization of what is involved with MS, Miriam was thrilled that at last there was a reason for all the weird signs she had been experiencing. She was ready to accept whatever treatment she needed as soon as possible. She had to wait to find out what could be done with her insurance. Hopes for future jobs might be stifled by pre-existing condition policies. Miriam resolved to continue working part time. Her ambition to become a national Forest Ranger through the Masters Degree she had been pursuing were dashed.

Prior to leaving with her husband for his Rotary Convention in Brisbane, Australia, Hilary remembers that Miriam's neurologist planned to do just one more test: a spinal tap on Miriam to rule out Multiple Sclerosis. During her long plane trip to Australia, Hilary read about MS and discussed it with Robert. Neither had any close acquaintance with MS. Upon arrival in Brisbane, both Hilary and Robert experienced jet lag, however their excitement at having arrived added extra adrenalin to keep them going long enough to visit the convention hall. No sooner had they stepped inside than Hilary's eyes caught sight of a banner across the top of one of the hundreds of booths, "Rotary MS Fellowship." Hilary made a beeline for that booth. After meeting with a gentleman representing the booth and reading the literature, Hilary realized that Miriam indeed had MS. All the odd symptoms that Miriam had been experiencing over the years came together to solve the mystery of what had been plaguing her.

Hilary cried. The gentleman at the booth hugged her. He seemed to know straight away that Hilary was inquiring for a close friend who was being diagnosed at that moment. Since that time Hilary and Robert have been part of the Australian MS Rotary Fellowship and have received support and information that have helped immensely to understand this odd disease that takes on many forms. No wonder MS is so difficult to diagnose.

The "jerky eye" was referred to as "optic neuritis." The strange tingly feeling and numbness that Miriam had in her right leg from time to time was also a common symptom of MS that may lead to diagnosis. Miriam's type of MS is referred to as relapsing remitting. With this type of MS, one may enjoy remissions where it may seem that one does not have anything wrong at all, and then without much warning, it may surface. Multiple Sclerosis means "many scars." The scars are from the body attacking its own myelin sheath covering the nerves at their synapse, disturbing the messages so important to the functioning of the body. Hence, MS has many varied symptoms.

Initially, Miriam's insurance dictated her treatment choice. Copaxone was an injection to be administered daily just under the surface of the skin. Miriam hates needles. This was really a horrible fate, but she told herself that it was not a death sentence. She learned that with treatment, those with MS could live an average lifespan. Most of all, her determination and dreams to complete the highest point of each state in the US helped her to face her foe. Miriam waited over a month before a nurse could come to train Miriam, Hilary, Robert, and another friend to administer the injection. Miriam was pleased with the prospects of this treatment because it would allow her the freedom to travel independently. The others were trained in order to give Miriam injections in her back where she could not reach. With daily injections, Miriam would need many choices for injection sites: stomach, upper thigh, under and on top of upper arm, hip, and back. The nurse gave instructions and treatment began within a few weeks.

Miriam's shots did not cause her to feel any side effects until about a month had passed and she began to have injection site reactions that were bright red inflamed areas as large as golf balls. When her physician diagnosed her sores as an allergic reaction, Miriam had to discontinue Copaxone. Eventually she changed to Avonex, an intermuscular injection to be given weekly.

Miriam was pleased with the fact that she would not need to give herself the daily shots, however, she knew that Avonex may cause flu-like symptoms within the first 24 hours following the weekly injections. Her Medicare plan stipulated that the shots must be administered at the neurologist's office. Miriam would no longer have freedom to travel from her home town for more than a week at a time as she would be tied down by her weekly visits to her neurologist's office. This was very disconcerting for someone like Miriam who had been climbing the highest peaks in different states and different countries.

As with most life-changing conditions, Miriam asked, *"Why me?"* This was the third strike against her: Discrimination against her as a deaf individual (particularly when seeking employment), falling off Mt. Hood, and now learning that MS would restrict her beloved activities. After a brief period of mourning, Miriam called up her stubborn determination and set goals for her daily life. She chose Monday mornings for her regular Avonex injections, anticipating her flu like symptoms would last through the day, but the good news was that she would have six very good days each week. Nurse Patty who gave the weekly injections had a wonderful sense of humor. Both Miriam and nurse Patty loved to tease one another and make the best of the weekly visits. Although she did not know ASL, Miriam could read her expressions and natural gestures. Miriam would beg for mercy for the intermuscular shot to be done as carefully as possible. An interpreter was not needed when the appointment was only for administering the weekly dose.

Why did Miriam get MS? What are the odds of her getting it over anyone else? Four times more women have been diagnosed with the relapsing remitting form than men. MS is diagnosed mainly around ages 30 to 40. MS is more common in those who suffered infectious mononucleosis or Epstein-Barr virus when younger, usually during the teens or twenties. MS is most common among those of Northern European ancestry. MS is more prevalent among people living further away from the Equator, where natural Vitamin D from sunlight is lacking. All the above fit Miriam.

Research for MS is growing by leaps and bounds and there is hope for a cure. One research reports higher amounts of aluminum excreted in the urine of those with MS. Next we are waiting for a definitive explanation. Do those with MS ingest more aluminum in their diets or cook with aluminum pots or do they simply excrete aluminum from their bodies more than those without MS? Research is ongoing in hundreds of areas. Another common factor among those who have been diagnosed with MS is genetics. There have been cases of twins and some siblings sharing MS. However MS is not contagious. Miriam's family has no knowledge of any family member ever having had MS or any condition resembling the disease.

Since the initial diagnosis, when the first MRI showed 5 lesions on Miriam's brain, Miriam received more MRIs to assess the progress of her the condition. It is extremely difficult for tests to locate spinal cord lesions, so the brain is closely monitored. After a year on Avonex, Miriam's 5 brain lesions actually shrunk to a smaller size. Had Miriam refused treatment for the aggressive form of MS that she has, statistics indicate that her lesions would have either remained the same size or increased their size and/or numbers. Miriam is pleased with Avonex and she and her neurologist Dr Keller agree that this is the best treatment for her.

Dr. Keller was so pleased with Miriam's progress and return to good health that she gave in to Miriam's pleading and consented to her traveling to Australia to volunteer for the 2005 Summer Deaf Olympics. Miriam had already participated playing tennis in two

Summer Deaf Olympics representing her home country Canada. She won ribbons in both the Los Angeles and New Zealand Deaf Olympics. As an experienced leader, Miriam qualified to volunteer in the Australian Games. She had to provide her own transportation. Her only misgivings were related to the fact that she could not take her Avonex injections with her to Australia. She would endure three months untreated while out of the country. She would pay for the missed medication.

The trip satisfied her traveling desires. Initially, the group Miriam was assigned to meet was American athletes. However, their arrival was delayed so she was sent to assist the Italian athletes. Their sign language was as fast as their spoken language counterparts. Given a little time, Miriam knew that she could communicate with them, and before long she was able to instruct them on where to go and what to do on arrival and preparation for opening ceremonies. Without any Italian volunteers Miriam was the most level-headed person to assign to the group. She said that they had lots of smiles and naturally she smiled back.

After the closing ceremonies, Miriam joined a tour group to see Australia. In spite of the heat, Miriam kept up with the group as they hiked trails in various locations to take in the sights. Her favorites were Ayers Rock, the Great Barrier Reef and watching the penguins come to shore in south Australia where 12 Apostles Rocks jutted out of the sea. Miriam was the only deaf person in her guided tour. But there were people who wrote notes to Miriam discussing facts and other communication along the way.

It wasn't long after Miriam returned to Corvallis that the first of her three major MS attacks occurred. Hilary describes seeing Miriam's right leg look like that of a gumby bendable toy. Her optic neuritis returned and it was impossible for Miriam to navigate her own home. Everything moved in her environment. Hilary rushed her to her neurologist who ordered that Miriam be hospitalized for three days and receive IV infusions each day. Miriam would not consent to hospitalization. Instead, she wobbled her way into the infusion department where she was surrounded by around 6 other patients, mostly those receiving chemo treatments. Two large fish tanks with odd-looking fish helped soften the scene. In spite of her misery and pain, Miriam had the attention of all those around her as she explained all her plans for her upcoming climbs of Wyoming and Mt. Rainier. The others were enthralled and cheered Miriam for her continued success. Midway between Miriam's exciting story-telling, she attempted to make her way to the restroom pulling along the IV pole, but her legs would not hold her. She had to be wheeled in a wheelchair. The other patients looked on. Upon Miriam's return to her seat, she resumed her tales picking up where she left off.

Miriam stayed at Hilary and Robert's house where she could be looked in on as her physician requested in lieu of hospitalization. Each day Miriam's health worsened until about two days following her third IV infusion. Miriam's friends were very concerned that her two month trip to Australia had compromised her health. It was upsetting to see such a strong young lady so very ill. Miriam knew the price she paid for her trip, but had she known, she would have gone ahead with the trip anyway. Her insurance situation dictated that she be tied down to a once a week visit to her home-town neurologist's office, somewhat like a felon needing to report to his probation officer. Miriam is an independent person and cannot live that way.

Miriam purchased her own private insurance in order to help pay for her Avonex and obtain the freedom to administer her own weekly shots. To Miriam her freedom was worth her out-of-pocket expenses. Miriam began traveling to give MS advocacy presentations. Now she could give herself the injections Sunday evening and sleep through part of the 24 hour flu-like symptoms, rather than having to wait for a week-day appointment at her doctor's office, and then spend her Mondays being ill.

Miriam faced her second major MS attack following her climb of Denali in Alaska when temperatures on the mountain made it difficult to keep her Avonex syringes at refrigerated temperatures, not too hot, not frozen. Her first two weekly injections went well during her climb, however Miriam's attempts to inject herself the third week on Denali were unsuccessful because the medication had changed consistency, having been stored at the wrong temperature.

She went ahead and continued up the mountain. Hilary remembers various guides saying that climbing is 75% mental and 25% physical. The 75% was going strong until approximately 14,000 feet elevation when her numbness on her right side extended to her abdominal area and around her back. In the past, her numbness was mainly felt in the right leg. Miriam continued to 15,500 feet before succumbing to her villainous MS. This was the first time the numbness extended to everything below the waist, making it difficult to time when to relieve her bladder or bowels. This was Miriam's second major MS attack.

Multiple Sclerosis manifests in many forms. Even after a definitive diagnosis, a patient and doctor look at each ailment in an attempt to determine *"Is this MS-related or something else?"* When Miriam's health problems worsened in 2007, she went to various specialists to determine the problem and ended up having surgery for a paraesophageal hernia. She and Hilary planned a Spring Break trip to California between their teaching terms. Their plans were cancelled once Miriam realized she would have a drain tube from her hernia repair outside her body for five weeks. She had been plagued with gastric reflux problems that her previous surgery reopened.

Miriam was unable to swallow and after repeated visits to the ER in the middle of the night, it was determined that her throat was closing up on her, preventing her from swallowing normally, and this was MS related. She reported extreme pain shooting up her left arm into her chest area that eventually was diagnosed as swelling around the heart area. Miriam became severely dehydrated and needed to be put back in hospital on intravenous feeding to restore her strength. This was Miriam's third major MS attack or exacerbation and it was the worst. She lost 40 pounds through the three-month ordeal. As with the first and second attacks, Miriam had been forced to suspend her weekly Avonex injections while recovering from her surgery. Now she knew that she would be unable to bounce back following surgeries as she had in the past. A surgery may aggravate the body enough to make the MS flare up particularly in situations where Avonex therapy must be withdrawn. Miriam now realizes how very important it is that she continue weekly injections of Avonex without interruptions. She has been free from her MS caused vertigo for the past three years that she has been on Avonex.

Hilary and Miriam's other friends worked hard to help her during her transition back home until Miriam's parents were able to come from Canada to stay with her during a long slow recovery. Miriam had to take a leave of absence from spring term 2007 teaching ASL at Western Oregon University.

Miriam at the Black Mesa, Oklahoma high point

Black Mesa, Oklahoma: Rattlesnake Country

Hilary White's Perspective

I consider myself fortunate for having been invited to join Miriam again on more state high point climbing adventures. We had originally planned to cover Arizona, New Mexico and Oklahoma. At that time, we were disappointed to learn that forest fires forced closure of trails to both Arizona and New Mexico's highest points, but we figured we had just enough time to drive to Oklahoma, camp, climb, then drive back to Albuquerque to fly back home to Oregon. It was June 15, 2002.

In Albuquerque, we were already near the north end of the state making it an easy straight shot for Oklahoma's panhandle. Fortunately, our destination, Black Mesa at 4,973 feet, was at the very end of the panhandle, just across the border east of New Mexico.

As we headed east, we tried to make the best of our trip in spite of having missed out on the other two states. I knew that Miriam's strong determination could get her down when facing disappointment. We were crossing territory that both of us had never seen. This would become another adventure. Miriam, an excellent spur-of-the-moment traveler, quickly pulled open her map to chart the course and visit places of interest along the way. She told me that our next stop would be Capulin Volcano National Monument. Miriam is fun to travel with, so it was great seeing her get herself back into a good mood. We laughed when we saw a lone antelope in the midst of a cattle herd.

There were hardly any other vehicles along the desolate portions of northern New Mexico. No cars means we can chat in ASL all we want. This may sound scary to hearing people, but believe it or not, deaf drivers have proven to be safer than hearing drivers by statistics taken from The National Fraternal Society of the Deaf years ago through their insurance program.

When communicating in ASL while driving, the passenger is equally responsible to keep his/her eyes on the road. We had to watch for jack rabbits.

Miriam was mesmerized by the sight of an antelope gracefully loping across the open land. She was reminded of her Grazing Land studies for her Masters Degree. She could remember what she had read about these great expanses of open grassland which are productive only during the rainy years. Now dry and desolate, we could imagine the lush grassland that lured settlers to farm this area. Many settlers suffered severe drought and it became a “dust bowl.” Although buffalo once roamed here, it was now just dried out grazing land, home to prairie animals and plants.

As we pulled up to Capulin Volcano Visitor Center, we checked out the displays and by chance ran into a family who knew sign language. They had also heard of others attempting to collect as many state high points as they could. That was a pleasant surprise, way out in the middle of nowhere. It was interesting driving up the volcano, completely circling around and around the cone resembling the shape of construction zone cones. When we arrived at the top, 7,877 feet, we saw into the crater.

Miriam was not feeling up to par, so she told me to go ahead and hike along the trail into the crater while she watched from above. It was quite a view across barren landscape. We could see some smaller volcanic formations in the distance. It felt good to get out and stretch my legs, however I knew that Miriam normally would be doing the same thing. This was another of those odd symptoms that we later found out to be her MS gradually surfacing.

Prior to crossing the border into Oklahoma, we entered an entirely different type of landscape that was nothing like anything either of us had ever seen. This was where dinosaurs roamed and it looked like the appropriate scenery. Tall rock formations jutted out of the land. Plenty of trees and caves in the rocks provide sanctuary for animals. The lovely Cimarron River flows just north of here.

Crossing the border, Miriam cheered because this was the 50th US state that she had *"touch finished"* of all the travels she had taken over the years with her father in their old van and then later on her own. As a born Canadian, that is pretty remarkable! This would be Miriam's 40th state high point, however. She had driven across the US three times. Despite her strong Canadian roots, Miriam became a US citizen in 1995 when I stood in as her witness at her Naturalization Ceremony. She considers herself a dual citizen.

We stopped at "The Merc" in the small town of Kenton to ask for directions to nearby Black Mesa where we would search for Oklahoma's highest point the next day. We were warned against entering that area due to the high population of rattlesnakes. The owner of the store carefully lifted a wooden box from his shelf labeled "Baby Rattler" and opened it before we had a chance to back off. Inside was a pink rattle that a baby shakes. What a tease! We knew that we should attempt the snake infested trail during the cool early morning hours when the rattlers are still under rocks or underground. The store owner asked us if we had ever heard a rattlesnake sound its warning. Miriam indicated she was deaf and I told him I was hard of hearing so he grabbed a real snake's dried up rattle from his shelf and shook it next to my ear. He told me to memorize that sound, but that it would be faster and much louder. He said he could not shake it as hard and fast as the snakes do. We inquired about restaurants and he told us we had two choices, his Merc or a house located in Black Mesa State Park. He gave us directions.

We drove to the nearby State Park and found a campsite without rocks nearby for snakes to hide under. It was a nice place under a tree beside the stream. Miriam decided not to pound in the tent stakes so we could have a quick morning get away prior to sunrise, particularly since there was no wind. We left to check out the other "restaurant." On the way, there were many cattle that stared at us curiously as we drove past so we realized this was not a well-traveled road. White rounded pebbles along the roadway were the perfect nesting ground for Killdeers. We had never seen so many apparently sick or injured birds with broken wings! We smiled at their antics and slowed way down so as not to hit them. In the rear view mirror, Miriam could still see them flapping alongside the road and many more performers were ahead of us. Perhaps they do not have many opportunities to distract predators away from their eggs other than the occasional cow. It was quite a show of nest defending.

At last, we arrived at the "restaurant" that happened to be an old house. There was no sign but the door was opened so we peaked inside the open door to see a family. They told us we were at the right place but the wrong hours. No hours were posted, but that was alright. We knew we could go to "The Merc" for buffalo burgers. Probably that was the whole town talking to us as we ate our giant burgers! It was more like a fellowship than a restaurant. The townsfolk said, *"So you are some of those crazy state highpointers, where are you from?"*

They all warned us of the rattlesnakes, trying to get us to change our minds. They pointed out the dinosaur bones on the shelves and told us of the paleontological and prehistoric sites we could visit there in the Badlands. They told us the history of Kenton and the train robbers. They told us where to look on our hike up Black Mesa for the large cool caves used by outlaws to hide with their horses before waylaying the trains. *"Oh you are in the panhandle now and we are all descendents of those rough tough cowboys. This is the Badlands!"* they admitted. They reminded us to return once we summited to receive our certificates.

The sun was still up as we drove into the campground for an early rest since we would rise before dawn. Miriam parked the car and told me she would use the restroom and meet me back at the tent. I had my eyes focused on the ground by my feet watching for rattlesnakes wondering if I would try sleeping with my boots on. How would I leave the tent if "nature calls?" I was afraid that one might be under or around our tent. The campsite was not far away, but I stood in the vicinity of our tent and could not find it. Hmmm, where did it go? Oh my gosh, someone must have come and stole our tent! We had just been told about the outlaws. As Miriam exited the restroom, she remembers seeing me waving my arms wide to get her attention from the distance, then signing, *"Tent gone, someone stole tent!"*

Miriam thought that was impossible. She looked around and saw it upstream drifting along like a big balloon. She waved back to me pointing out the tent above her. I looked and answered, *"Do you suppose that is ours?"*

That night, Miriam was also paranoid about having to step out of the tent in case of rattlesnakes. She was afraid of getting bitten in the behind in the middle of the night. We kept the flashlights where we could quickly find them. All of the other campers were in RVs. We were the only tent campers.

We did not realize that this was one of those odd time zones where part of the state is an hour ahead of the other. The small town of Kenton is the only place in Oklahoma that observes Mountain time. So when we left to drive to the high point, we had to wait an hour longer for sunrise and napped in the car. As soon as our eyes could possibly see the ground without the help of flashlights, we gingerly stepped along the trail. It was very unsettling. We did not have to worry about altitude sickness, falling off cliffs, or bad weather. The most dangerous state was said to be Rhode Island. Wyoming, Washington, Montana and Alaska are the other forbidding state highpoints. But our hearts were beating and our adrenalin running full force here in Oklahoma at 4,000 feet elevation as if we were attempting the others.

There was a type of cactus that when dried out, it lays on the ground hollow with diamond-shaped patterns closely resembling rattlesnakes, one of nature's tricks! We had 8.4 miles to go round trip. Miriam's determination won over her fears to accomplish this endeavor. Her eyes are far better than mine, I was depending on her eyes and she was depending on my ears. I was in the lead, afraid that I might wake up a snake under a bush and scare it out to bite Miriam close behind me.

Although this was an abominable trail, Miriam was impressed with the clear posts marking our way so we would not become lost way out there away from civilization. She also enjoyed the beauty of the yellow and pink flowers along the way. Low scrub brush closed in on the single file trail. Should one of us get bitten, our thoughts were both visualizing getting the other person to the nearest hospital miles away. Miriam had a poisonous snake-bite kit in her day pack just in case, although we both knew that the best choice is still to get to the nearest medical facility as soon as possible. We both had two trekking poles that might help us. Snakes are attracted to warmth while hunting prey.

Eventually we began to climb switchbacks until we arrived on the mesa. Miriam, with her good navigational skills, explained that we had a ways to go across the mesa. Although still early in the morning, the sun shone down on the treeless mesa. We did not stop to talk much because we needed to concentrate on watching for snakes. What a surprise it was to see an antelope looking right at us. Both of us were also spellbound before the antelope leapt away. It wasn't long before I saw fresh rattlesnake droppings, a light green color, the same consistency as that from the large python that my son Nathan had at our house. I smelled the same smell and saw the same scat on the path in front of me I had seen from the months the snake was at our house. We knew the snakes were awake now with the bright sun warming them.

We kept moving about 20 minutes further before we saw the large monument marking the high point as well as the distances to each of the nearby states. Here at the tip of the Oklahoma panhandle, Colorado and New Mexico weren't far away. We signed the registry located inside an ammunition box before heading back to beat the summer heat. Miriam loved the view from the top of Black Mesa,4,973 feet, she treasures her photos showing lovely 3 D views in all directions.

We did not waste any time returning, but took the same caution watching for rattlesnakes. Two other people were heading toward the high point. Again, the cactus "skeletons" fooled me into thinking I was seeing diamond back rattlesnakes. Then just short of our round trip, I heard a very loud noise that sounded similar to that of the rattle The Merc owner shook by my ear the day before. It did not sound as if it were right by us, but I know they can move fast, so I told Miriam and we just kept going. We did not run, there could have been more, it was hard for me to detect from which direction the sound was coming. When we jumped into the warm car, Miriam asked me to turn off both my hearing aids. I was confused but followed her instructions. She yelled very loud to relieve her tension. We did it! When we arrived at the The Merc we were given an informal celebration by the owner and townsfolk as our certificates were awarded to us. It was very touching.

We crossed back into New Mexico and stopped at Clayton, a town where there was a KOA camp. We set up our tent and paid our fee. The office referred us to the old landmark hotel with saloon below. It looked like a bar from the old cowboy westerns, well preserved from the past. Photos covered the walls of events that had taken place in this little town, most particularly the hanging of some miserable outlaw. As we ate our meal, the TV in the saloon flashed warnings of a tornado while Miriam watched a baseball game. It wasn't long before the game was replaced by full screen warnings to get under cover. We asked the waitress for the bill and she told us to hurry home. We told her we had a small tent at the KOA. She said, "*No honey, you will not last the night in a tent, you will be lifted up and blown away!*"

We rushed back. Miriam ran into the KOA office as the lady was about to close up. It was just our luck that there was one cabin left to rent for the night. We were very thankful. There was no tornado that night in Clayton but a lightning storm blasted through. We both slept very well and noticed the ground outside was drenched in the morning.

We stopped in Las Vegas, New Mexico, to visit Miriam's Gallaudet classmate, Ken Litherland's place. Miriam had never seen the nice back-country cabin where Ken lived with his wife and two daughters. They had to work so asked us to stay and babysit their daughters while they were away. A large forest fire was dangerously close. Ken gave instructions to open the gates to free his horses and cattle in case the fire came that close. We smelled the smoke but could not see the fire from the cabin. Firemen carried hoses through Ken's property and assured us they would let us know if it came time to evacuate. We enjoyed interacting with the girls as they were both fluent with ASL. It was a nice ending to having completed one successful high point out of the three we had hoped for.

Patriotic Miriam waves an American flag on top of Boundary Peak, Nevada

Boundary Peak, Nevada: Scree is No Fun!

Miriam made two attemps to climb Boundary Peak, Nevada, before she was successful. This chapter is written primarily from her viewpoint and taken from her journal excerpts.

First Attempt to Climb Boundary Peak Miriam Richard's Perspective

It was early June 1998 when I first drove from Oregon to Nevada to attempt a climb of Boundary Peak. As the name implies, Nevada's highpoint is located on the border with California to the west. After driving through northern California with my friend Leslie's dog Tilly Jane, TJ, I crossed the border into a very desolate desert area of Nevada. I pulled over and slept the night in my car, leaving a window open for TJ to breathe fresh air.

I waited until daylight to find the service road (SR 773). There was no sign to indicate where SR 773 was located. I ended up backtracking several times trying to decide which dirt road would take me up to the trailhead. After driving partway on both roads, I made my choice as to which might be the road I wanted. It was dry, dusty, rocky and sagebrush scratched at the sides of my car like a Brillo pad. I could feel large rocks hitting underneath and the sides of my car, I could feel the strain of the axle as it hit the rough road repeatedly. I was afraid the axle might break and I could be stranded out there in the desert. There were times I would feel my wheels spinning as I pushed the accelerator to urge my car forward when it became stuck. I really wished I had rented a 4-wheel drive vehicle. The eight mile road took about an hour to pass through.

When the road came to an end, I got out to have a sympathetic look at my car. The blue paint was covered with dusty brown silt. I put off checking the scratches and dents until later. TJ wagged her tail as we started hiking through sagebrush. I let her stay in the lead to scare off any snakes or other creatures that might be lurking out of sight. We walked through a dried-up river bed for a mile and a half before ascending a snowy slope. I did not realize until later that the mountain was made up of loose scree. Poor TJ began postholing, her long legs dropping deep into the snow. Although she has climbed Mt. Hood with Leslie and was in excellent shape for a black lab mix, TJ got down on her side on the snowy slope and told me to give it up. I had wished I had brought along crampons to clamp onto my boots but they were back home in Oregon.

Second Attempt to Climb Boundary Peak
Miriam Richard's Perspective

I offered a nice surprise to Hilary for her March 25th birthday. I would pay for her to fly to visit her first cousin Rita in Volcano, California in July, 2002. My plan was to rent a 4-wheel drive vehicle from the Sacramento airport, visit Rita and then go on my own to conquer that foreboding peak in Nevada. Having tried it before only to find the snow prevented me from ascending, I realized that July might be a better time to climb.

On the way to Rita's house, I enjoyed having Hilary along to chat and share her sense of humor with me. She marveled at the fields of fruit and old gold-miners' whistle stops. We both thrive on the adventures that add to the highpointing trips. She shared with me her memories growing up with Rita. Their grandfather, fathers, and Rita and Hilary all have some degree of hearing loss, however only Hilary uses ASL. Rita agreed to meet us in the town of Volcano since the roads are complicated. A sweet old lady sitting on a bench greeted us. She offered to sell us a bag of beans. Hilary made the purchase and it was not long before Rita drove by. The lady jumped up faster than Hilary and aggressively waved at Rita.

As Rita and her friend Kathleen prepared the dinner, they told us that the lady who sold Hilary the beans was the unofficial Mayor of Volcano. She knew everyone by name and spent most of her days sitting on the bench waving at the townsfolk.

Rita and Kathleen also told us that the old wooden building across the street from the park bench was the old jail built over a hundred years ago. The carpenter who built the structure was also its first inmate. Hilary and I laughed and suggested the carpenter might have built an escape route.

I left Rita's house the next afternoon heading east to Nevada. I was grateful for the high clearance on my rental jeep. I had paid additional insurance coverage in case of dents, scratches, or other possible problems from the rough dirt road. The vehicle was so high that it missed the low brush that had caused considerable paint damage to my low sedan. I parked at the trailhead and began my ascent at 5:00 in the morning. The sunrise was a gorgeous orange glow. I expected the day to warm quickly so I scurried along quickly through the scrub brush.

Looking at Boundary Peak from below, it does not look too difficult. This time there was a new trailhead sign: "Boundary Peak, 13,143 Feet." Three miles round trip did not sound bad at all. What I did not expect was steep scree slopes nearly impossible to climb. I felt as if I was on a pile of marbles as I mustered all my effort to clamber up the loose volcanic rock. I could not believe how long it was taking me to make a little bit of forward progress. Later, I read that this measly three-mile climb came with an altitude gain of 4,140 feet, much more pronounced than most of the other high points.

I was glad I had plenty of sunscreen and water as well as a cap to keep the sun out of my face. But I was getting nowhere. I became frustrated and yelled at the scree. I could see no paths or any other way of getting around this slope. I cried. After tremendous effort, I made it to the top of the slope, but saw that there was still a long trek across the ridges of several mountains. I determinately decided I would not cry anymore and push on in the soaring heat. About a half hour later I finally saw a rounded pile of rocks and registry box. It was the 4th of July, so I pulled out my American Flag that I had carried in my pocket. The 100 degree heat was unbearable. I felt dizzy. I took some time to think before heading back. Ironically, California's Montgomery Peak, only a few steps away across a saddle was higher than Boundary Peak! However it was not California's highest peak. I had already topped that peak. With all my efforts to mount this miserable high point, I felt Montgomery Peak mocking me.

My eyes were playing tricks on me as I headed back. Again, I attributed this to the intense heat and did the best I could to make my way back. There is no trail. After sliding down that horrible pile of rubble, I tried peaking over the scratchy bushes to find the shortest route back to the jeep. Taller people would be able to see over the bushes but I could not get a bearing on my location. I cannot believe that it took me 12 hours to go only three miles. I admit that I hated this mountain high point more than any of the other 49 state highpoints. As I drove back on the dirt road, because of nausea, I put the windows down rather than use air conditioning. My right eye was jumping around worse than the bumpy road. I knew I was losing it and decided to check into the nearest hotel to rest. I found a place in Nevada and slept until checkout time at noon the next day.

The drive back to Rita's house took me the rest of the day map reading and navigating different roads. My jerky eye made it difficult to see the fine print although I have 20/20 vision. I would later learn I was suffering from Optic Neuritis, a common symptom of MS. Later, Kathleen shared her perspective of seeing me after I returned to Rita's house:

> *"You returned flushed and exhausted. I was a bit apprehensive about my ability to communicate with you, as I didn't know sign language, and Hilary and Rita were away when you arrived from the climb. We shared some nutritional meal items, and we communicated through writing.*
>
> *I have always felt humbled in your presence, as there is a numinous quality that pervades*

your being. After eating and hydrating, your dire need was to rest. I will never forget ushering you into our guest bedroom and pulling down the bedspread and sheets while you waited close by. Once the bed was prepared for you, the most generous smile of appreciation flooded your face while you uttered a sincere "Thank you." I held the sheets up while you climbed in, never losing the pain of exhaustion, or the smile, from your countenance. I gently covered you with the blankets and watched in awe as you almost immediately passed into sleep state. I quietly came out and sunk into my living room chair, flooded with tears. I tried to muffle my crying before remembering that it hardly mattered. What did matter was my profound recognition that I was in the company of the most courageous and spiritual being I might ever know, I was honored beyond words, and enlightened for a lifetime."

The next day, the town of Volcano, population 100, had their annual parade. Although I did not feel well, I went along with Hilary, Rita and Kathleen to watch the excitement. The lady who sold green beans from the park bench was not in her usual place. I looked around for her. Once the parade began, the lead car was an old 1930's car with the "Mayor" sitting in the passenger seat waving exuberantly at the crowd. With a town that small, the parade had to circle around twice because it wouldn't have been very long otherwise.

Miriam trying to hold back her tears on Kings Peak, Utah, on one of her most difficult experiences of a lifetime

King's Peak, Utah: A Difficult Journey

FIrst Attempt Summiting Kings Peak

Miriam and Hilary drove from Idaho through Utah in order to reach the trailhead for their climb to Utah. It was a round-about drive, but the trailhead access was the southwest corner of Wyoming. They stopped by the Ranger Station in Wyoming to inquire about the trail making sure there were no changes such as recent fires. Evanston, Wyoming was the nearest town to the trailhead. They had to leave the paved roads to travel on three forestry roads for about 20 miles.

Somewhere out there in the middle of nowhere, they crossed from Wyoming into Utah. Sometimes those gravel roads have sign markers that are obscure or missing. Crossing a state border in such a place can make directions more complex as numbering systems change. After having driven so far, they were relieved to enter Henrys Fork Campground. Both hungry and on a tight budget, Miriam scavenged in her trunk for tomato soup to cook on her little camp stove. Soon the climbers were dining. Hilary remembers her meal to be the best tomato soup she had ever had. Although store-bought, food always tastes better when camping.

As they sipped their soup and ASL conversation made no sounds, they looked up to see a large female moose standing nearby. Initially, there was no eye contact made between the moose and the humans. Miriam felt they were watching a stage play as the moose entered their "dining room" and slowly walked off. Both felt goose bumps going up their arms. They felt that this was a good sign of another exciting adventure.

The next morning on August 21, 2000, the backpackers set off at sunrise. The trail is 28 miles round trip. Miriam's calculations allowed for 3 days as long as everything went smoothly as planned. A full day was set aside for the summit day. The trail gradually meandered upwards into lovely lush bushes and forests. Their goal was to arrive at Dollar Lake before dark.

It was cool under the trees and shrubbery on either side of the trail. Now and then an opening between the trees allowed them views of the stream. They did not have to lug along heavy jugs of water this time. Instead Miriam would use her water filter to obtain water from the stream or lake for drinking and cooking. As they came to an open meadow, Miriam spotted another moose.

Miriam closely follows her map. She knew they would be crossing a stream. With heavy packs on their backs, crossing the rough-hewn logs would be a challenge. The other alternative was to wade through the water across the rocks. Miriam had fallen on the first day of her 14-day solo-backpacking trek on the Wonderland trail along the perimeter of Mt. Rainier where a bridge was down. She did not want a repeat of that incident so she chose to balance across the logs and she led off as Hilary checked her options.

At last Hilary made up her mind to cross after Miriam, trying not to look down at the water as she kept her pack centered on her back and held her arms out for balance. There was no railing to hold.

Elkhorn Crossing is a mixture of meadow and forest. Hilary was remarking that this was one of the loveliest sights she had ever seen. Miriam kept her eye on the mountains ahead and it wasn't long before she spotted Kings Peak. They had just been exposed to over 12,000 feet without any altitude problems in Idaho. Miriam knew that climbing again to high altitude soon would be beneficial since they had already built up their red blood cells. The hike continued so gradually uphill that they hardly noticed a change in elevation. Deep in their thoughts, they did not notice a cowboy riding along behind them. Border collies were herding a small group of sheep. A puppy was riding in the saddle. So far away from any human habitation, it was a rare sight to see. They fumbled with their cameras but the visual memory will always remain.

It wasn't long before two bull moose appeared in the distance. Hilary remembered her encounter with a large bull moose in Alaska when she and Miriam backpacked at the foot of Denali several years ago. She had her bear bells and bear spray recommended by rangers, looking out for something big and black, not expecting a moose camouflaged by the shrubbery. They were only 4 feet apart with their eyes locked on one another for what seemed an eternity until the moose decided that leaves would taste better. Hilary had read that moose can be more dangerous than bears.

They walked through a patch of skunk cabbage growing in mud. With the added weight of their packs, they jumped to the dry spots on the trail to avoid getting caked with mud. Both had their eyes out for Dollar Lake. They missed it, but after setting up the tent at the base of Kings Peak near another tent, they looked down and spotted Dollar Lake in the distance. Miriam headed over to the water in the canyon and filtered some water. Hilary took off her boots and soaked her feet in the cool water. The weather was perfect, everything was set for tomorrow's summit bid.

Two men coming down the trail from Kings Peak entered the tent set up near theirs. The men had pins on their hats, badges and shirts with Highpointers Emblems. This was the first that Miriam was to learn of the Highpointers Club. Miriam cannot remember the man's name, but he wrote the Highpointers web site on scratch paper for Miriam to look up. The men had successfully summited another and Miriam and Hilary hoped to do the same the next day.

In the middle of the night when Hilary stepped outside the tent, she tried gently zipping it without disturbing Miriam. However Miriam felt the tent shake, turned on her headlamp and asked Hilary if she saw stars in the sky. Hilary did not remember but she unzipped the tent again to have another look. With the rainfly attached just in case, Miriam could not view the sky from inside the tent. Hilary returned informing Miriam there were no stars. Miriam signed *"Darn!"* She knew that clouds meant rain or lightning. She did not want her climb jeopardized. They had a narrow window of time before Hilary had to catch her plane from Salt Lake City.

After an hour or two of sleep, Hilary and Miriam were ready to climb but had to await the showers. They peered out the door of the tent watching for a break in the weather. They bolted for the trail as soon as they could and followed a young couple up over Gunsight Pass into Painted Basin. They were awed by the huge colorful boulders and the great expanse as the trail dropped down into the basin. The trail was easy to follow and marked by rock cairns.

All of a sudden a huge bolt of lightning zapped nearby. Hilary hid her metal trekking poles under a boulder that she would pick up on her return trip. The hair on her arms was raised, she knew this was out of fear or from the electricity in the air. She had read that a metallic odor of ozone would also warn of charged ions in the air. She made her way along with her heart beating fast and her hearing aid turned off so as not to jolt her out of her hiking pants. As the lightning hit again and again, it was amusing to Miriam to see Hilary jump while at the same time, it was upsetting that their chances for summiting today may be compromised. Climbers should never be on the mountain after dark. Time was lost already to wait out the heavy downpour. Miriam felt the loud booms of thunder and knew it was close. When three big tough boys passed them, Miriam signed to them they were crazy to take chances with lightning. They brushed her off saying they were not afraid and continued on oblivious to the storm.

Miriam and Hilary kept going forward until they saw a young couple turn around and head back towards them. It was at this time that Hilary and Miriam had to make a major decision. The lightning was hitting more frequently in the painted basin and on Kings Peak. They were not aware of any strikes in the vicinity of their tent. They hid down under some boulders with the intention of waiting out the storm. After a time, they were rain soaked and with much chagrin, decided it would be too late to summit if they had to wait until the lightning stopped altogether. The clouds were black and there was no end in sight. Very reluctantly, they sauntered back to the tent. The men from the Highpointers Club were gone, Miriam remarked how lucky they were and how she wished they had allowed one more day to summit. Hilary had to get to the airport. The rains stopped and they headed back down the trail.

Hilary tried hard to lift Miriam's spirits by telling her that this is not a bad place to have to come to for a second try. They did not talk much on the way back. They stopped halfway to set up the tent for the night. Early the next morning, they visited the Oregon Trail Museum in Wyoming. They were impressed with the museum setting, grounds and the collection. Driving back across the border into Utah, Miriam dropped off Hilary at the Salt Lake City airport. She narrowly missed her flight not hearing her gate call. The passengers moved to board a gate with a different number than that on Hilary's ticket. She thought it was another flight so she remained in her seat until an attendant came to have a look at her ticket and beckon her onto her plane home. She hadn't bathed for days and hoped she did not smell too badly.

Hilary felt sadness that they were not able to summit Kings Peak and she would miss the opportunity to see her brother in Colorado. Hilary loves adventure, but she wants to be around to see her children have grandchildren some day. She felt she had let Miriam down by being cautious. After dropping Hilary off at the airport, Miriam drove all the way to Loveland, Colorado to Hilary's brother Brian's house. Miriam had already met Brian and his family several years ago when she and Hilary went to Colorado to acclimatize Miriam for her Aconcagua Climb in South America.

Second Attempt Summiting Kings Peak

Miriam arranged a trip to summit several mountains while traveling with her parents. Kings Peak was the first stop. Miriam, Hugh and Marjorie Richards share their account of this in this chapter and subsequent chapters.

Hugh Richards' Perspective

After deciding to go on this trip, I felt that I should condition myself. I borrowed a backpack from Miriam and carried it on two to three-mile hikes daily. I made the pack heavier after a couple of weeks by filling jugs with water to add the amount of weight I could carry. Eventually I was walking eight miles and the pack weighed about 30 pounds, but this was on level ground at sea level. I am diabetic, and we had to think about what I could eat. Since I would be expending a great deal of energy, it did not seem that a high blood sugar from a meal of mostly carbohydrates would matter because I would soon work it off with the strenuous climb. I did not worry too much about what I picked to eat as long as it had a lot of calories and was low in fat.

The first day of climbing, we drove from Wyoming to the trailhead in Utah, about 20 miles from the RV camp. We parked the car, loaded up our packs and started to climb Kings Peak. After about two hours, we met two hikers who were watching two moose in a small pasture. I talked to the people and exchanged pleasantries. They asked me where I was from and I told them Canada. After we had left their company, I began to think I should not have told them where I was from less they break into our car because they knew we would not be back for three days. It was on my mind the whole time until we returned to the car. I was thankful I had worried needlessly. We climbed all day until about 2 PM when we came to Dollar Lake, a distance of about 7.5 miles and difference in elevation of 1,345 feet.

This was our first camp. We would stay here overnight and climb the mountain the next day. We could see the mountain plainly now as it was a nice clear day. We were at 10,785 feet elevation level. I had no idea how poorly I had prepared myself. I was gasping for breath every 20 feet. Miriam thought I would be all right the next day and that I would be acclimatized by morning. We pitched the tent and made the camp then ate a meal and went to bed early for the climb the next day. While climbing the first day, we met a group of boy scouts and the scoutmasters who were on horseback--very nice people. We did not know how nice until the next day. We got up early at 5 AM on the second day and made a meal of rolled oats and bagels. We started to climb again heading for Gunsight Pass. I had not acclimatized as much as I needed. I was gasping for air every 20 feet. We came to a very steep climb, I said to Miriam that I did not think I could make it any further. I was going to be slow. I gave her a share of the water I was carrying and reorganized the pack. She set off on her own up this very steep climb. I watched her until she disappeared. Then I headed back to our base camp at Dollar Lake.

Miriam's perspective from Gunsight Pass, Utah

I arrived at Gunsight Pass at 11,888 feet at 6:30 AM and parted with my father. I had two older guide books describing two different routes ascending Kings Peak from here. One went across to the right and down, around and up while the other was the main trail heading straight up. I decided to take the short cut that would save me one mile. The trail had rock cairns marking the way at the beginning, however it eventually changed to loose scree on the steep incline so I did not detect any more guide posts or cairns past that point. I could see the false summit, or Anderson Pass ahead, thinking it was the true summit of Kings Peak. Instead, I was 5.5 miles off course! By the time I realized this, I was devastated! I had no choice but to continue the way I had come.

While scrambling up towards Anderson Pass, I grasped the larger boulders, but they slid down the mountainside just as easily as the lightweight pebble-sized scree. There were moments when I reached out to grab what I thought would be a good firm hold, but as the boulder-sized scree moved, I pulled myself away as it rolled down the steep incline. I was lucky I was not going down with it! From the top I could see Kings Peak off in the distance and could not believe how far I had to go!

The descent was not an easy slide down the scree. Instead, I had to carefully plant my feet. For some reason, I had chosen not to bring my trekking poles. Only my feet could test the footing. After descending 1,000 feet, I saw the group of Boy Scouts my father and I had seen our first day hiking in from the trailhead. They quickly recognized me but saw that I was hiking alone now and they showed their concern. They indicated they had just come down from the summit of Kings Peak. I gestured to them that I would begin climbing it. They told me that I was the last one to climb for the day. I went ahead, I just had to.

There was no trail that I could find from this direction so I had to just make my way up Kings Peak like a grasshopper for about two hours. I clambered along in spite of the black clouds hovering overhead. Any high elevation summit becomes dangerous in the late afternoon. Both my mind and body faced incredible stress. When I saw the summit flag waving at the top, I cried, knowing that my goal of summiting was quite different than my final destination. I could not see how I could return to my tent without my headlamp or flashlight. How would I see where I was going? I had come a different way. I told myself that I was stupid to have gotten myself into such a desperate situation. This was my first major mistake of my life. What was I to do alone way up here? I took a self-portrait of myself with the flag while attempting to smile. I look at that photo now and see the strain on my face.

After I had taken my picture, I turned around and the Scout Leader was right there like an angel. I could hardly believe it that he had taken the scouts down to Painted Basin and took two more hours to climb back to reach me! I was so grateful to him! He radioed for a horse rescue and began guiding me back down the mountain. I had a horrible blister on my left foot from having come all this way so I limped back down the mountain. I believe it took me about four hours to reach the Painted Basin in my poor exhausted state.

Stress brings on MS symptoms and perhaps some of those came into play. I had been sweating from the heat, then as the late afternoon clouds rolled in, my sweat contributed to the cold. I was invited to warm up in a tent at the Painted Basin area and plopped down at 9:20 PM. They covered me with blankets as I waited the horse rescue for about 30 minutes.

As I came out of the tent, I was surprised to see that it had been raining and there was lightning. I was concerned for the horses. It was rough going for them to step over the sharp rocks in the Painted

Basin area in the dark. Two of the Boy Scouts walked in front holding the reins guiding my horse and the Scout Leader's horse. At one point, my horse lost its footing and slipped down onto both front knees. It wasn't until 12:30 in the morning that the scouts and horses dropped me off at my tent.

Hugh Richards' Viewpoint

I waited all day until some other climbers started to return. I went back up the trail towards Kings Peak and asked the returning hikers if they had seen Miriam. Eventually I talked to someone who had seen her. They told me she was still struggling to reach the top and one of the scout leaders we had met the day before was helping her. I was very relieved as it was 4 PM. I worried about her for three hours when around 7 PM, one of the other scout leaders came by and told me they were going to get her on horseback as she was in a state of collapse. I thought Miriam would be back any time now so I made supper and waited. I ate my supper, as it was getting cold. Sometime later, the scouts informed me that she wouldn't be back until 11 PM. I was really worried now. I asked if she was hurt. They told me she was just very tired. When they finally made it back, I thanked all of those concerned and I rolled her into her sleeping bag. I heated supper for her. She was trembling so bad she could not eat very much. During my frantic efforts to look after her and get her food, I knocked over the stove, which was still hot and burnt a hole in the tent.

The next day we broke camp and headed down as we had left my wife Marjorie back in Lyman and she expected us later today. We loaded our packs. I tried to take most of the load but there was just too much. Miriam and I started down. After an hour or two, it became too difficult for Miriam to carry a load so I began to relay the packs down the hill. Eventually we made it down and drove back to Lyman Wyoming. WOW, what a time we had, the beauty of the scenery, and the struggle--I wouldn't have missed it for the world.

Marjorie Richards' Perspective

When this trip was first suggested by my daughter, it was my intention to let my husband and daughter go on their own. I was pushed and prodded by my husband until I finally gave in and said I would go. They wanted a driver. So off we went, my husband the cook, me the driver, and my daughter the climber. What a combination. We each had a specific function.

The first day we left from Chilliwack, B.C. and drove to Corvallis, Oregon in our motorhome. On the way, we saw a van do a roll over on the highway just south of Bellingham, Washington, then a motorhome off in the ditch and two more car accidents along Interstate 5. This was not a way to start a long motor trip. Anyway, I drove very carefully so we would be sure and get through at least the first day.

When we arrived at my daughter's home in Corvallis, she was very excited to start the trip. She had everything ready to go. She had been getting ready for months. One thing about her is her determination. Once she sets out to do something it is just a matter of time before it is all planned out and organized and finally finished.

We all helped get her things into the motorhome and she checked her father's backpack, inspected his hiking gear and made ready for the departure the next day. That night, we got to bed early for our start in the morning. The first day we drive along highway 20 through Oregon State to the Idaho border. The smoke was dense at times from all the forest fires and you could feel it in your lungs. My daughter helped with the driving so I did not have to drive the whole way. It made it nice and I was not nearly so tired as I usually am. Usually, I am the sole driver. That night we stayed in Boise, Idaho at Mountain View RV Park.

The next morning we were up bright and early about 7 AM on the road. We were headed for Lyman, Wyoming. This was to be our first stop for climbing. We drove all day through some pretty dense smoke. The forest fires had been quite bad during the summer months. We arrived in Lyman in late afternoon and started looking around for a campsite. The one closest to Kings Peak Utah was reserved so we went to the other end of the town and got a pretty good site there. Our only problem was that it was going to be farther to drive the next morning to start the climb. Miriam said that there was no need to get there too early in the morning because they would only climb for about four hours and then stop to set up camp for the night. The steep climb would be the following day. After breakfast the next day off they went with the car. I was left to hold down the motorhome for four days. This was a long four days.

On the fourth day, I waited with their lunch and they did not come. Then I wondered what had happened and it was nearing supper and I had heard nothing. I was beginning to get worried. When they did return, Miriam could not get out of the car. I wondered why. Then they explained about her getting lost and walking for hours and her rescue by horseback by the scouts. Bless those scouts. Her poor feet had such big blisters. I felt so bad for her. I bathed her feet with baking soda and warm water, fed her and bundled her into bed. She looked just exhausted. But, she said she had a good time. She was to climb the next mountain in a week. I was wondering how she could possibly do it with feet in the condition of hers.

Miriam takes in the scenery atop Granite Peak, Montana

Granite Peak, Montana

Majorie Richards' Perspective

We continued on with our trip, setting out the next day after Miriam summitted Kings Peak. With Miriam still not walking and with her feet elevated all day, we drove on through Rawlins to Casper Wyoming. Finally, that night we got as far as Buffalo, Wyoming and stayed at the Big Horn Mountains Campground. The next day we drove on to Columbus, Montana. Here we stayed at the Mountain Range RV Park. Since we got to Columbus early in the day, we drove around to find the road to the Montana Climb. It was off the highway quite a bit but a nice drive through the countryside.

After an hour or so, we turned around and headed back to the campsite to make ready for Miriam's climb the next day. A good supper and her pack all ready to go, we got to bed real early. We were up the next morning by 5 AM. We had about a 2 ½ hour drive on road that we were not really familiar with, so this accounted for our early start. We got going and made pretty good time until we made a wrong turn. Then we had to backtrack to find our way. The signs were something to be desired. Not too explicit. Eventually we found the dirt road to turn off on. This was an experience because of the large pot holes and cows roaming on the road. Impossible to make any time. So with careful maneuvers on a very narrow road at times and some one lane wooden bridges, we eventually arrived.

The other members of the climb were there. Three men and my daughter. They were all older, somewhere between 45 and 50 years old. The guides and people who carried the supplies had not yet arrived. So we had plenty of time. After about a 30-45 minute wait, the guide team arrived. Much to my relief, there was a girl in the group that was going with them. They checked Miriam's gear and went on to each member of the group doing the same. She was ready to go. After loading up and some redistribution of the various loads each was to carry, the group set off. We were to be back in four days around noon. My husband and I left and drove back to Columbus.

Over the next three days, we rested up and explored the area. On the third night, there was a big fire in the little town of Columbus. The population of this town is 1,600. The building that was burned housed the local pharmacy and had been there for more than 80 years. This was an historic building in this town. This was very devastating. Later, we heard on the news that it was arson. Every fire truck for miles around was on the lone main street of Columbus. It almost burned down the entire main street of this small community. Local residents told us it would raise the cost of drugs as the grocery store with a small area for over the counter medicines could raise its fees. The nearest pharmacy now was in Billings over 40 miles away. It was a sad day for the residents.

On the fourth day, we left after an early lunch for the drive to pick up our daughter. It was a little easier this time to find our way. We arrived around 1 PM. No one was in sight. We waited and waited and waited. It was nearing 3 PM. We were starting to become worried. Where were they? Finally, the three men returned and told us it had been an extremely emotional climb. Our daughter's blisters had come up again and she was having a difficult time walking back to the starting point. The carriers returned with the supplies. Still we waited. About 4:30 PM., our daughter limped in. She was red faced and completely exhausted. *"Oh, but I had a good time."* This was astounding to me as I could think of several things to do to have a good time and I would not look like this or be this exhausted. After retrieving her things and saying our good byes, we laid her out on the reclining seat in the car. Before we turned the first corner, she was asleep. Back at the motorhome, we continued to bathe her feet and bind up her blistered feet.

Miriam Richards' Account of the Climb

I joined a guided climb with Jackson Hole Mountain Guides on a trip designed to go 23 miles in four days on a Class 4 strenuous technical climb. I waved goodbye to my parents, then started off along a gradually climbing trail toward Mystic Lake. Along the way, a cat came out of nowhere and followed along behind me. Mystic Lake is a gorgeous lake in the middle of a large valley. This is where the cat left us, heading off in the Ponderosa Pines.We stopped at the Phantom Creek Trail for our lunch break.

Following lunch, we headed up 26 switchbacks reminding me of our Mt. Whitney, California climb. Once we passed the treeline, large smooth boulders rounded a ridge. I loved the natural beauty of this breathtaking spot. I could see glaciers above, trees below, and "Big Sky Montana."

The place we stopped for the night, around 11,000 feet elevation, had a lovely cool fog blow in, reminding me of an Oregon coast fog in this landlocked state. It played with my eyes, allowing occasional glimpses of the landscape, and then hiding it from my sight.

The next day we moved from 11,000 to 12,000 feet. My favorite part was seeing mountain goat babies. When I saw some white goat hair on the ground, I picked it up and put it in my pocket.

As we walked along, the men in the group talked amongst themselves as I looked all around me, happy to be climbing again. Then all of a sudden, the guide waved to get my attention and pointed up at a mountain peak that looked like it had been shoved straight up out of the mountain. It was overwhelming. But when the guide gestured that I would be going up that, I thought at first that he was joking with me. I watched his expression and realized he was serious. *"Impossible,"* I thought. I had read descriptions from several books and looked at pictures of Granite Peak, but none of them did justice to the real face-to-face look at Granite

Peak. I felt so very small in comparison to the enormity of what was ahead.

That day my guide was worried about the weather. Black clouds moved through high above us pushed by high winds although it was not windy where we were. The next day we left our tents at 3 AM to make our way across boulder fields that I detest all the way to the foot of the enormous rocks. I had a close up look at what I was to climb and it resembled a huge breaching whale shooting straight up out of the water. Now I knew what I was getting myself into. The guide showed me a note asking, *"Are you up for it?"* I said, *"Yes! Go for it!"* We crossed a narrow snow bridge. No mistakes could be made here, it was a long way to fall below. We all had ropes and harnesses and crossed one at a time.

We began our class 4 climb with the guide in the lead. There were places where I could not quite reach because I have short arms and legs so the guide would give the rope a little tug to help. I smiled as he lifted me just enough to get me out of a bind. I was determined to do all the climbing myself otherwise. A little further on, I felt a gentle tug on the rope and a little confused, looked up to see my guide take my picture on a steep pitch with a small lake way down below.

Finally I made it to the top at 11:30 AM to a stunning scene. I reached the big sky of Montana, 12,799 feet! I was happy. We stayed a while to eat lunch at the top before rappelling down. After dropping to the bottom of the pitch, the guide handed me a note, *"I was impressed with you. The other three clients were crying, scared to death."*

By the time I arrived back at camp that night, it was 8:30 PM and I was the last person to get back to camp. Dinner was handed to me. I took the grub with me into my tent and was soon asleep. I had put in a long day and could not stay awake another minute.

We descended 6,000 feet the next day all the way back to the trailhead with very sore feet from my blisters. One impossible climb was over and done with.

Hugh Richards, whom Miriam called "the best rattle-snake defender." He was proud to summit his second high point in North Dakota

The Dakotas

North Dakota, August 17, 2002
Marjorie Richards' Perspective

The next day we picked up and drove on to Theodore Roosevelt Park following highways 90 and 94. That night we stayed in the park near Medora, North Dakota. American state parks are so much more improved than the ones we are used to in British Columbia. Most of them have full hook-ups for RVs, such as electricity, water, and sewer connections. Where we come from in our provincial parks, we are lucky to have a bathroom within 100 feet and a tap with running water, if you have a bucket.

In 1883, Theodore Roosevelt established a ranch on the grounds where the National Park now exists. There are interesting museums on the grounds. The following day we drove around the park. There were prairie dogs running everywhere. We came upon buffalo roaming free on the road and grazing the land. A wonderful place to visit.

The next day, we drove to Amidon, North Dakota. We drove into this town on a Sunday. Across the road was a police car. I asked my husband to go over to talk to the police officer about directions. He started across the road and came back laughing. I thought it was strange. My husband told me it was a mannequin in the car dressed like a sheriff. As we sat and watched, you could see the cars slow down going past. I guess they were fooled as well. We decided to park the motorhome in the center of town and my husband and daughter went off to climb White Butte. This was to be a two hour hike as White Butte was 3,506 feet in elevation. This was a short 2 mile hike for the climbers. They returned in less than two hours and we were off again. Then we drove on to highway 85 and picked up I-90 to Spearfish.

This was a good break for the climbers. The lady at the campsite told us of a scenic roadway leading up to Deadwood. So we took her advice and after lunch started out. We passed some beautiful waterfalls and high cliffs. This is reminiscent of the cliffs west of Salt Lake City.

It was a long drive and we were beginning to think we would never get there. Then we ran into road construction and detours which slowed us even more. It was poorly marked as far as finding the road which would lead us to Deadwood, our destination. Finally, after seeking directions, we arrived. Deadwood has a population of 1,800, with an elevation of 4,532 feet. The town is a deep gulch and the residents live on the steep sides of the canyon. It was a gold-rush boom town in the late 1800s. We wandered around visiting the historic buildings some with winding staircases that you might expect fancy ladies to strut down. In the middle of the main street, they had a staged gun fight. This drew a large crowd and went on periodically throughout the afternoon. We played a few casino games and had supper in a modern hotel. The lady at the campsite had recommended the hotel for it was to have crab legs and all the trimmings. We were not disappointed.

Hugh Richards' Perspective

We headed for Theodore Roosevelt State Park, North Dakota, along highways I-90 and I-94 to Miles City where we bought bread, milk, and eggs. On again to Medora and the Park.

The large prairie dog town had a museum and a small house which was part of Theodore Roosevelt's ranch. The museum had on display all types of flora and fauna. The buffalo where just down the road, all fine specimens.

The campground had a lot of trees and brush between each site, and I wondered about the consequences of fire. We unhooked the car and took the circle drive saw many buffalo, a coal seam, prairie dogs, beautiful scenery of the badlands type.

The next day, we headed for North Dakota's high point, White Bluff, about fifty miles south. We came to a small town and saw what looked like a highway patrolman sitting in a car. I went over to ask directions. To my surprise, it was a mannequin with blue shirt on and a peaked hat. What a laugh on me! We found the road from the directions in Miriam's book. Following the instructions in the guidebook, we hiked up this hill called White Bluff, our biggest concern was they said watch out for rattlesnakes so we carried long sticks, fortunately we did not see any.

We continued on state route 85 south to Spearfish on I-90, found a campground set up camp, had lunch. We then headed up to Lead and stopped at the lookout. We really were surprised to see how much of the old mill had been removed. Thankfully, we have photos of the way it looked ten years ago.

We went to Deadwood, wandered around looked all the old saloons and gambling halls saw a mock gunfight on the street. We went down to the end of town played some slot machines, had supper, and returned home.

Miriam Richards' Perspective:

North Dakota's highest point lies on a farm. My dad and I stopped to knock on the door. As the door opened, our heads dropped down to look at the short woman who opened it. As we handed her $20, she said one sentence, *"Watch out for rattlesnakes."* We drove along the bumpy dirt road before arriving at a barbed wire fence where a post on the fence corner could be removed and set aside for us to step through before replacing it.

Father had worked on a trekking stick carving it little by little on the trip in preparation for this trail, knowing it was infested with rattlesnakes. We hoped we were there before the snakes woke up. Father took the lead with his stick poking through the thick dry grass from right to front, to left and then side-to-side without any hesitation, just tromping along in a rhythmic determined fashion. I scurried along close behind him trying to keep up with his pace until we arrived at the White Butte summit, 3,506 feet. This would be my father's 2nd state high point and my 44th. Dad hurried back to the car just about as quick as he could.

South Dakota, August 20, 2002
Marjorie Richards' Perspective

We headed towards South Dakota to Custer. We camped at the Flintstones' Campground at Custer. This was great for kids. The restrooms were in the shape of Fred and Wilma's house with rounded doorways. Very unique. They had a Flintstone show for families in the evening which seemed to be fairly well attended.

Once again, the climbers went off to Mt. Harney. This time they left early in the morning and returned sometime after lunch. That evening, we wandered around the town doing the usual touristy things. Visibility was not good here as there were still many forest fires in the area.

The following day we took the car and visited Mount Rushmore. I had not been there for 10 or more years and it had greatly changed. The parking facilities had greatly improved. Also, the entrance to Mount Rushmore was lined with the flags of all fifty states. A very impressive site. They had a movie of the creating of Mount Rushmore and the trials and tribulations the men encountered as they carved the rock. Fortunately, the movie was closed captioned so my daughter could understand and appreciate the documentary. About three or four days before our arrival, President George Bush had visited the site. In a way, we were fortunate as we probably would have had a difficult time accessing the area had we been there at the same time.

The next day we visited Wind Cave National Park. Wind Cave was discovered in 1881 and was formed in one of the vast limestone layers underlying much of the area. Strong wind currents blow alternately in and out of the area suggesting its name. The long corridors and galleries are decorated with unusual boxwork and frostwork formations that are illuminated by light. Here they were not able to provide an interpreter for my daughter so I did the best I could to explain what the guide was telling us. This was made extremely difficult at the point when they turned out the lights in the cave and we were in total darkness. However, it was truly enjoyed by all and we had a very good day.

The following day, we went to see Chief Crazy Horse. It is located four miles north of Custer in the Black Hills. You could see this sculpture from the road but we decided to go in and get a close up view. It turned out that there was absolutely no anticipation of ever having deaf visitors. No closed caption, nothing. I made a formal protest over the fact no consideration was given to the deaf visitors who may wish to view the site. Once again, deaf people were overlooked. The mountain carving is still in progress and so far only the face portion has been completed. An interesting day.

After seeing the sights around Custer, we drove over Togwopee Pass elevation 9,658 feet to Dubois,Wyoming. A very steep and beautiful Highway 26 heading northwest. This night we had an extremely well planned out campsite. A lot of forethought went into the laying out of the sites and grounds. There were log cabins for motel guests with tall trees all around. Even horses for those who wished to ride and a stream for the fishermen.

The following day we headed through Casper and on to Jackson Hole. There we stopped to talk to the guides who had taken Miriam up the Montana climb. They were not prepared to take her on the Mt Gannett Wyoming climb. She was told her conditioning was not adequate. This was due to the experience they had with her on the Montana climb. So with her money refunded we left. She was extremely disappointed. But, considering her condition and her poor feet, I was relieved that she would be able to rest up. We wandered around Jackson Hole and had our lunch while there. After lunch, we got back in the motorhome and proceeded west.

We headed for Twin Falls, Idaho, on to Jackpot, Winnemucca, and Reno, Nevada, then home.

Hugh Richards' Perspective

We headed for Custer, South Dakota, which was not a long drive, the air is full of smoke there are many forest fires burning nearby. We set up camp at the Flintsone's RV park in Custer. After setting up, we drove out to see the trailhead for climbing Mt. Harney, South Dakota. high point 7242 feet. The next day, Miriam and I climbed it, and it was more like a strenuous walk. The route up Mt. Harney was built during the 1930's by the relief corp. Periodically, we came upon steps and fences. At the top, there is a lookout tower about 25 feet. high build of stone. You can see where they let the wooden beams into the walls as you go up the recently installed metal stairway to the viewing platform. What a view! We could see the fire near Keystone a town at least 30 miles away to the northeast.

We visited Mt. Rushmore, and what an improvement. The Avenue of Flags with all the columns is very impressive. Took lots of photos, very smoky. The Keystone fire is just over the ridge you can see it bellowing up black smoke as the trees catch fire and explode, making black smudges in the white smoke.

The next day, we went to see the Crazy Horse Monument. It is very rough. It will not be finished for many years. We went to Cave of the Wind Park in the afternoon. This was impressive, but not as big as others we have visited. At the entrance, there was a small hole in the ground the wind just blew out of it hence the name.

Later, we headed for Jackson Hole, Wyoming, a long drive, and camped at Dubois. One of first campgrounds laid out by someone who knew where to put everything. Tomorrow we will get to Jackson Hole to meet the planners of the next climb and talk about canceling it and getting Miriam's money back. Everything worked out to our satisfaction. We headed for home.

Miriam Richards' Perspective:

My father and I left to hike the trail to Harney Peak, beginning with Trail #9 at 6:30 AM. The trail was very nicely organized, one of the nicest highpoint trips. As we walked through a metal staircase tunneling upwards, we spiraled around emerging into the daylight. South Dakotans built this lookout structure on their highpoint 7,242 feet many years ago and it is still sturdy. When I gazed way down and over the side of the lookout, I spotted one lone mountain goat resting peacefully on a boulder below.

Miriam with Ken Litherland's family and Allison Hamstreet on top of the New Mexico Summit

Arizona and New Mexico: Fun With Friends Excerpts from Miriam Richards' Journal

Hilary and I went to Arizona in June 2002 with the intention of climbing Humphreys Peak but were turned away by a closed trail due to a forest fire.

I contacted Allison Hamstreet, a deaf friend who lives in Scottsdale, Arizona asking if she would be interested in climbing with me in late September, 2002. That gave her three months to practice getting in shape for the climb. I explained to her that the trail was not a technical climb, but would be high altitude, 12,633 feet. Allison agreed to go with me.

Allison picked me up at the airport and drove to Flagstaff where we stayed the night at a Motel 6. The trailhead was only about a 20 minute drive from Flagstaff. We were the first climbers to arrive at the trailhead sign. When Allison stepped out of her car, I waited for her to change into her boots. She did not bring any boots with her, just the tennis shoes she was wearing.

The trail began as a nice long walk in the park. It was beautiful and well kept. Eventually, a gentle slope brought us to the foot of Humphreys Peak, not far from a ski resort. We could see the ski lifts. The trail headed gently up, then gently down until we reached the saddle at 11,750 feet. From this point on, the trail narrowed and became very rocky. Foot placement took full concentration. Allison's tennis shoes did not have enough tread to grip onto the rocks. She slipped a few times and fell, gashing her knee. I told Allison that I did not recommend she go any further without boots. I was afraid for her safety. She had mixed feelings about turning back due to her eagerness to climb to the highest point in her state and realizing she could slip off a narrow ledge.

I continued alone, climbing about an hour more before I reached a wooden pole about three feet high marking the summit, 12,633 feet. In the distance, I could see smoke from the Grand Canyon

Fire and imagined snow on the slopes below. I asked another climber to take my picture and headed down attempting to catch up with Allison. Allison was already in her car waiting for me. I enjoyed seeing her again but felt sorry that she could not share a summit victory with me.

Before returning to Oregon, I took Allison to a sporting goods store and bought her a good pair of hiking boots. I invited her to join me on a climb in New Mexico in the summer of 2003. That would give her 10 months of conditioning and opportunity to break in her boots prior to meeting me in New Mexico. Allison accepted my offer.

We set off in July, 2003 for New Mexico. I want to take this time to say thank you to Carla Garcia and Henri, both deaf friends from Gallaudet University, for their week-long hospitality while I was in New Mexico. Also Ken Litherland, a deaf classmate of mine at Gallaudet University who has climbed higher than any deaf person worldwide. He was on his way to the summit of Mt Everest when he turned around to help a friend who was succumbing to altitude sickness.

Allison and I met Ken Litherland, his wife Carol and their daughter Christina from Las Vegas, New Mexico. They really wanted to climb Wheeler Peak, New Mexico with me, the highest point of the state. Neither Ken or his family had ever climbed the highest mountain in their own state, nor, although he was a highly experienced climber had they even considered climbing it, so it took me, an Oregonian, to lead them!

When Allison and I drove from Albuquerque to Taos Valley Ski area on July 4th we found a long lineup of cars in the town of Arroyo Seco where a special celebration for July 4th was to begin. It was cool to see people with pets in the parade. A horse was pulling a fire truck. We waited and proceeded slowly through the town. We checked Alpine Hotel to see if they had a vacancy for one night and the clerk said yes and booked us a room. The area is around 9000 feet elevation which gave us time to adjust to breathing the thin air. Later we bought a ticket to ride the ski lift and view the lovely countryside. It was a nice cool ride. We noticed that Wheeler Peak was fully covered by black clouds. As I took a picture of it I studied where we would hike on the trail. We were satisfied with the conditions for the next day climb. We shopped a little and bought a T-Shirt saying "13,161 feet Mt. Wheeler." We walked around the area and bought a lot of drinking water for the next day.

We were up at 5:00 AM and got ready for the climb. We met Ken, his wife and daughter at 6:00 AM and drove to the William Lake parking area. The first trail was 3.5 miles one way to Wheeler Peak. We began our climb at 6:15 AM. The beginning of the trail was nice and easy with a gradual altitude gain. My favorite part was being able to look up at the amazing view of the mountains with an orange sunrise. Luckily we hiked in a shaded place because we were on the right side of mountain.

We arrived at William Lake, which was much smaller than I visualized from the maps. Three friendly people from India decided to hike with us. The mile from William Lake to the summit was pretty difficult: steep with some lose scree. The altitude combined with the physical exertion and the heat caused me to have difficulty breathing during the ascent. I was impressed to see Ken's daughter hiking pretty well even though she was only 7 years old. Wow! In addition I was pleased to see that Allison had improved over her climb with me in Arizona the year before. The others were ahead of me because I was out of shape because of two emergency surgeries recently. But I thought I was hiking quite well considering. The key is mental and my stubborn spirit motivates me to keep going.

I saw a cute brown marmot standing in front of me. I thought that he or she would run away from me but the critter remained nearby keeping busy with stashing food under its rock. Later that scree on the trail reminded me of similar scree on the Nevada trail that I hated. It pained me to take it step by step breathing hard all the way. Gradually I arrived at the summit full of joy and extended my hand in a "high 5" slap to congratulate Ken and to the three people from India who leap-frogged back and forth around me on the steep portion of the trail. Carol, her daughter and Allison also joined in offering high 5's. We took pictures of each other and signed the registry book. I kissed the benchmark. I estimated around 50 people summited that day. We all were so happy because Ken's wife, daughter and Allison made their first highpointer in New Mexico. I thought about how amazing it was for me to have reached 47th of 50 state high points. Wow, I cannot believe that I did it so recently after two surgeries. At the same time the weather was perfectly clear and sunny. We reached the 13,161 foot summit at 11:00 AM on July 5th. At the top of the summit, we saw heavy smoke in the Pueblo Taos area.

Once we were all satisfied with our time and had fully absorbed the glory and view from the top, we headed back 7 miles on Bull-of-the-Woods Trail, making the trip a loop. We did not realize how long the new trail would be. All of a sudden, what a nice surprise: within a very short time it was snowing! I was thinking the snow appeared to tell us *"Congratulations, you summited successfully."*

After the light snowflakes fell, they were gone as quickly as they had appeared. There are so many mini flowers with such a lovely variety of colors. I recognized columbines. I love exploring the wild outdoors. I was pleased how good the trails were, with a full panoramic view of the mountains. I told Ken that New Mexico is very similar to Montana's geology. Allison hiked downhill quickly while Ken, Carol, Christina and I hiked slowly enjoying and exploring the view. It is always such a delight to interact in ASL with a family where all use sign language.

Later Ken decided to run down to catch Allison for transportation reasons. Hiking alone I took the wrong trail but it led to the right place! It was odd that I arrived first, before Ken and Allison, although both were well ahead of me. They could not believe it when they saw me. The whole trip took us 11 hours to hike. We started to smell the smoke we had seen: a forest fire. Tired, we ate dinner. Ken's family asked me to stay at his place for one night.

The next day Ken invited us to ride his John Deere mini truck as he herded all the cows together to move them to a different pasture. Ken and Christina rode horses while I jumped at the chance to drive the 4-wheeler. Later Ken let me ride his horse for a few minutes and that was cool!

Carol and their daughters and I went to Las Vegas for a Mexican Latino festival. Christina performed four different dances in spite of her long hike climbing with us the previous day. At the same time I enjoyed fully immersing myself into interacting with all the Latino people at their festival, a real Mexican cultural event. We drove to Ken's parents for dinner and farewell. It was fulfilling to have free-flowing ASL conversation with Ken's parents. We drove back to Sante Fe and stayed overnight at Carla's. We decided to buy natural green apple champagne and celebrate together. Carla was amused that I wore my USA boxer shorts as I popped the cork on the champagne. We laughed and cheered. Overall I enjoyed my one-week vacation in New Mexico. I am happy that climb is completed since the trail was closed the previous year due to fire. Hilary and I flew into Phoenix with the idea of conquering the highest mountain in Arizona, and then flying to Albuquerque to climb Wheeler Peak. Both trails were closed completely due to fires. It was not all in vain since we drove to Oklahoma and completed the climb at the panhandle where it overlaps northern New Mexico.

Miriam on top of Gannett Peak, Wyoming, her 48th Summit

Gannett Peak, Wyoming: Miriam's 48th High Point

Miriam made reservations with Jackson Hole Mountain Guides (JHMG), having selected the "Deluxe Gannett Peak Expedition" because this is a technical climb and a long distance trail. She was the sole client provided with two private guides and a cowboy with horses and mules. The trail is very strenuous as it rises up through the Wind River Range displaying steep walls of beautiful rock formations along glaciers.

Miriam flew alone from Eugene, Oregon, with a changeover in Denver, Colorado before landing in Jackson Hole, Wyoming. As Miriam exited the plane, she spotted a Hispanic man holding a sign displaying her last name, "Richards." She waved to the gentleman to indicate that she was the person he was awaiting. As she rode through town, pleasant memories surfaced of her summer job working at Grand Teton National Park. She had missed this scenic land and felt happy to have returned to Wyoming.

The driver dropped Miriam and her bags off at the JHMG office. She searched for a hidden dark location to set up her one-man tent behind a tree by the building for the night. This was in the city. Needless to say Miriam was ill at ease and hardly slept until she felt her tent shake at 5:30 AM. It was her guide, Laura. She told her to have her equipment ready for inspection in time for a 6:30 AM departure. Miriam and Laura had met two years ago on Granite Peak, Montana's highest summit. At that time Laura was a porter. Now she was a guide. She introduced Miriam to her fiancé, Trevor, the other guide.

They rode in Laura's pick-up and stopped at Smith's Food Store and gas station. Laura drove them two and a half hours while Trevor slept. Miriam's eyes were wide sightseeing the beautiful Wyoming geology. She saw several antelopes leaping around in the open. Eventually they arrived at Bald Outfitters Company for horse transport. She watched as her heavy backpack was hoisted onto a scale for weighing. A mule would carry her pack. A horse guide tried to find a saddle to fit her since the straps were too long for her short legs. He replaced her saddle with another for a better fit. Her horse's name was Russia because of his white and red colors resembling the Russian flag.

These sturdy horses are suited for the high altitude; they plod along over the large rocks causing a bumpy ride. They are wider than most horses, stretching the legs of the riders in an unnatural position. Miriam had reasoned that if she carried her backpack up the trail, it would have taken her forever to hike the 20 miles while a horse could carry her over such rough terrain quickly. Miriam did all she could to hold onto the saddle horn as the horse navigated many large rocks and boulders. After five and half hours bouncing along on Russia and having to be alert to shifting her body with the horse as it stepped up onto the big rocks, then down to the ground again and again, her body was sore, particularly her bottom and Miriam was looking forward to hiking on her own two feet.

They stopped at noon for a lunch of dried tomato and basil, lunchmeat, onions, cheese, dip and crackers. The food tasted very good. The weather was sunny, winds on and off. Miriam took pictures. Then they rode another three hours.

Miriam loved seeing the many of features of the terrain, which included waterfalls, small lakes, streams, and incredible shapes, and colors of rock formations. She was mesmerized by the variety of wildflowers crowded in alpine meadows.

The cowboy guide was smoking heavily alongside Miriam while keeping an eye on Russia who gets aggressive at times and likes to run off if given the chance. Miriam had great difficulty dismounting him. By now her legs were quite sore. She found it difficult to walk again. It was 4:30 PM when they arrived at their destination.

The cowboy left immediately to return his horses and mules to the starting point all in the same day. Stock animals were not permitted to remain overnight in the Wind River area due to protection of wild animal habitat and many domestic animals cannot tolerate over 10,000 feet elevation.

Miriam was greatly relieved as she set up her tent and took a short nap to get her mind off her pain. After waking, she strolled around the valley. The guides cooked delicious veggie pizza for dinner and served tea. Miriam sat finding the names of the mountain peaks from her map: Fremont and Jackson Peaks from her vantage point.

The first night Miriam slept at 10,300 feet elevation. Her body had to adjust to this rapid rise in elevation since she came from approximately 300 feet elevation in Oregon the day before. Horse rides can move people to higher elevation gains more rapidly than they would naturally climb on their own. She knew she needed to drink water to help her body become oxygenated.

Miriam saw another JHMG guide named Steve accompanying two clients who slept in the same area for the night. The Wind River trail is very popular although remote. Laura approached Miriam to explain that they would hike four and a half miles to access Timbercross Camp the next day. She asked Miriam to teach her the fingerspelling alphabet before going to bed. Both guides were very friendly.

Excerpts from Miriam Richards' Journal August 11-18, 2004

During the night I slept very well and by morning felt better adjusted to the high altitude. I woke at 8 AM and after drying the tent in the sun Laura taught me how to pack my backpack items in the correct order. I enjoyed the potato with melted cheese that Trevor cooked for breakfast. I drank the green tea that I'd brought.

We left our first night campsite at 10 AM. We began hiking on our own feet carrying our own packs past Island Lake. I spotted a long-tailed weasel on the rocks. The Titcomb Basin Trail was easy and relatively flat for 4 ½ miles along Titcomb Lake. The beauty of the lake view, waterfall and rock formations made it a photographer's paradise. Above me, I saw Twins Peak, The Sphinx Skyline Peak, and Bob's Tower. But it was a special honor to see my own peak, "Miriam Peak." Guide Laura pointed out names of flowers. Skypilot smelled awful. Indian Paint Brush was a bright red/orange color. Alpine Aster, Elephant Head and Lupine were purple. The Primroses had a hot pink color while the Cinquefoil was yellow. All the flowers had splendidly unique shapes.

After stopping to filter and refill our water bottles, I learned that a climber with a different guide decided to quit at this point. Reveling in my strolls along the rivers, I only looked forward and upwards. I identified Dinwoody Peak from my map as I ate my lunch before heading to our next campsite at Titcomb Basin area. I set up my tent next to a huge rock in order to prevent winds from disturbing my sleep. At the same time, I enjoyed watching a chubby pika eating grass. I took more pictures of this Wind River Valley and did some reading. Mosquitoes appeared everywhere. Highpoint Adventures by Charlie and Diane Winger explains the difficulty of hiking across Bonney Pass with its many loose rocks. I was looking forward to the next day's challenges.

On the next day, August 12, 2004, I woke up and thought how nice it was waking up to see Titcomb Lake so quiet in the morning sun. Not long after departing the camp I realized just how challenging it was to hike across the loose rocks in this high tundra with my heavy backpack. Many highpointers have the good fortune to cross this area when snow covers the loose rock making for smoother stepping. I did not complain, but my gut was saying *"This is impossible!"* I called upon my strongest mental and physical abilities to conquer this difficult terrain and drank water continuously.

Soon I saw snow patches mixed among the boulders and loose rock. I admit I was beginning to feel quite nervous during this 1,000 feet elevation gain, constantly climbing from 10 AM until 4:20 PM. My body was very tired but I had no trouble breathing even as the air became thinner. Spotting some pika, I was distracted from my struggles. I kept telling myself to keep going until at last we arrived at the Bonney Pass Summit. Laura beckoned me, wanting to push on to camp at the bottom of the glacier tonight instead of tomorrow. She told me I was too slow climbing today.

Besides the loose rocks and 12,800 foot elevation, my heavy backpack ate up my energy. I have adequate experience having backpacked many years over rough terrain as well as my 14 day solo trek around Mt Rainier. I have worn out 8 backpacks in my lifetime beginning with an old metal outer frame. Over the years I have shopped for better fitting packs to match my body as well as my equipment needs. I suspected that my MS was a factor at this point causing me some sensory issues but I was not dwelling on those thoughts. I was working on my positive mind set. I did not sign up for this guided trip naively. I had read and reread the pack of papers in advance. I had reviewed the expectations for each day's allotment. I felt the total trip was realistic. When Laura spoke with me, I knew that with 8 days set aside for the climb we could afford the time to stop at Bonney Pass as scheduled. This place was perfect for me with the 360 degree view including Miriam Peak and Mt. Gannett. The body recovers faster when the mind is at peace. I begged Laura to camp here and she consented.

I set my tent among the many rocks to block the wind. Two men approached from the direction of the summit. As they drew near, I could see they were twins. They told me they had set their goal to complete 48 state high points, excluding Alaska and Hawaii. Some highpointers choose that route. It was inspiring to meet the twins and nice of them to share their happiness with us.

As I played cards with my guides, we began to see clouds approaching. I lost at "Hearts" and headed for my tent praying for good weather tomorrow and strength for me to continue.

I woke at 7 AM the next morning. My prayers were answered for a sunny day with partial cloudiness. I loaded my backpack. Now at last I put the crampons on my boots after having lugged them all this way. We slid down Dinwoody Glacier, saving a great deal of time. This is called glissading. My ice ax acted as a break to guide the direction and speed of descent. We arrived at Ferrace Camp by 11 AM, having the rest of the day for rest. This is referred to as acclimatizing. As with major mountain peaks, setting aside a day to allow the body to become accustomed to the thin air may mean the difference between success and failure at high altitudes. Food and snacks must be chosen carefully to prevent altitude sickness. We ate hummus with 8 grain crackers. Foods containing fats such as nuts, although high in protein, require oxygen to digest. The body needs the oxygen in the muscles at this altitude. Tonight, I was the winner at "Hearts."

August 14, 2004, I woke up and thought *"What a terrific day for summiting!"* This will be my 48th state summit. I woke at 3:30 AM and dressed for the final climb. I was amazed at the seven shooting stars in the night sky. My dreams and prayers were coming true. I was ready to leave by 4:30 AM. Trevor announced that we must reach the summit before 12:30 PM, a rule that goes with most summits this high. We would be limited to 8 hours. In my mind, I questioned whether or not I could make it. This made me nervous. My emotions began to fire up and I could feel my heart racing. We were ready to start. We left our tents and backpacks. My pockets were filled and I carried my ice ax with the strap wrapped around my wrist.

Arriving on top of the glacier at 5:30 AM, the guide was surprised and pleased that I made it so quickly. My next climb was to be from the bottom to Gooseneck Pinnacle, but my headlamp was fading out. Sunrise was at 6:30 AM at the same time we viewed a crescent moon. The red glow on the mountains added to the stunning sight that spurs my love of the outdoors and experiencing the elements.

Ahead was Pinnacle Glacier with 40 degrees of steep climb with 800 feet elevation gain. I was astounded by the size of the bergschrund, a large crevasse in the glacier. From there we climbed for 2 more hours to arrive at the top of Gooseneck by 8:30 AM.

My guides praised me for doing such a good job. Plenty of time remained to reach the summit. Laura said that we could reach the summit in two hours.

Even with sharp crampons on my boots, there were thin places on the glacier where a step resulted in my leg sinking down into the ice: postholing. The guide was above me on boulders with ropes assisting my glacial crossing. My mind prompted me onwards with reminders that the summit was so close I could taste it. I continued praying as I stepped gingerly across the ice. I admit I was scared. So far Gannett Peak was the most difficult of any of my 47 previous state high points. I do not know how I endured this beating, especially now that I knew I had MS. What I was doing seemed next to impossible. I refused to look down the viciously steep slope I had just conquered. I postholed four times. It was not easy to pull my own leg out of the hole. It had to be done quickly before the ice locked me down. It takes great strength pushing with the opposite leg to free the other with the help of an ice ax.

My mind fought with my body enduring such excruciating physical stress for two more hours until Trevor told me that we were almost to the summit. As it became a reality, I cried for joy at having accomplished such an impossible climb. What a joyful moment! Unbelievable summit! I signed to God thanking him for my successful summit. This was indeed my time to cheer. I made it to my 48th state highpoint! This was my first major victory since my diagnosis with MS. At this point I had been awaiting a course of treatment involving the drug Copaxone. I had no MS drugs with me on this trip.

Once I got my bearings, I saw a big silver pipe containing the summit register. Inside I wrote down *"Deaf Woman, age 39, Corvallis, Oregon, Miriam Richards. Praise the Lord for summit. I truly thank you Laura and Trevor JHMG Guides for big patience. Excellent! Hurrah."* I took in the fantastic view 360 degrees around the mountains in perfect weather. Trevor pointed out that we could see the Grand Tetons in the distance. About 60 miles away from us, the highest Grand Teton was a mere 36 feet shorter than

Gannett Peak. We took a rest before descending to our campsite. I took one last view and farewell.

Of course my heart raced again due to the fear of descending such a steep embankment as we headed back on a route meant to get us down quicker although it was risky. Afraid I would fall on down the mountain, I focused my concentration thinking positively towards having a safe journey down. We left the summit at 11:30 AM and after much glissading and slipping on loose rocks that fell onto the snow I arrived at my tent at 4:30 PM. That was 12 hours on my feet. I yelled *"Hurrah done! Whew!"* Trevor gave me a high 5 as he congratulated me on my 48th State Highpoint summit. We all hugged.

I took off my wet boots and set them on a rock to dry. After hot cocoa, I went straight to bed having endured a long emotional and physical day. I said to myself, *"Congratulations, you did it!"*

This morning, August 15, 2004, I did not enjoy climbing. I got up at 7:30 AM and ate a bagel with cheese. I gave my tent to my guide because my pack was too heavy. We left our campsite at 9 AM and walked back over the glacier trail. Trevor climbed very fast with his long legs stepping across soft patches of snow onto sturdy boulders as I struggled along with my shorter legs maneuvering across the uneven ground. I saw 6 climbers with a yellow lab heading toward the summit. I was so impressed with the yellow lab having made it this far. I continued for 2 ½ hours in the miserable soft snow with loose boulders and became overtired. At last we arrived at the top of Bonney Pass. My energy had run out. My guides told me we must descend. I took a short rest before descending and took in one more close up view of Gannett Peak.

The descent was not much of a reprieve from the ascent. I would have handled the clambering more easily without my awkward backpack listing to and fro throwing me off balance. I fell several times and my guides took some of my things from my pack to lighten my load. I cannot believe the strength of my guides. My pole got stuck into a big rock and broke. I told Trevor to go on without me because he did not like to climb so slowly. So Laura and I continued for another two hours. I stepped so slowly because my knees hurt. I told Laura that I would never again walk on Bonney Pass. I saw flowers again, waves of them and they lifted my spirits. When I saw the flower appropriately named Elephant Head for it's trunk-shaped nose it made me laugh.

At last we arrived at Titcomb Camp. All of a sudden the weather changed into dramatic showers, black clouds everywhere. I was relieved at the opportunity to summit with perfect weather. As I was setting up my tent quickly to keep the rain off me I noticed a small black shape slowly slink near me, some type of mole. I put Ben Gay on both knees to ease my pain. Tomorrow we will hike along the easy flat trail. I was pleased to be nearing the end of my Wyoming trip. Two mountains remain: Mt. Rainier and Denali, Alaska!

I woke to step outside briefly and met a 76 year old climber with his guide heading toward the summit in the downpour. I showed him my banner and he photographed me. Later I was to learn that the bad weather continued for two weeks so it would have been impossible for them to continue over Bonney Pass.

I felt too lazy to carry my 45 pound backpack the next morning, August 16, 2004. I hiked slowly for 4 ½ miles taking me two and a half hours. I needed frequent stops to rest. I used up my strength on summit day and there was little left to keep me going. We stopped between two lakes and crossed a river with my one remaining pole. I took pictures of a lake and was pleased when I saw the slides I had taken gave me the added reflection of the mountains. It was interesting to see the variety of color tones of a colony of ants. We arrived at Indian Pass and camped that afternoon. There were rain showers off and on. Laura set up a tarp overhead. My whole body was feeling strange irritating sensations that I believe to be MS symptoms. I felt sick and took pain pills hoping my symptoms would settle. I looked forward to returning to Oregon and having a nurse instruct me and my friends how to administer daily Copaxone injections. I was not looking forward to the long horse ride tomorrow. I knew that would be the last hardship of this climb. I looked forward to a hot bath at a hotel after 8 days of no bathing. During the night, it was windy and rainy with more thunderstorms and constant lightning flashes. I felt badly for the 76 year old man whom I met heading for the summit in these conditions.

On the next morning, as we were waiting for the horses, I took some time to view the mountains, analyze geology, and watch other groups hike. Not all people come to this pristine wilderness to summit, many come to enjoy the sheer beauty. Many pika were running around the field. Bad weather continued. Trevor left to hike back 20 miles while Laura and I waited for the horses and mules until 3 PM. We wrote notes under the tarp as it rained.

Finally the cowboy arrived with 6 mules and 3 horses. As he organized the backpacks into the mule saddle, I noticed how much he fit his role of a cool tough cowboy. I could only imagine the skills required to get all 9 animals up the rough trail for 20 miles in a lightning storm before guiding them back, what a long day for him! As we headed back, I immediately noticed the discomfort of my legs that would last 6 hours straight. After riding two hours, my horse got a hoof bruise. He stepped off the path onto the soft grass giving him less pain. I tried to gain control of him but he wouldn't cooperate with me. The cowboy decided to give me his horse George, a very tough horse, while he rode mine.

George was easier for me to control, giving me the chance to watch the pika play. The cowboy had to stop three times to organize the mules and cinch the ropes and shuffle their loads that would get off balance from their high and low steps around the rocks. I realized George knew he was nearing his stable when he galloped the last leg of our journey. We arrived at 9:30 PM. It was only with great effort that I dismounted. My legs had locked into position due to so many hours on a wide horse. It was so painful I could barely walk. Trevor gave me a high five slap saying *"It is over!"* He loaded our backpacks into his truck and drove us to dinner before driving to the JHMG office to drop off gear and equipment. It was midnight at the office when Trevor, Laura and I signed my banner. Trevor asked if he could keep it to mount high on the wall of the office to honor my name as the First Deaf Woman with MS to successfully summit my 48th State Highpoint. I accepted the deal. I hope the banner remains there forever to inspire others. They dropped me off at a Super 8 hotel where the clerk carried my backpack to my room. The bed felt good as I lay down but I could not sleep at all that night as I adjusted to a different environment.

The next morning, August 18, 2004, I took a bus to Town Square for shopping. I entered Teton Mountaineering and a store clerk asked me if I needed help. I said *"No, thank you"* as she caught on to the fact that I am deaf. She was thrilled to sign and introduce herself. She helped me to find a nice pair of pants. They have become my favorite hiking pants. I ate a Buffalo Burger for lunch. The bartender signed *"pop?"* and I signed *"yes."* I was amazed to find a town so receptive to sign language. In most towns this is not the case.

Just as I entered the airplane prior to departure we were informed that the weather in Colorado was very bad. We would have to wait one more hour. I realized I would miss my connection to Eugene. Upon arrival in Denver, it was disconcerting that I would have to pay to stay in a hotel after having arrived too late for my flight. I frantically searched for an alternative and found a flight to Portland. I tried to page Robert to let Hilary know, but she had already left for the Eugene airport. I rented a car from Portland and arrived in Corvallis at 4 AM. My baggage was delivered to my house the next day. Hilary could not hear the public address system at the Eugene airport, so a lady found her to tell her that I had missed my flight. Robert had described what Hilary looked liked when he spoke to the lady by phone so she could find her. What an adventure story.

Miriam with her two RMI Guides on Mt. Rainer

Mt. Rainer, Washington: Three Attempts

Six years before her first attempt to summit Mt. Rainier, Miriam hiked the Wonderland trail around the mountain alone. This was a significant feat. Below, she recounts her hike in vivid detail.

Wonderland Trail Hike
Excerpts from Miriam Richards' Journal

On August 14, 1998, a sunny day, I left Longmire and said goodbye to Leslie, who worked as a carpenter/ranger at Mt Rainier National Park in Washington State and started off along Wonderland Trail. It is 75 % uphill and 25% downhill. My backpack was approximately 60 pounds and my body so tired from having just finished painting a house that I had to take a four-hour nap. I hiked and rested often. My mind wandered to many topics as I walked along. I saw a Nutcracker bird, two frogs, a snake, and mice. I passed Rampart Trail and continued until I reached the first river crossing. The first river crossing was a short bridge in the middle of a place where two rivers converge. It did not make sense that a bridge would be in the middle while water flowed on both sides of it. I assumed the rivers must have laughed at the bridge as they changed direction some years ago. It scared me because it was hard to hike across the major river without a bridge spanning both. I tried to think positive as I leaped across looking for large firm rocks to ford my way while balancing my heavy pack. Unfortunately I stepped on a loose rock, lost my balance and fell on my left side-- getting half my body wet. I struggled to get up from the icy cold glacial water. I felt very upset this first day to have this mishap at the start of the trail. Oh well, I had no choice but to go on because of my stubborn mindset to prevail.

I continued hiking with my whole left side soaked as well as my left boot squishing water as I walked. Then I checked my backpack and found that I lost a water bottle! That is the most important survival item. I had just one water bottle left. I had to be extra careful to ration my water for the day so I would not run out. Of course, I felt very disappointed, but hoped I would meet a ranger so I could ask for another bottle. I told myself to think positive and look beyond what happened. Thirteen more days remained before my scheduled completion of the Wonderland Trail. I slept at Devil's Dream Camp #1 and strung all my wet clothes between two trees; my sleeping bag was mildly wet. Later I searched for water and luckily I found a pond. I saw 1,000 tadpoles in the water. Amazing! I filtered the water by running it through my water-purifying bottle. I ate my dinner and slept without a tent. I chose not to take a tent because it was too heavy for me to carry with the other supplies that took priority. I covered myself with a homemade window screen I had rigged up to fit over my face as mosquito protection. I pulled my tarp up to my neck as if it were a blanket. I love sleeping out in the open air! I crave solitude. I'd hoped for the best. It worked fine.

When I woke up the next morning, it was cloudy and cool, without much sun. I picked up my backpack and set off. Soon I met a ranger, a godsend! He asked me if I had made it across Kautz Creek. I told him that I fell and lost my water bottle. He paged his wife in Indian Henry Cabin, two or three miles further up the trail to ask her to give me a new water bottle. It was so nice of her to offer me some water along with the water bottle. I was happy and felt so relieved! I took pictures of the ranger's wife and their cabin and thanked her very much. The mountains framing their cabin made a lovely picture.

I continued to walk. It was hard to resume walking again on the second day. I hiked slowly as my left knee hurt. An area in my left chest and lung were painful maybe due to my backpack being too heavy. Two backpackers sharing the load is more efficient because only one set of pots and pans is needed, only one stove, cooking fuel, tent, tarp, water filter, first aid kit, matches, binoculars, and camera. Hilary was in England visiting relatives. I missed her.

Normally there is a give and take sharing the load. A solo backpacker must foot a much heavier load. I have no fear facing the challenge of solo backpacking and there is a spiritual feeling to being alone in the wilderness, a time for self-reflection. The trail was now 50% descent and 50% ascent. Lots of chipmunks, and two cute marmots for company as I tried to balance my heavy load crossing loose rocks that hurt my feet.

I spotted a narrow bridge ahead. Three Chinese boys backpacking passed me walking fast. Wow! I felt like an old lady plodding along. Many wildflowers in all directions made every view a painting! My mind thinks about different issues minute by minute. One moment I felt sad for no apparent reason and a moment later I felt fine. I was so tired and some areas of my body ached while others hurt with a sharper pain. I hoped I would have enough energy to endure the complete trip. I cooked my dinner at a wilderness camp at the North Puyallup River, read books and pulled my tarp over me at 9:00 PM.

I hiked on August 16th to a cloudy and rainy day in wet socks, boots, and shorts, I got thoroughly upset. What an afternoon! For the last three nights mice had bothered me. I didn't sleep well and the tarp leaked into my left boot; it was full of water. I hurried to pack and left camp. I hate low plants that are so full of water they cause wet boots and shorts. There seemed to be no end in sight.

I hiked at a faster pace hoping to shake off some of the water the plants were brushing on my pants. Eager to get out of the aggravating wet bushes, I understood what it was like to be a sheep being herded through a sheep dip. I hated the feeling and became short-tempered and screamed, not even bothering to look around. I repeatedly twisted the water out of my socks. I hurt my left knee again. I saw a big hawk and chipmunks.

At the 3.6-mile point, I had reached the halfway point. I met the three boys again and they just waved at me. They were as wet as I was. Because it was so wet and cold, I continued hiking without any breaks or lunch. Then I passed another boy. I stopped at North Pullage camp and searched for an individual camp. It was damp so I decided to move to the group camping area. There was a small place to hide with dry ground shielded by the trees. It started to rain and I tried to set up the tarp but it made me upset. I yelled *"Why me? I am innocent!"* By the third day I had expected sunny summer skies. While I wrote my journal, it kept raining. I tried my best to keep myself warm. No one was here to accompany me. I must to do everything myself without asking anyone to help.

Tomorrow it would be five miles to Golden Lake cabin (ranger house). I hoped someone would be there and I would have an opportunity to get warm indoors and dry my clothes and socks and boots. I wished I had brought a tent and rain pants. A coat would have been better than a poncho. I hoped I would make it through tonight and not get hypothermia. I was so chilled. I am using my special propane fuel to help me get warm, careful not to use too much like "The Little Match Girl." The Wonderland trail really needs to be repaired or change its name to Misery trail.

It was sunny the next day (August 17th) for a very short time. Then it turned cloudy and cold for the remainder of the day. The ranger cabin was uphill, a very long steep trail. I passed four men who appeared to be out on a day hike. I had hoped someone would be in the ranger cabin but no luck. It was hard to dry my wet clothes, socks and boots. I had planned to dry them by the heat from the gas cook stove. This day I was not feeling very happy. There was not much to think of but when I got there the empty ranger cabin next to Golden Lake was nice. For the first time I slept very well as it was warm enough this night. I slept under a cabin roof overhang. Oh good! One mouse on my head bothered me. Perhaps it was intrigued with touching my long hair and smelling my bad breath. I saw birds, a snail, and a pika. The trail was much better than yesterday. I became chilled and needed to warm myself with more heat from my stove fuel. I hung my clothes on the ranger's windows. Tomorrow I would hike 6.4 miles to Mowich River. By the map, the trail is supposed to descend.

The morning of August 18th was cloudy and I was fogged in all day. The descending trail was easy, similar to Mary's Peak. When I woke up in the middle of the night as nature called, I saw clear stars. I woke up around 7 AM. Soon it was sunny but thick clouds moved in within an hour. I hiked and saw several lakes and small birds flying. There was not much to see due to the dense fog. I felt alright. It was so quiet. I made up two different stories in my mind while hiking. One story was about how, at my workshop for the DeafBlind Retreat camp during the last week prior to my continent high point trip, I would add a climbing tale about my upcoming South American trip. Some ideas I thought of were to demonstrate the ice axe, boots, and crampons – letting them touch and get an idea as to what mountaineering is all about.

A second story came from my silly imagination. Because I have seen many trees that have fallen everywhere, I realize that being deaf I could not hear any cracking sounds as they fall down. I have daydreamed that as a big tree hit me, my two trekking poles hit my collarbone and my stomach and I had extensive internal bleeding and had to reach for my whistle to blow for help. Four backpackers heard my whistle blow to warn them. Immediately they came running toward me. I used my finger to write the words in the soil: DEAF, HELP, HURT! Two backpackers ran to a Ranger Cabin six miles away as the two other backpackers focused on my immediate medical needs. I was going into shock but one backpacker urged me to stay awake as much as possible. I wrote letters with my finger in the soil and fingerspelled sign language ABCs to teach them as they struggled to keep me awake. Later they introduced their names by sign language. In the meantime, the two other backpackers yelled for three rangers to dispatch a rescue team. They got a horse to race and help me but it was a three-hour wait. Initially, they arrived and used a chainsaw to cut the heavy tree. Then rescuers put an IV in my hand. They lifted me into a rescue stretcher and carried me back to the ranger house where there was open space for the helicopter to pick me up. It zoomed to the hospital and the doctors said that it was amazing that the tree did not hit my neck paralyzing my back. They performed surgery on my collarbone and my stomach. It took a month to recover. Two months later, I would be back to normal and ready for the highest point in South America, Aconcagua. I am stubborn and don't give up. That was my made up story to keep me busy. Perhaps these imaginings help to prepare me for what I might face.

I crossed Mowich River by bridges. There was lots of open space at Mowich River Camp, however the ground was too rocky to sleep on. There was a great sheltered cabin. It was good sleeping inside and avoiding the rain! My wet clothes were hung up all afternoon. I really hoped they would dry! I met two other backpackers in the shelter and I said and waved *"Hi"* but there was no communication in return. I would attend to my own needs and myself. I sat on the rocks watching the river flow while I read and relaxed. I had not seen any wild flowers this year compared to last year when we hiked the Skyline Trail lush with their beauty.

Pah! Pah!(ASL sign with voice translated as "Hurray! At last!") August 19th came with sunny and blue skies. Warm!!! That night, again a cute mouse crawled into my backpack and I caught it in my flashlight beam. It was so funny! The mouse was confused as to which direction to scurry due to the bright light blocking its vision. Good drama unfolded. I had no worries about the mouse inspecting my backpack since my food items were carefully cached in a tree every night. Then I dozed off and again mice came to see me closely. Perhaps the first one beckoned his friends to have a close up look at a real human without a tent. I yelled at the curious mice.

I slept all night and woke up to repack my backpack. Then I started trudging up steep hills for 4.5 miles. I was sweating profusely. I stopped for several breaks. I passed six people. Finally I saw Mount Rainier again and arrived at Mowich Lake, a nice campground and nice lake. I went to the ranger house to pick up food for the next five days, but no luck, no one was there. I was hungry for lunch. I had to eat a cereal bar. Only two GU packets and the cereal bar remained. Then I washed my dirty clothes and socks and washed my hair as well. I felt much better and hoped the clothes would dry faster before sundown.

I was happy that the ranger arrived at 3 PM. Hurray! I got the two food boxes that I had given my friend Leslie to drop off at this ranger station for the next portion of my backpacking loop. I gulped my delicious late lunch. It was funny that Leslie put a fish toy in my food and a treat of three bags of chocolate drink. At last I was relieved and went to Mowich Lake to relax and read. My boots finally dried out completely!! There were about 20 people camping at Mowich campground. I thought I would lie down on a picnic table if the sun permitted. If it started raining, my strategy was to sneak under cover of the ranger house roof. I could walk inside my sleeping bag without the burdon of a tent, I was quite portable. This late afternoon it remained sunny. I saw a very cute marmot within 50 feet of me. I also saw two pika today.

The next morning was sunny and partly cloudy. Last night again mice bothered me twice but I didn't mean to drown the cute mice in my water bucket. When I emptied the water, I did not expect frozen dead mice to fall out. Sorry, poor innocent mice--the next time I will empty the water before going to bed. I was awakened around 4:45 AM due to raindrops on my face. I said, *"Oh no not rain again!"* I put the tarp and net over me. But the rain lasted only a short time.

Then I packed my stuff and hiked very slowly, taking my time. Three young boys passed me twice and they hiked so fast 5.5 miles of steep descent. Then 3.2 miles of nice stable trail with little ascent across rural wooden bridges was a welcome relief. I saw several slugs and one bird. My backpack was heavy with my renewed food and fuel for five days. I strung up my tarp as a canopy hoping it would work out well tonight. I prayed for no rain.

I watched three backpackers attempting to walk over the narrow suspension bridge anticipating doing the same tomorrow morning. Carbon River Falls was very nice. I was betting that another mouse would come crawl on me. Imagine, I thought, I already had completed seven days of backpacking! The total mileage so far was 42 miles. I had seven more days to go.

I thought about a sign I saw "Backpack into wilderness? 1) Freedom 2) Challenge 3) Responsibility." Yes, freedom to have solitude and do what I want and my time to explore. Challenge my physical ability and mind, test my endurance and stamina. Responsibility is taking care nature/animals and being ready and alert for the next day. I read from four books daily: 1) Into Thin Air 2) Altitude illness prevention and treatment for South America 3) Parables of Hope for Disabled 4) Daily Devotions for the Deaf.

After reading and sitting on the hill where I had the best view watching people crossing the suspension bridge, I left at 5:10 PM planning to walk across the bridge for practice without my pack. But when I noticed the sky was full of black clouds, decided to back off.

I walked to the river to replenish my water supply. Then I saw two women setting up their tent with a huge tarp. One of them tried to throw a bear bag over a tree branch. When I offered my help, she said something to me. I told them I was deaf so she called another woman who knows sign language. *"Hi"* was the sign she knew, that was all. I offered my help to throw the bear bag but they told me *"No thank you."* So I left them alone.

As my dinner was cooling, I became concerned about the weather for the night. One of the women, Sarah, came to me when she heard a thunderstorm coming. She was so nice to offer a place for me to sleep under her tarp. I accepted and told her my tarp was the worse for wear. They introduced themselves to me and I read my book until nightfall.

As I was lying comfortably under the tarp, I remembered having seen six women camped out beside Carbon River. Suddenly at 3:00 AM there was a very dangerous thunderstorm near our camp. I felt comforted with the two women who provided extra protection for me and began to pray for the six other women to be safe. I trusted that God would take care of us. I felt calm and had no fear. The thunder shook the ground making huge banging noises for an hour. I kept praying that it would stop. A very heavy rain dropped out of the sky. I was concerned that a lightning bolt might hit a tree causing it to fall on us, but nothing happened. I praised God and thanked him for protecting us that night. I had never experienced camping out during such a severe thunderstorm.

I woke at 7 AM on August 21st, earlier than usual due to lack of sleep again with mice tickling my sweater cap. I wrote a note to Sarah to thank her for saving my life and for preventing me from getting seriously wet. I waved goodbye to the women and was on my way by 8 AM. This morning, there was fog and low clouds in the lower and upper elevations. It was sunny and partly cloudy.

Then it was time to walk across the narrow suspension bridge soaked from all the rain during the night. I carefully walked across and made it to the other side. Whew! What a long upper trail! I took it slowly as there was no hurry. I trudged up, up, up until I noticed the clouds and fog below while above me it was sunny. I passed eight backpackers going down.

I chanced to meet a lady backpacker who happened to know sign language. She is a school teacher in Klamath Falls, Oregon and she graduated from Oregon State University. We chatted a short time and then I proceeded. As I headed back uphill, I spotted 14 marmots with one darling new baby. I saw many small birds, jade bugs, two one-inch frogs, and several chipmunks. I saw the back of beautiful Mount Rainier. That made me happy. The trail was exceptionally pretty this day. My body was so weary and my shoulders hurt due to the heavy backpack. I saw sparkling Mystic Lake and found there were thousands of tadpoles. Wow! I walked toward the Mystic Ranger cabin because I wanted to sleep under the eaves. No ranger there, so I waited.

I was about to take a short nap due to the fact that I felt so tired. A lady stepped on the porch board, enabling me to feel the vibration and wake up. She looked and said something to me. I told her that I am deaf. I was surprised that she knew a little bit of sign language. Normally when I mix with the general public shopping, traveling, presenting at workshops, or participating in athletics, it is rare that I would happen to meet someone who knew enough sign language to carry on a conversation. We had a short chat and she told me she was a speech therapist for deaf children. She said she and two other ladies needed a permit to sleep overnight at Mystic Lake. I explained that the ranger was not there. *"Do not worry, you take my permit tonight because I want to sleep here under the eave due to the fact that I have no tent. I can't afford to get wet again tonight. You never know."* She told me that if I needed help or anything to come and see her at the camp. I said sure. She was so happy.

I stayed at Mystic Lake two nights as a break and to catch up on much needed rest. I had completed 45 miles. Now 48 miles remained with five days left. Wow! My body was still in good physical shape. Although I am skilled at reading topo maps, I did not quite realize how steep the terrain would be. It wasn't until after I completed the full 93 mile loop that I learned I had climbed over 20,000 feet total accumulated elevation gain (6100 meters) over my journey several years later.

I needed to get water for drinking and dinner before dark. I walked to camp Mystic #1 to check and see if everything was all right with three ladies. They used my permit and invited me to join them for two hours of company. Fortunately, Alex knows basic sign language so it was easy to chat with less note writing back and forth. This was welcome company for me. The ladies worked for a hospital for children. One is a speech therapist, one is a psychologist, and one is an occupational therapist. Alex is a Canadian working here for six years on a visa. Nancy moved often from Iowa to Chicago to Detroit to D.C. to Washington State. The other lady was shy--I forgot her name, but she was born in Washington.

As we chatted, we met another backpacker, Aaron, from Fort Bragg, California, who had been on the trail 9 days. He told us a story about his aunt. One day the aunt and uncle went camping in the Sierras in California. So they camped far away in a big tree. Lightning hit the tree and it fell down opposite them. Close call! But the electricity from the bolt shot through the tree roots underground to his aunt's feet, burning them. His aunt woke up and screamed. His uncle said *"Hey don't worry everything will be all right."* But by the next morning they could see that she got a mild burn to her feet. That was an interesting story and relevant to us after having had a thunder and lightning storm so close to us.

I learned that Alex had climbed Mount Baker, Mount Rainier twice, and Mount Adams three times. Wow! We spotted three cute deer passing through the campground. I was getting up to leave but Nancy begged me to wait to take a picture of us as fond memories of the trail before my departure. Within a few minutes I suddenly felt so isolated again since my 8 solo days prior to meeting the ladies. I told myself *"Do not worry, solitude is a good experience. Then when one meets with good company it is more special."*

I set up my thermo pad to turn in for the night. Quite unexpectedly the ranger showed up at 8:30 PM. He knew that my expressions were apologetic for breaking the rules camping beside the cabin but gave me his consent to sleep under the eave. I slept on and off until finally the night sky cleared with stars overhead.

The next morning (August 22nd) was sunny and warm. I woke up as a result of the curiosity of a marmot crossing the porch boards. The ranger asked me if I was okay and if I slept well. I told him I was fine and there were no problems. The ranger left to do his routine. I took my time eating breakfast and sipping my green tea. Four ladies appeared and asked me to take a picture of them. I obliged. How sweet it was of one of the ladies to give me a candy bar. Two of the ladies continued backpacking while the two others stayed one more night and planned to hike up to the glacial area. She told me that she would wave to me when they get to the top of the glacier. I told her I would watch for them and asked her to be careful and wished them good luck. They grinned at me in reply. Later three new men appeared and said *"Hi"* because I was sitting on the porch of the Ranger cabin. Perhaps they mistook me for a ranger?

I decided to move to Mystic Lake and stay all afternoon for lunch, read, and relax my mind. I took time to breathe in the fresh air.

Another family of six people appeared. After reviewing my goals and plans, I thought I would try to cover 10.9 miles to the next overnight at Sunrise Camp. I had spent five hours that afternoon 12 to 5 PM sitting next to Mystic Lake. I had a suntan after having applied sunscreen three times. Scoping out the area, I saw approximately 20 people hiking around the lake. I could not believe it when I saw that a man caught three fish, one was a beautiful trout over 12 inches. I wished I could fish too. Oh well, nap for an hour, read book and watch the landscape. The verse for today told me to get away from the world's problems and spend more calm and quiet time to gain spiritual peace. What a perfect day and I thanked God for the blessed day. I needed that.

As I promised myself, by 5:00 PM I took a short stroll around the lake and saw about 5,000 tadpoles busy swimming. Amazing. I saw just as many busy ants! Then I filled up my water bucket to cook dinner. I cooked pasta with tuna fish while re-packing my backpack. I poured some of my white gas into the ranger's bottle because it was too heavy to carry. I loved watching chipmunks scurrying. The ranger wrote a note saying *"more clouds developing tonight, will have showers through the morning, may clear by afternoon."* I just hoped no rain would fall tomorrow because there is no shelter available at Sunrise. If rain was heavy, I might ask someone to let me sleep in their tent. I would wait and see how the weather would turn out tomorrow. I slipped into my sleeping bag at 9 PM and read from my book Into Thin Air.

August 23rd was cloudy, windy, cold like snow with showers. What a long day to hike! I left the cover under the eave of the ranger cabin. I could not figure out why my body was still weak, I simply did not have enough strength. I walked slowly. Now that my Multiple Sclerosis has been diagnosed, I look back and realize why I was so weak at the time. I passed two ladies in their 60's and saw them again. One lady fell down. I offered to help her up but she said she was fine and thanked me. They planned to camp out at Granite (5.5 miles). I told them I was heading to Sunrise, 11 miles. They said *"Oh what a long day! You better hurry up!"* I agreed and said goodbye. I hiked slowly while thinking positively. Suddenly, I became chilled. I kept going, drinking some water and eating GU.

I passed several backpackers and saw a blue glacial cave. I passed by Granite camp and then had a short break. I kept going to the top of the rocks where it felt so very cold and windy. I put on a fleece coat under my raincoat. There were low clouds all the way up and I was barely able to see the view. There were four marmots again. I decided to take pictures but startled when a ranger surprised me. I said *"Hey your walking is as fast as running."* He said *"Oh my backpack was too light, making it easy to walk fast."* Then I let him go and said goodbye. He disappeared into the clouds.

"Keep going," I told myself. I was surprised to see the two men again. It confused me as to where they hiked. One man told me that I was coming close to Sunrise. I stumbled up to him. I kept going until four trails crossed. I was confused as to which trail I should go on. Two ladies who had a map directed me in the direction of Sunrise Camp. Whew! I only needed to make it down one more mile. Finally, I spotted several rangers working to plant vegetation. It turned out I had walked in the wrong direction but added on less that one quarter of a mile. They beckoned me to come with them because there was not a proper sign or arrow. So I turned back and followed the workers to Sunrise camp. The extra distance with a heavy pack was difficult, but when I finally arrived I knew I had survived another major hurdle.

It had been a long 6 ½ hours making my way to Sunrise Camp. My body was so chilled! I shivered badly. It was so cold. I set up my tarp and went to the bathroom. I started my period so no wonder I got so cold throughout my body. Then I went to the shallow lake to refill my water and fire up my gas stove. I made tea first to warm my cold body, then I ate soup with rice and a can of chicken. I drank more tea and let the gas stove burn all night to keep my hands warm. I had plenty of white gas so I used it up all night knowing I would get more white gas tomorrow at White River camp and it would last for four days of cooking.

I had three or four more days to go. Worse, Sunrise Camp was located at a high elevation of 6,300 feet. It made sense that it was very cold at this elevation. I had to force myself to think positive to keep myself warm. My body shook on and on. I drank hot tea every hour until dark. I was looking forward to finishing my backpacking trip in spite of the intense cold and rain. I was beginning to feel lethargic and I could not wait to take a hot shower and sleep in a house. I was surprised that I had endured 10 days in the outdoors without even the shelter of a tent. I must be strong. Two hours remained before dark. I hoped I would make it tonight without succumbing to hypothermia and asked God to keep me warm tonight.

At last the blue sky I had asked for arrived on the next day! I did not sleep well the night before because I slept without protection at high elevation in the cold. Both of my hips hurt due to my thin sleeping pad. I had no choice but to follow my schedule and get up, hoist my pack on my back and put one foot in front of the other. I was rewarded by the nice view of Emmons Glacier. The descent was too steep and hurt my feet. I kept myself going only by creating different dreams to distract myself from my misery.

Two ladies paused and were puzzled as to what was causing the noise emanating from me. I was amused by their funny facial expressions. I carried two bear bells along to let any bears know of my presence. This was especially important as I hiked alone. Hearing people are heard more easily by their chatting or whistling. They may also hear the presence of bears. I walked toward White River ranger cabin and spotted a trashcan. This was a cause for celebration. After having to carry my trash for five days and cache it for five nights, I could finally relieve myself of the stinky burden.

I continued to the ranger cabin to pick up my last four days supply of food. But the office was closed. Suddenly, by coincidence I ran into my friend Leslie who was making a quick stop at the National Park cabin as part of her ranger duties. She had dropped off my last supply of food and fuel here over a week previously. We both found it incredible that we happened upon one another after having said goodbye 11 days ago. Leslie was concerned about me and she asked me how everything was. I told her that I made it but it was a tough trail with annoying weather and more up and down steep trails than expected. She looked at me amazed, *"You made it all this way within 11 days!"* She saw that I lost weight and admitted that I looked awful. Then she told me to just get in her truck and she would drive me back to my car where I left it in Longmire. I said that I had four more days to go to hurry and finish. She questioned whether or not I would make it. I assured her that I was determined to finish what I started.

Leslie, who can sign and voice, made several calls as to where my food had been stashed. She showed me a 1926 ranger cabin that they had restored. She drove me up to another ranger cabin asking where my boxes of food had been cached. Another ranger, Debbie searched for my boxes. She followed us back to the White River Cabin where she located our food behind the cabin. It was in a special garbage bag can well hidden for Wonderland Trail hikers to use in advance of their trips. Although that excursion wasted 1½ hours, it was a welcome rest and distraction.

I repacked food into my backpack and started to hike again. It was a late start because it was already noon. I started feeling nauseous due to my period. However, my energy was gone with none left to hike any further. I stopped for many rest breaks. I had to move on although I could hardly stand on my tired and blistered feet. It was especially difficult with my heavy menstruation. I lectured repeatedly to myself urging my tired body onward. I had to continue with only five more miles left. Although that may not seem very far, I was battle worn. The trail was very neat, wide and the best so far. I saw several waterfalls and struggled to hike although it took me five hours. It was a long trail.

I saw the ranger and he told me that I had one more hour left until I would reach Summerland camp. In my mind, no way would I make it. No energy remained to hike but I had no choice. The last portion was an uphill trail until I finally reached the camp! My intention was to sleep under shelter but three rude boys would not allow me to sleep. When they saw me arriving at the camp, they waved me off away from their area as if they owned the place. I became upset. I was crabby because of my period, and I needed a warm place, I almost cried out because I was shunned and had no place to go for shelter. I had no choice but to put my sleeping bag out in the open area to survive with my tarp pulled up blanket-style. I hoped for no rain especially not tonight. Both my feet had juicy, painful blisters, and by this time I had tied my boots onto the outside of my backpack and resorted to sandals. It was difficult to walk with sandals across the sharp gravel trail.

I used my gas stove for two hours to help warm up. I wished so very much that I had brought my tent. Be patient, I told myself, three more days to go. I hoped I would survive. Much to my surprise, Summerland camp had the best clean toilet house. Now as I approached the end of my journey, clear visions came to my mind of my trials and tribulations over the past 11 days alone in the wilderness. I saw myself fall down in the Kautz River the first day, losing my water bottle, wet for three days, mice bothering me, difficult trails up and down, thunderstorms, cold nights and sweating from the heat and weight of the pack. This was a great challenge for me. However I was nearly across an almost impossible barrier. Summerland camp area was superb. The Frying Pan Glacier was beautiful. Wildflowers along the slopes were various colors and shapes. There were many squirrels and birds. I noticed the fog rolled in. I hoped I would have a chance to sleep well this night. It was a good thing my friend Leslie gave me an extra fleece jacket so I carried two, one for my chest and one for pants. Again, I urged myself to think positive and struggle to the last.

I was surprised how fast the night went. I slept well because of the extra fleece Leslie gave me. August 25th was sunny with partial clouds. I got up late at 8:15 AM and left at 9:30 AM. I walked like a caterpillar and took my time across several glacier trails. Tomorrow should be less than five miles to Indian Bar. It is a beautiful area from the summit to Indian Bar. I saw three marmots. Unexpectedly, I saw a mother bear with her cub within a half mile distance. It was hard to get a good look at them from that distance. They walked so fast in a different direction. I took several breaks and a lot of pictures. Across the top, I thought to myself, it looks exactly like The Sound of Music. The area was alive with the hills. The view was magnificent! I felt like I was on top of the world and all around amazing green and purple flowers as I meandered. It was a surprise to see the bear and her cub only 500 feet from me!

I had assumed the mother would be taking her cub in the opposite direction. She surely smelled my strong odor! They crossed in front of me and I froze. I could hardly believe it! I scrambled for my camera without taking my eyes off them and took a picture. They keep walking fast acting as if I was just another part of the wilderness. The cub tried to run to keep up with its mother, so cute! I was so happy to have witnessed that special moment, knowing what a threat a mother bear can be protecting her cub. I strolled along until a lady backpacker caught up to me. I told the lady about the bear and her cub. She said, *"Are you serious!"* I told her yes. She walked quickly and hurried on.

I passed a lot of waterfalls this morning along the way. Then I spotted Indian Bar cabin. The bad news was that the shelter had a bad smell of urine. It stunk. I asked the lady who had passed me if she would mind that I join her spot to camp. She said it was okay and offered me some potato chips. I set up my tarp next to her tent. Her name was Teri and she had come from Buffalo, New York to go backpacking for 12 days.

The area was full of beautiful wildflowers. It was wonderful to see that. My feet still hurt and my left thumb was raw. The skin had opened up. My back and shoulders hurt badly. I seemed that I had had enough backpacking on this trip. But there were only two more days to go. I wished I could fast forward time. I am looking forward to having two days bed rest this Friday and Saturday before going to the DeafBlind Retreat camp for one week as a volunteer. I told myself, *"Come on, you can do this Miriam! You will be fine within two days. You will make it with God's help."*

It was sunny and partly cloudy over the mountains by morning. I had not slept well the night before. The funny mice bothered me three times. Two guys helped to fix my gas stove, and then I ate my dinner and read. I didn't like the grueling hike that went deep down then came back up. Roller coaster trails. My feet still killed me. My hip, rib, and shoulders were getting rubbed by the straps. I had more than enough pain in different areas. Later I saw Mount Adams with clouds down below. As I hiked, my mind told me to hurry and get to Nickel Creek Camp. I felt extremely exhausted due to lack of sleep and pain everywhere. My backpack never seemed to change; the heavy weight was a daily occurrence. I saw butterflies, bees, a frog, and birds.

Upon my arrival at Nickel Creek camp, all I wanted was to be quiet, dip my feet into cold water, set up my tarp, cook dinner, read, and go to bed. Thinking over my plans for the next day, I hoped I would make it from Nickel Creek to Longmire, which would leave me 14 miles to complete my trip tomorrow. I was scheduled to sleep one night at Paradise Camp but I changed my mind because I wanted to finish so badly. I wondered if I could handle the final 14 miles all in one day. My dream was to crawl into a real bed, be warm, drink Dr Pepper, and have a good shower. So far, I had no shower for 13 days. I stunk like a skunk!

August 27th was to be my last day of my longest backpack trip! What a long day for me! Again, I could not sleep well. The mice crawled on my face and gave me a mild bite on the right side of my neck. I got up earlier than usual and two guys from Ohio introduced themselves. One works for Hewlitt Packard in Ohio and the other had just completed 6 months backpacking the Appalachian Trail. I was impressed. They were so friendly and concerned about me. I waved good-bye. Then I walked, walked, walked, and sweated profusely! I was so happy because it was my last day. I passed several waterfalls and lakes. My feet had become really sore and painful. I stopped by Reflection Lake for a short lunch break. I had to force myself to keep going.

I knew I would soon face civilization when I saw several cars on a road paralleling Wonderland Trail. I stopped at Paradise camp to chat with two men who were happy to see me so I joined them for a short break. They offered me a bottle of water, two candies, and an energy bar. It was so nice of them. We had a short chat and then said good-bye. I crossed several bridges. At last I was approaching close, closer, and when my eyes beheld the small town of Longmire, my emotions welled up inside me, almost crying but I held onto myself. After this major milestone, I envisioned throngs of people cheering to congratulate me, but not a soul welcomed me back. I signed to God, thanking Him for protecting me on my journey until I completed my goal successfully. At last, I finally arrived at Longmire! I returned to the real world.

I walked to Leslie's ranger house where I would sleep two nights before we would head off together to the DeafBlind Retreat. The first thing I did was to take a nice warm shower and I looked forward to sleeping in a real bed. The next day I did not expect to have an upset stomach all morning. Why would this happen to me now? My left foot was so painful after having lost three nails. I suspect that maybe there was a little broken nail inside.

I cleaned my backpack and went with Leslie to Alder Lake for a swim and kayak ride. Leslie introduced me to a young woman named Eva, the mother of two children. Her daughter was deaf. We chatted with them all afternoon. We went out for pizza dinner that night. I kept patting myself on the back for completing a brave solo 93-mile trip in 14 days. I assumed that I would be ready to climb Aconcagua, South America in 1999.

First Attempt to Summit Mt. Rainier Excerpts from Miriam Richards' Journal

On May 23, 2004, I left Corvallis with an interpreter around 1 PM and drove to Rainier Mountaineering Inc (RMI) in Ashford, Washington. The trip took us about four hours. While driving, there was concern about the weather. It was mixed rain and heavy black clouds but then changed back and forth to partly sunny skies with a lot of puffy clouds. Once we entered Ashford, we went to the RMI office and met the manager who confirmed my reservation. A total of 14 climbers registered and six guides would be provided. I relaxed and walked around the outside of the office area and went out for dinner to a restaurant named Copper Creek that looked nice, quaint and cozy. I stayed in the climbers bunkhouse. It was very neat, spacious and cost $30.00 per night. The room had no door so I had to change clothes in the bathroom. While I was laying in bed I looked through the bunkhouse window at the tall green forest framing the star-lit night sky.

I had a good night, got up the next day and ate a bagel. Following breakfast, I met the group at 8 AM. The coordinator guide counted 14 climbers, three of them women. My guide, Ryan, introduced himself and said he would work with me. He double-checked my gear before departure in the shuttle bus. We rode from Ashford to Paradise. The RMI manager sat next to me and told me that he had heard so much about me. We arrived in Paradise and many of us headed immediately to the restroom. A combination of anxiety and fluids for acclimatization necessitated more frequent urination. The group was split into group A and B. I was to go with group B, designed for a slower pace.

We climbed from Paradise Inn beginning at 11 AM and arrived at Camp Muir at 5:30 PM. I knew Camp Muir from having climbed there with my friends Leslie and Hilary several years back. At that time, Camp Muir was our final destination and I had not yet been laden with MS. This time I felt great for 2.5 miles and later started to feel the weight of the heavy backpack. Two guides took some things out of my backpack. We had breaks four or five times. I was behind by three minutes. Guide Ryan trained me to learn to breathe in a rhythm that was not easy for me. It was very warm, clear weather, then within a very short time a white out fully obliterated our view! I needed to focus on my own slow pace. I thought that I was the last person to arrive at Camp Muir but I was wrong, there was one guy behind me. I felt good and commended myself for my pace. I kept asking God to help my strength and safety throughout my climbing expedition. The building designed for climbers at Camp Muir is a big square box, that is it. If I needed to use the toilet, I would have to go outside to the toilet pit. Our chef guide cooked spaghetti with garlic for our first night. I drank a lot of tea. The guide lectured about the roping in procedures we would be implementing during our climb. We practiced and learned how to tie a prusik knot. It was fun putting the knot to use. After our rope course, all climbers got into our sleeping bags. I had a difficult time sleeping due to the hard wooden floor.

All of the climbers got up at 6 AM the next morning (August 25) and went outside for stretching exercises to prepare our bodies for the physical demands ahead. I was impressed with the splendid panorama. It was a perfect sunny morning. I saw the black shadow of the ridge when the sun came up. That sight inspired me to stand up for a few minutes. I took pictures. The climbers got ready for our rope course outside where we learned to use an anchor for belay practice. Then we worked on three skills: 1. Self rescue 2. Rope guide 3. Harness/crampon review.

Guide Ryan told me that I had done a good job and I would be fine. The head guide told us he had a gut feeling that a weather front was coming and he could not promise to guide us to the summit the next day. He would have to make a last minute announcement early in the morning between 1:00- 3:00 AM if we were to go ahead with the climb. We rested in order to be mentally prepared. Oh boy! I admit that I was a little nervous and excited. I kept saying that I would be fine and climb for fun and do my best.

The next day proved to be a disappointment for us! We would face a strong storm, wind, sleet and snow for the next five days, canceling our summit attempt. Plans changed and we continued learning climbing techniques through courses inside the building. I noticed that other climbers were disappointed since they were also hoping to climb the summit. I could not believe what I saw with my own eyes: the dramatic change in the weather from perfectly sunny to a fierce storm. The guide told us that we should go outside to learn how to tolerate cold, windy, blustery conditions for an hour. I was relieved to retreat back inside for warmth. I did not enjoy that experience and at the same time found it difficult to use the pit toilet while wearing a harness along with climbing pants. I had to repeatedly use the toilet all day due to drinking a lot of water to better oxygenate my brain.

We learned more about using Topo Zone with a compass. I had difficulty understanding how to use the Topo system through an interpreter. During the night there was a short time when the weather cleared and I could see the moon and stars during one of my numerous trips outside. I was lucky, they told me, that I did not have to hear all the loud sounds created by both the weather and snoring sounds. The hearing people had trouble sleeping due to the echoing noise. I did not hear any noise. The nights are always very quiet for me. However, I remembered when Leslie, Hilary and I camped one night in a tent at Camp Muir and the canvas dome tent slapped us all night as the wind blew. Motion can be more disturbing to those who are deaf. However, constant motion such as a boat at sea is soothing.

On August 27, 2004, the unfortunate lousy weather continued. I became restless along with other climbers. One climber explained to me that the barometer tells us that the weather will be bad all week due to the pressure. The head guide announced that he was sorry that we couldn't climb the summit due to weather. I said *"Darn it!"* That means I have to come back another time. It would be hard for me to save such a huge sum of money for my next climb. I paid in advance for an interpreter and myself. We descended and I had trouble walking because the fresh snow was too deep. I fell down repeatedly and was frustrated. All the climbers went home silently. I went back to RMI to book a second attempt on Sept 16-19, 2004. I will try again!

Second Attempt Climbing Mt. Rainier
Excerpts from Miriam Richards' Journal

On September 15, 2004, the day before climbing, I drove to Auburn, Washington, to stay with Danielle's parents at their home. They had a nice house in the Mt. Rainier area. Danielle was one of the clients climbing Mt. Rainier during my first attempt. It was good to see her again and have a place to stay prior to our second attempt climbing with RMI. That night, we saw on TV that Hurricane Ivan was ravaging the southeast with gusts of 160 mph and sustained winds of 130 mph. We went to bed and had a good sleep.

The next day Danielle's mother cooked breakfast for us. We left at 5:30 AM and saw a raccoon, dog and deer. Our gear was inspected at RMI. We hiked out of Paradise at 10:45 AM. I was not used to seeing bare ground until 7,200 feet. In the past, I climbed on snow almost from the beginning. The hundreds of steps at the beginning were hard for me and I had to step really high with my short legs while my backpack weighed me down. We took breaks on three occasions. Weather was cold, windy and snowy. I did not see many people climbing. I saw a chubby squirrel searching for food.

Our guides told us we would stop to camp now instead of going to 8,800 feet due to poor weather—white out. We stopped at around 7,900 feet. Oh boy, my hands were so cold as I hurried to set up the tent in the valley protecting us from the wind. It surprised me that the trail was easier than in May 2004. I was amazed! I liked my new parka jacket, fleece jacket, rented crampons, gaiters, and shell pants. I liked the shell pants because there is more room and easy access to pull them on and slip them down.

All of us got into our tents to warm up and drank hot liquids. I hoped I would not have to get up to go to the bathroom during the night as it was very windy. This evening was for relaxing and napping off and on. I prayed to God for better weather tomorrow and crossed my fingers. I really wanted to summit and finish.

The next day was a repeat of more back luck with weather similar to what happened when I climbed last May. The snow was over two feet; we could not go to the summit. It looked like I must postpone my goal to 2005. It ended with us staying in the tent all the next day and night. We slept like bears hibernating in the winter. My body hurt because my sleeping pad was not thick enough and the duration of sleeping and lying down was too long. We just ate, slept, ate, slept, ate, and slept! Of course, I hated this and I was disappointed. It wasted my money twice now. My sharp boot crampon cut my finger. Ouch! It was cold, windy and snowing outside. There were only three climbers with two guides on this mountain. No one else was here. Our Camp Muir summit was cancelled. I wasn't sure what to do about my next RMI trip.

I wondered if a friend would be willing to guide me for free. I hated to make another reservation with no promises about weather conditions. I honestly felt hopeless. Then I shook this feeling off and started thinking about my need to work hard to earn money. The next day I met my parents in Rochester, Washington, before going home. I planned to work at the winery, driving a forklift, and referee soccer so I could save up for another summit attempt.

Third Attempt Summiting Mt. Rainier, Washington
Excerpts from Miriam Richards' Journal

What a surprise it was to receive a grant from Balance Bar to cover my RMI fees! I was so relieved and worried less about my budget. I am truly thankful to Balance Bar for the grant to help make my trip successful. I used the money for my training at a local athletic club and acclimatized in Switzerland on the Mont Blanc trail with REI Adventures. I felt that if the weather would just give me a window of opportunity, I would have my body in the best physical condition possible. The Mont Blanc trail was similar to that of Mt. Rainier.

I arrived with an interpreter on August 16, 2005, in the town of Ashford again to sleep at Mountain Inn Resort after 8 PM. The bedroom was quite small for two people, somewhat like a tent. I asked the owner if they could cook breakfast early. She said *"No, we only serve breakfast at 8 AM."* I had mixed feelings: nervous, excited and worried about weather. I did not sleep well all night and the soft bed hurt my back.

I got up the next morning at 6 AM, dressed, and ate an apple and a Balance Bar for breakfast. I drove to the RMI building. I paid for the interpreter's rented plastic boots while I reviewed my gear. Oops! I can't believe I forgot my pole baskets for use in deep snow. At the last minute I bought new poles providing me with better shock support. Before coming to RMI, I bought upgraded crampons, overmitts, gaiters, and freeze dried food at an REI store. I purchased a new digital camera for my future lectures. I needed the new technology that would provide me with easy installation into computer programs. During my trip to Switzerland with REI Adventures, I noticed that most tourists have digital cameras. My outdated camera with 12 rolls needed an upgrade.

The same two guides, Ryan and Shawn, inspected my gear. We left in an RMI van at 9:30 AM. I took a picture of me with the guides before ascending. This time I wore my Balance Bar t-shirt to let my sponsor know that I climbed Mt. Rainier. I wanted to inform people that Balance Bar sponsored my trip. Ryan asked me to lead so I could set my pace. I strolled and observed the view full circle 360 degrees. At the beginning, my body had difficulty adjusting. Later my body warmed up and gained speed. I felt good about my physical endurance. We had four short breaks. The weather was just right, cool and sunny. I loved the panoramic view the most. The hiking trails were mixed gravel, stairs, screened over rocks, snow, and boulders. I preferred hiking on snow than anything else.

Our guides searched for a place to camp at 8,300 feet. I enjoyed viewing three famous mountains: Mt. Adams, Mt. St. Helens, and Mt. Hood, referred to as "the diamond triangle." I had review crampon training, walking "Duck," "French," and taking three steps, then blowing air out. We hiked on rocks with crampons. I disliked that the most. It is difficult walking on rocks. Ryan said the practice was designed for us to trust our crampons. Ryan announced a last minute change of plans for the next day. We were originally scheduled to hike from 8,300 to 9,800 feet, but he wanted us to go up to 11,000 feet. Once we arrived at Camp Muir we picked up helmets and harnesses.

The next day, August 18th, I could not believe the bad weather came back just as it did for my first and second attempts. It was windy and rainy. Of course I was upset and disappointed, ready to cry, and I asked why it happened a third time? Ryan came to say *"Don't worry soon it will be clear."* I was unsure as to whether to trust Ryan's judgement of the weather. We had to stay in our tents all morning. I had no choice but to go back and sleep until 11 AM. Later Ryan said that we would go ahead and hike to Camp Muir. I left the camp at the 8,300 foot level at 11:30 AM and arrived near Camp Muir at 3:30 PM with a 1,700 foot gain. That was not bad while stepping onto snow. Because of continued poor weather we decided that we had better stay and camp where we were. We camped at 9,900 feet waiting for clear weather until the next day before going on up to 11,000 feet. Oh, I forgot to mention that a little bird jumped onto my hair. I was surprised. Maybe the bird was trying to tell me that everything was all right. The bird said *"Don't worry"* because it knew I was not in a good mood due to bad weather. I had three days remaining.

August 19th, I woke up and zipped open my tent door. At last I was able to see sunshine! My eyes were shocked. We left at 9:30 AM and arrived at Camp Muir 10,080 feet. I stood and stared at the beautiful scenery around the area. I started to feel in a better mood than the night before. I felt my body start pumping adrenaline. One group arrived from the summit. One of the men asked me where I was going. I told him that I was climbing up to 11,000 feet to camp on Ingraham Flats. He said, *"Wow, go for it!"* I put on my harness, helmet, and avalanche probe. I was ready to ascend to 11,000 feet. This was my first time going more than 10,080 feet on Mt. Rainer after two previous attempts. Pah! Pah! (ASL for *"Yes! At last!"*)

I slowly ascended because of the danger of falling rocks that this area is notorious for. One medium–sized rock fell and rolled toward our area, narrowly missing us. I did not like stepping on the scree trail at Cathedral Gap. As we crossed Cathedral Gap I had difficulty breathing due to the high altitude. Ryan said that we would hike 45 more minutes before arriving at Ingraham Flats Camp. We finally arrived, giving each person a high five as if to say *"Yes finally!"* It was a beautiful blue glowing glacier where we camped. Wow. Ryan said that the rule for bowel movements is that it must be put into a blue bag because of the precious environment. Only 3,000 feet were left to reach the summit. The night was full of beautiful stars and a full orange moon. I begged that the weather would be the same tomorrow.

All night I had to use the toilet several times because the guide ordered me to drink a lot of water to get more oxygen to my brain. This time I was lucky to have perfect weather to climb to the summit. The guide woke me up at 3 AM and we left at 4 AM. I climbed toward Disappointment Cleaver, the most difficult trail I had ever experienced. The trail has a mixture of snow, deep scree, and boulders that must be negotiated with very sharp crampons clamped onto hard plastic over boots.

I saw beautiful blue deep glacier in every direction. One area of the glacier was split into a deep crevasse. I was petrified over the idea of having to leap across the wide gap with my short legs but Ryan set up a belay rope and I overcame my fear and leapt over the crevasse. Whew! I was struggling to breathe three times with each step. I clearly saw Mt. Baker, Glacier Peak, and the city of Seattle. I whimsically sent thoughts to my parents living on the other side of Mt. Baker that I was climbing. We met other climbers who reached the summit and passed us. Ryan bragged that his client is deaf and has Multiple Sclerosis. One of the climbers in that group signed *"beautiful!"* and waved his hands above his head in ASL (silent clapping meaning *"congratulations!"*). Wow, that was very cool!

I became exhausted, my energy was low. Ryan suggested I leave my backpack. I kept saying *"Come on, come on, go for it!"* Finally we reached the summit at 11 AM. I was overcome with joy! Surmounting this goal of mine took all my thoughts and energy over the past year. With every odd job I worked, my mind was always right here on this summit. I had only a short break before having to descend. I was so worn out. By noon we descended back to our camp. It was hard stepping into the soft snow slipping downward with each step forcing me to work hard with both knees. Sometimes I fell into the snow. Again I had to step onto rocks with my crampons part of the way. I spotted a small bird flying higher than our 12,300 feet. That impressed me. I saw a black crow too. It took 12 and a half hours round trip. That was a very long day for me with my MS. Now I have proven to myself that am I ready to climb Alaska's highest peak.

We arrived at the tent and Shawn offered wine to everyone to celebrate my 49th highpointer. I was not thrilled to hike down from 11,000 feet to Paradise in one day. The next day I made it all the way down safely to Ashford and they gave me a certificate of congratulation. I said *"Pah! Pah!"* I finally conquered Mt. Rainer this time!

Miriam at 15,500 feet on Mt. Denali, her highest elevation of all her state summit climbs

Final High Point: Denali, Alaska
Excerpts from Miriam Richards' Journal

I went to Colorado for the third time to acclimatize in May 2006, at Brian's house in Loveland as a home base. I rented a 4-wheel drive and met my friend Lindy Deane at the Denver airport. She was surprised to see me with my short hair cut. I explained that I donated 12 inches to Locks of Love for children who lost their hair due to cancer. We drove to the trailhead of Mt. Elbert where I would lead Lindy on her climb. The last time I climbed this mountain, I was alone and it was August. My purpose was to acclimatize myself for my upcoming Alaska climb while reuniting with my good friend from Maryland.

My body was not performing as expected. I was disturbed by my MS symptoms of tiredness and weakness on the right side, both common MS symptoms. Once we reached the treeline, I told Lindy I would wait for her there and she could go ahead on her own.

Lindy climbed quickly through the snow. She is always in good shape. Once she arrived at the top, she looked around for the actual high point. Snow covered the mountain all the way so the benchmark and registry were buried beneath. Lindy was unsure where to go, there were no other climbers, but footprints went in all directions.

Scurrying down through the trees while lightning was flashing, Lindy and I returned to our rented vehicle. I could barely see the road with all its bumps in the blizzard that hit as we drove off.

The next day, we drove up Pike's Peak to visit some interesting rock formations and cultural and history sites. After dropping off Lindy at the Denver airport, I returned to Brian's house and did some landscaping for their back garden and around their house. Two days later, I picked up Hilary at the airport. After spending the weekend with her brother and family, I guided her on Mt Elbert, my second time summiting Colorado's high point. Hilary said to her family *"Miriam is acclimatized. She had already summited Mt. Elbert by herself six years ago, yet her happiness upon touching the same summit for the second time was as if it were her first. She is truly happy on mountaintops."*

Then we went to Estes Park to hike more trails at high altitude in preparation for my Denali climb. My endurance was at its best. I love carpentry work, so I helped Brian build his shed.

Anchorage May 23, 2006
Excerpts From Miriam's journal

I flew into Anchorage where I spent the night with Lyn and Jim Stirling, Hilary's relatives. They treat me like family on all my visits to Alaska. I rode a shuttle to Talkeetna. I paged Hilary on the way with my Blackberry pager:

> *5:42 PM: Shuttle driver lady says 8 French Military soldiers with us to climb Denali.*
>
> *7:46 PM: Hi again stop break 45 minutes oh no I want to arrive Talkeetna now, I must be patient. Lady driver says 1 hour and 15 min. Soldiers go drink beer, I sit van and wait.*

That was the last transmission I was able to send or receive until after my climb. Hilary and my parents had to just wait and be patient for three weeks.

I arrived in Talkeetna and met my guides Kathy Cosley, Joe and Mark at the Alaska Mountaineering School (AMS) office. I paid $23,000 for the three guides, airplane flight, food, National Park permit, and sled. The first time Kathy and I met was on my quest to climb the highest mountain in each continent during my Aconcagua, Argentina climb in 1999. Kathy knew me well; she was fully aware of my climbing style and my MS and had confidence in my abilities. Kathy has led treks and climbs worldwide. She and her husband co-authored a book on climbing techniques that reads as clear as a textbook. Prior to meeting me in Chile, Kathy started learning sign language as soon as she knew a deaf climber would be a client. I am impressed with the communication skills she learned in such a short time on my behalf.

Kathy selected two young guides from AMS to accompany us. I felt comfortable with them and their skills. I was physically and mentally prepared for the next day.

The next morning my guides inspected my gear. My sleeping bag and mittens were not sufficient protection for a Denali climb so I rented a sleeping bag guaranteed for –40 degrees protection, and overmitts. I loved the sleeping bag but never used the mitts, which were not good for fingerspelling. Kathy explained that with 21 days and a limit of three black bags of 7 pounds each for food, we would need to separate items ahead of time. The AMS building is perfect for climbers coming and going. It is clean, spacious (like the state), stocked with a variety of good climbing food, and well organized. I relaxed, then checked in at the National Park office. I paid $200.00 for a climber special use fee. I viewed an uncaptioned slide show with a review of the rules. The day was calm and the organization process smooth. A cat resides in the office along with a short black dog named Luke who loves to play basketball. I was very thirsty, perhaps from the dry air, so drank a lot of lemonade.

I was to be dressed in my mountaineering clothing and ready to go by 4:15 PM. As the propellers shook the small Talkeetna Air Taxi, my heart pounded nervously. However, the pilot looked like a pro, so I sat in front ready to enjoy the ride. The airplane had such a different movement than any I had ever experienced. It was very light and lifted softly up and down as if it were floating on a cloud. The weather could not be more perfect: sunny, blue skied with contrasting white snow covered mountains. I sat quietly and stared at the mountains for a long time. Our little air taxi reached an altitude up to 8,400 feet. The three guides sat in the back. We had around 40 minutes flying time, then we came close passing between the ridges of the mountains before pulling out and down into a hair-raising swoop over the beautiful glaciers.

I felt such an inner peace. I was silent while I savored a vision so powerful and overwhelming. The Air Taxi landed smoothly on The Southeast Fork Kahiltna Glacier. We had to disembark and unload our gear immediately so the plane could take off as soon as possible. Joel handed our permit to a National Park Ranger stationed on the Glacier. Kathy happened to know two women rangers as friends. We brought our gear to the tent area. I looked up at the awesome mountain valley at 7,200 feet. We took it easy all afternoon. Mike passed my inspection as a good chef-guide. During the evening I taught them basic ASL. It remained bright most of the night except from 2-4 AM. Kathy and I read in the tent. I was glad to have rented a Marmot Col sleeping bag because it was more spacious and warm than the one I used on Mt Rainier. It makes me feel like a hibernating bear.

On May 26th, we got up at 6:00 AM. It took two hours to pack, eat, and get ready so we departed our base camp at 8 AM with all our gear. I had my first real experience of pulling a sled while our group was roped together. First we descended Heartbreak Hill, 500 feet wearing plastic boots. My guess is that we trekked around 4.5 miles to the 7,800 foot base camp. We walked on Kahiltna Glacier—incredibly massive! I felt so small in comparison to the vastness of the glacier below the looming mountains. We enjoyed perfect weather with a nice breeze. I fell twice and struggled to get up because I stepped in soft snow causing both my legs to go deep down into snow. My guide Kathy was in front of me and was quick to cinch the rope as the assistant guides behind me followed suit. I crawled to safety with the added weight of my snow-covered backpack. Once I had fallen, the experience made me very tired. It was difficult to get back up with a heavy backpack. Kathy made the decision to put on our snowshoes and pull our packs in the sleds.

As I stared into the white snow while stepping to a steady rhythm I envisioned my shadow to be a Peruvian lady with a hat. We continued in a nice slow paced march stopping for a break several times. Joel loves the ASL sign for *"WOW!"* So far we were ambling along well and arrived at Camp 1.

Kathy inspected the ice beneath with a special pole before setting up our campsite. Mark placed ice blocks around the tent area to block the wind. I had to level off the snow by assisting with a shovel before placing our tents. Guide Joel made an impressive toilet area for poop. They asked me how to sign *"poop."* They think it is funny. I stood admiring the awesome mountains and blue glaciers around our camp at 7,800 feet. I saw a black crow. Suddenly it became very windy. I asked Kathy *"What's up tomorrow?"* Her goal was for us to move to 9,800 feet. Ski Hill would be a difficult steep upgrade. I had a satisfying and invigorating day.

I slept well that evening. By 6 AM it was still windy. We would wait for another hour. This was my first experience having a bowel movement outdoors in the ice room. That was an experience I will never forget.

One thing that climbers do is put duct tape on what climbers call the "pee" bottle and clearly label it "pee" with a heavy black marking pen to be sure to not filter water into it. Sometimes one or two people in a climbing group will do all the filtering for everyone. We line them up and take turns doing this. They want the "pee" bottles kept separate to be sure not to mix with the water bottles that look the same if not labeled.

My "pee" bottle for inside the tent was full so I was forced to go outside. We broke camp and left at 9:30 AM. It was cumbersome carrying my pack 2,000 feet up the hill. We continued step by step ever so slowly. When I looked ahead I thought that this hill would be impossible for me while pulling the sled but I surprised myself, I truly made it! I would say I hefted my backpack plus my 35 pound sled for 2.5 hours. I felt as if I were in a trance from the routine of staring down at each snow step I took from 9:30 AM to

4 PM with only three short breaks. I had a little trouble with my nose running. I caught a cold and developed a cough. I had to spit and blow my nose.

Later in the afternoon I fought against the heavy wind pushing me back. The worst part was the icy wind hitting my face. Ouch! The biting wind froze my body and clothes. But Kathy told me to keep going. I was suffering but knew I must persist towards base camp 2. Somehow my tummy told me it was time for a bowel movement.

This was totally unexpected. I knew that bladder and bowel dysfunction were among the effects of MS but did not fathom it would happen to me while I am still young and healthy. The central nervous system sending messages to the brain has some misfiring spark plugs as they jump the nerve synapse. The message telling the brain that it is time to go potty was delayed by the lack of feeling or numbness spreading around my middle. I did not expect this to happen until I was much older or when my MS was more progressed. My three guides at the last minute set up the tent in the middle of nowhere because of the bad weather. I waited, cowering my head from the wind and zoomed into the tent. I tried to keep warm and needed to clean up the residue from my unexpected bowel movement. Kathy brought a hot drink and snack. Later we ate lentil soup and spaghetti dinner. The wind died down. Kathy told me that I would not have to pull the weight of my sled the next day.

The next morning (May 28th), we got up to a clear blue sky and left at 10 AM. We walked slowly over a long distance hill from 9,800 feet to 10,000 feet. While I hiked I constantly thought of all those people who support and pray for me. I stared down at each of my meager steps like a turtle with a bright orange rope moving it along. GU is the best energy gel, giving a quick boost without the effort of eating. It slips easily down the throat when your jaw is too cold or tired to chew. I became frustrated with my developing cough and bad cold. I could not blow my nose with a handkerchief so I resorted to blowing my nose onto my overmitts.

My three guides decided to drop some heavy loads at 10,000 feet elevation. The purpose was to cache (bury) and pick them up later because of the steep incline ahead. I felt hot and layered down. I saw a chartered airplane pass us, wondering if they could see our small group of four. From 10,000 to 11,000 feet, the gain became more difficult. That hilly area was a hard part. I struggled to pull my sled up. Although Kathy had told me the night before that the assistant guides would help with my load, she changed her mind about the sled by morning.

I strolled very slowly while saying to myself that I must keep moving and be patient until arrival at camp 2. Pah! We arrived at last. Hurray... Kathy was so happy and hugged me. *"Good job Miriam!"* I sat on an ice block for a while as if it were a chair. Two other climbers volunteered to help dig the snow level for our tent. Kathy and Mike went back to get the heavy loads they had buried below. I retreated into the tent and read my favorite magazine "Guideposts" and my Into the Wild book. I searched for pills to kill my cold and cough. At Camp 2 I noticed that up to about 50 people could camp here. Each campsite had a lot of ice blocks because of the windy valley. Joel warmed up pizza. Yummy... I loved drinking warm orange Tang. I was exhausted and went to sleep at 10 PM.

I slept until 8 AM the next morning, and Joel decided to give me one day of rest and acclimatization while he and Mike carried heavy loads to Advanced Base Camp and returned the same day. Since I am not a superwoman climber, they knew that I could not carry heavy loads. They left at 9:35 AM to climb 40-degree Motorcycle Hill. I studied the trail and it appeared pretty difficult. I watched them climb as far as I could see them. It was one hour before they disappeared over the ridge. Impressive!

I took a good nap from 11 AM to 2 PM. I noticed clouds beginning to develop. I could not figure out how a black crow could soar higher than 11,000 feet. Amazing! Kathy was busy digging the snow because it was very slippery and icy for walking. She needed to level the soft snow covering our tent area where we walk. I told her that she was a busy bee while I was a lazy bee. She laughed at me. The National Park rule requires that guides must post a pole with a tag in each campsite cache burial area. If a guide should forget his tag to post on his pole, he would have to pay a high fine, the rules are very strict.

I was worried because I was wheezing. I took lung infection pills in hopes of solving the problem. I really wanted to get better before the summit. My hopes were to arrive at 14,200 feet the next day. Then I would inject my weekly Avonex shot for MS. That would provide me with more time to rest during the initial flu-like symptoms following each dose. I thanked God for bearable weather daily and prayed for good health.

The next day, May 30th, all of our plans changed. Mike and Joel were exhausted after seven hours carrying gear to 14,200 feet. They wanted to sleep. So I napped a lot and read my book all morning. Then they told me to get ready to go, WHAT! I started packing. I was puzzled. What were we doing? It started snowing and snowing. We couldn't see for any distance. After breaking camp, we stepped not more than 50 paces when all of a sudden Joel announced that he did not feel good climbing with poor visibility. We had to turn around and go back and set up the tent again at the same camp we had just left. I would have to unpack for an hour. It looked like a fire drill practice seeing how far we could get out and then back again. Snow drill practice!

I got into my tent to escape the heavy snow. I realized I would have to go ahead and give myself my MS injection now since we did not make it to ABC. Kathy asked me if she could watch me inject the needle. She saw the fluid inside the syringe as I plunged it through my skin into the muscle but it spilled out making a mess. We figured that the tip of the needle had frozen or the ingredients may have separated or changed consistency or could not flow through the tip due to temperature. Avonex could be refrigerated, not frozen or left in heat.

Kathy shook the tent repeatedly to keep the snow away from the tent. I appreciated the efforts Joel and Mike took to lug our equipment uphill.

It was still snowing the next day (May 31st)! Darn! We had to stay in the same camp for four days at 11,000 feet. I prayed, hoping it would be clear the next day. I wanted to move to 14,000 feet. I estimated around 60 people were stuck here waiting for an open window. I had only two weeks left until June 14th when my permit expired.

During the days I was holed up in my tent, one of the things that I was so fortunate to have brought along with me was a special urination funnel that is the best designed invention for women that was ever created. It is shaped to conform to our bodies so we can get it into a water bottle (clearly labeled) without having it spill over onto our sleeping bag.

Most climbing equipment is designed for men since they are the major consumers of mountaineering products. My friend Hilary had a terrible case of "shin-bang" after wearing heavy plastic climbing boots on Mt. Shasta. She was told that women suffer that problem wearing men's boots because our calves start lower. The front and back of the boot rubbed unmercifully onto her shin causing a three-year long wound. My hope is that as more women participate in mountaineering more products will be developed to meet our needs.

It was our guide Mike's 28th birthday. Joel made cheesecake with cherries and candles. We surprised him at 6 PM with other AMC people joining us. He smiled as we signed Happy Birthday. Three women joined in the festivities after hearing all the noise. After they introduced themselves I asked them questions. *"Small world,"* I told them, *"I saw you in the newspaper in Colorado."* They said yes. Pah! I felt honored to meet them in person and wished them good luck. It was a nice climber social. I got to meet three rangers. One ranger from Italy practiced sign language with me. Before he left, he said Cieso (it means good luck).

June 1st, the next day, I had to admit that I hated this day of harsh physical strain from 11,000 to 14,200 feet. It was difficult carrying a 25-pound backpack while gaining 3,200 feet. My body couldn't take the beating. I struggled. This was the wrong time for me to get diarrhea three times. It was a messy job for me to work hard to protect the environment cleaning up after myself.

Along the way, 13,400 feet, I told Kathy that I could not carry my backpack. I felt too weak. She explained that we had to go on; we could not just stop and camp in this area due to dangerous crevasses. She told me she was sorry but I had to carry my load to 14,200 feet. I shook my head *"No."* I mumbled to myself, frustrated. I begged God to give me extra strength.

Pah! I arrived at Advanced Base Camp 14,200 feet. I zoomed to the toilet pit. It took me nine hours 7:05 AM to 4 PM to climb Motorcycle Hill to Windy Corner, an endless climb. I saw a large army helicopter overhead. Later we were to learn that they came to rescue a man who had suffered severe frostbite higher up on the mountain. My three guides leveled the snow for our tent. I volunteered to help smash snow and set up the tent even though I was very exhausted. Mike said it was minus ten degrees F. I admit that I could not deal with the cold because of my MS. I had to stay inside my sleeping bag. The tent had light frost inside from our breathing. I estimated 100 people camped at ABC while we were there.

When I woke up the next morning, it was very cold. I looked forward to seeing the sun rise and warm my tent. At last the sun came out at 9:30 AM to warm us. I went outside to view Mt. Foraker. I chatted with the guides and read Between A Rock and A Hard Place by Aron Ralston, who had to cut his right arm to free himself from a fallen boulder. I was impressed with the bravery it took to do that. Reading distracted me from the cold. Twice I saw a helicopter drop food and supplies for rangers. It was interesting watching boxes lowered by rope and dropped into the snow. I met new climbers around our campsite area. I was not used to being so lazy, sitting around for days in the cold. I slept a lot because the cold weather forced me to stay inside the tent. At my home I always run errands to keep busy. Wow! What an impact it was for me to rest lazily for so long. My priority was to keep warm. I did not want frostbite.

Two days previously a man at 17,000 feet got bad frostbite on his hands and nose and an army helicopter rescued him. Frostbite is serious business. It is dangerous! The climber ranger showed me slides of frostbite prior to my climb so I would know what to watch for and know what it would turn into. I noticed that high altitude causes weird dreams every night due to less oxygen. It was very interesting. My coughing woke me during my sleep; I tried to catch my breath. Coughing in thin air with less oxygen is not easy. My body craves a lot of oxygen. I knew I had to be prepared to camp at 16,000 and 17,000 foot camps with less oxygen. I was not sure if I could face that because my body has changed since I got MS. I had to wait and see how things would go. I went outside for a short walk with Kathy. We visited new neighbors until night. No sooner had the Sun disappeared into the mountains than climbers were gone into their tents. All night I was restless because of my cough.

On June 3, 2006, Kathy and Mike went climbing toward the 16,000 foot level to drop a food cache while I stayed in the tent all morning. I got up at 11 AM and Joel taught me how to use the fixed rope and self arrest. We walked about the tent site. I exercised a little to test how I felt, working on my breathing. Joel saw me walking and told me *"good job!"* and I went back to my tent.

I remembered the first time Hilary and I came to Alaska to stay with her Uncle Jim and Aunt Lyn in Anchorage. Jim let us borrow his truck so we could drive to Denali National Park to go backpacking at Wonderlake. We left before 5 AM in order to arrive at the park in time to catch the backpackers shuttle. Traffic was light until we approached a roadblock. An enormous barge had fallen off a semi truck blocking both directions of traffic. There was no way we'd make the backpackers shuttle. Eventually a crane arrived to lift the barge causing more delays. I noticed a telephone line running behind the trees bordering the road when Hilary walked back there for another reason. I signed to her to ask if she could see the lines continuing as far as she could see. When she signed *"Yes."* I put Jim's old truck into the 4-wheel drive mode and headed for the trees. Now this is Alaska. I wouldn't try this in the lower 48. The ride was bumpy, we sank into mud holes but with wheels spinning we got out and made our way through the woods. Thick trees blocked our view of the highway so I guessed the distance past the barge and emerged to see the line of cars waiting on the other side. The people standing outside their cars waiting for the barge to clear seemed surprised when we drove out of the woods and back to the highway. Some cheered us, a bold move by two women from the lower 48 states!

Kathy returned and told me the bad news that because of the steep slope there was no place to camp at 16,000 feet. We had no choice but to climb from 14,200 feet to 17,200 feet. She told me that it would be too difficult for me to climb with a fixed rope across the split crevasse. Kathy knew it was hard for me to step high. She had just climbed the slope in deep snow and she is not much taller than I am. I said *"Oh really?"*

Kathy mentioned that from 16,000 to 17,000 feet we would have to climb a very long way on a ridge. Joel thought that it would be impossible for me to climb the entire way passing up the Headwall Camp at 16,200 feet with a 3,000 foot gain in one day. It would put an incredible demand on my physical capabilities. I was not as strong as before. I was not sure what to do, but I asked Kathy to let me try to gamble by attempting the climb and if not successful, turn back. It would break my heart to sacrifice all I put into this climb to have to give up without making one more bold attempt. But I am humble. If I cannot succeed, at least I came to see and taste the expedition as a true mountaineer. I already witnessed horrible weather, difficult trails, bad storms, met climbers who gave up, had harsh physical confrontations, stuck in a tent dealing with minus 10 degree cold.

I enjoyed seeing the beautiful glaciers, and mountains with ocean clouds. My other consideration was that I had contracted a cold and cough for two weeks that for the most part prevented me from getting better. I must remember that God and my three guides assured my safe journey. I realized that my MS could not deal with the extreme cold. I am more comfortable with hot temperatures. But maybe I will go back to climb Denali with better preparations. Who knows? What was important was my winning attitude. I received commendation for trying.

That night, a bad 50-60 mph wind crept in lasting all night. It was hard to sleep because the tent hit me repeatedly. The sun came out at 10 AM the next morning. I tried to give myself my second MS shot but it was frozen. I didn't feel good and my body was getting weak. The numbness that MS is notorious for causing was gravitating from my waist down. Kathy encouraged me to walk to the "Edge of the World" for a final picture. I told her that I would try my best. I made it to the "Edge of the World" at 2 PM. My troublesome cough made it hard to gasp for air. I took pictures of the 5,000-foot drop-off called "Valley of Death."

I asked Kathy to let me try to climb onward to 15,500 feet to see how I would feel the next day. They agreed to let me try to conquer an elevation higher than all the other state high points! Later we visited the three women from Colorado and chatted.

On June 5th, Kathy and I climbed from 14,200 feet to 15,500 feet all morning. I mumbled, *"What a hard steep headwall!"* I kept trying to triumph over each individual step as they were milestones. We gained 1400 feet within five and half hours. Kathy pushed me hard to reach my goal. I ate GU three times and drank a lot of water. Other climbers passed me and they patted me telling me *"Good job!"* for my effort. We arrived at 15,500 feet where there was a place to sit on a flat table of packed snow. I told Kathy that I had conquered a difficult steep trail. Kathy was cheerful and took pictures of me with an awe-inspiring mountain background. We left at 9 AM and arrived at the Headwall at 2:30 PM.

I wished I could camp at 16,200 feet, but this year the trail had changed to become steeper. It was very difficult to deal with my emotions having to give up my dream to complete all 50 state high points. I don't like having to say, *"I completed 49 and 3/4 high points."* I knew that it is not like me to come up short of my dream but I must accept the reality of defeat. Maybe I will return and try one more time without the guides. We walked down at a slow pace from 3 PM to 4:45 PM. As I descended, I was feeling overwhelmed by my emotions. I kept telling myself that I accomplished a great climb from the beginning 7,200 feet to 15,500 feet with a 8,000 foot gain! I sincerely appreciate all the effort my three guides put forth to support me all the way. They had their hearts on seeing me to the top.

Kathy announced that we would get up at 5:30 AM to leave camp ABC by 8 AM. I sighed. I am not a morning person. I noticed that my right lung hurt due to a persistent cough. I began to understand how difficult the Denali trail is. I recall my climb of Aconcagua, South America where I reached my highest elevation of 21,400 feet that beat Alaska's 20,320 feet. I wish I could trade those two. Oh well...

The next morning, Kathy urged me out of my hibernation because it would take three hours to pack everything. It felt as though we were moving in slow motion breaking camp in thin air. I started to pack my stuff but I felt there was something funny about my legs as I dug into the snow and ice that held down the tent. As I worked to free a rope attached tight with ice, somehow my body got numb and I tried to maintain warmth in my body by shaking my limbs one at a time.

My next problem was to carry my heavy backpack while maneuvering my balance. With my nerve synapses misfiring, my brain had to consciously maneuver my steps. This is very tiring for MS sufferers because it requires concentrated effort while others can just let their feet do the stepping without having to think about it. I knew that my two frozen MS shots were a key factor causing me to falter and triggering numbness from my tummy to my foot. I could not feel anything from the waist down when I descended. I could not determine when my foot came into full contact with the snow or whether my heel or toe touched first. It was tricky trying to determine when to lift the opposite foot. I got upset and asked Kathy to stop; I needed to take my emergency steroids now. Had I been home, my neurologist would have prescribed three days of steroid administered by IV. Although my emergency steroid pills were much less effective, they were better than nothing.

I could not deal with the cold snow storm and wind. I don't know how I made it. We left ABC camp at 8 AM and arrived at camp 2 by 1 PM. I got into my tent. I was chilled. Guide Joel brought two hot water bottles to keep me warm. My body functioned again from the steroid pills. I slept straight through the night.

June 7th was our last day to climb down from 11,000 feet to 7,200 feet without an overnight camp. At the last minute a client from a different AMS group joined us in our descent. He is the Mayor of a city in Massachusetts. He joined us on our walk back because he could not continue his climb; it was too hard for him.

Our descent would be a long one. When we were ready to leave we encountered the worst white out. We went ahead navigating by the red flag poles. Kathy was in the lead and could not see clearly. She had to stop to look at her topo map. She took what she assumed to be the right trail and indeed she led us out of the white-out unscathed! I was having difficulty with my grief because my time on Denali was over. Kathy told me that we stepped over 3000 steps in one day. Wow. How does Kathy know? She followed her GPS, counting her steps. She impressed me. I grabbed the opportunity to have one last look at the glorious mountains with glaciers.

We passed Camp 2 and then passed Camp 1 and hoped to catch the Air Taxi but we were unsure about taking off with the low clouds. Once we arrived at base camp on Kahiltna Glacier, Kathy went to see the Climbing Ranger to find out if we could ride soon. The waiting list was long. We waited for four hours and it was good news when the Air Taxi arrived and picked us up. I sat in front again as we flew between the ridges of glaciers. Once we flew out over the ridge, all of a sudden the land was green! My eyes were confused after spending two and a half weeks on white snow. I looked for grizzly bears but no luck.

After landing, I went back to the AMS office to clean up my equipment and take a shower. Joel dropped off the "poop" buckets at the ranger station and we went out for a special dinner. The restaurant was named Moose. The Mayor and I treated my three guides to beer. They loved that. The next day Kathy and I rode the bus shuttle back to the airport. Lyn and Jim were anxious to see us. Kathy hated to say good-bye as she held on with a long hug. She said she enjoyed guiding me and had an especially good time. She hoped she would see me again someday. Now Kathy has moved to France for a new life.

Having had to cancel the summit trip, I stayed with Lyn and Jim for a week and a half. Lyn and Jim took me to breakfast with their traditional Saturday breakfast group of friends. Then I went fishing at Kenai and Kasilof with a deaf guide. The best news was that I caught a 30 pound King Salmon in the Kenai River. I caught two halibuts at Homer.

I got a message from Hilary that I needed to get a notarized signature for an Energizer "Keep-going" promotion. I was selected as one of 10 finalists who were specially honored. You can check www.energizer.com to see my story, an essay Hilary submitted on my behalf. Click on the 2006 Hall of Fame Gallery. I really wanted to spend time with Jim and Lyn. They offered me their truck for my fishing trip, which was so nice of them. I bought a special hanging flower basket for them as a thank you. I gave them some of my red salmon too. Patty, one of Jim and Lyn's seven children was with us for her Fathers Day celebration. They gave me a cute bobble head moose. The day they dropped me off at the airport, Oops! I forgot my box of frozen fish at their house and they had to hurry to get it back to me at the airport. I got onto my flight in time. Whew! That was the last time I saw Hilary's Uncle Jim. He passed away within two months from cancer. I was grateful to have seen him one more time.

Guide Kathy Cosley's Perspective

I first met Miriam Richards in January of 1999, when she and her deaf friend Heidi joined an Aconcagua expedition run by Aventuras Patagonias, which was guided by myself and my husband Mark Houston.
At that time, I had never met any Deaf people, let alone guided them. I enjoyed the challenge and opportunity of learning to communicate with Miriam and Heidi, which we did by means of their patience, teaching me some basic signs, and also copious note-taking in the evenings for longer-term planning and briefing. Since that climb, Miriam has been in touch with me occasionally, updating me on her project of climbing the 50 U.S. High Points, and getting together for a short visit when she was in my neighborhood. We even attempted to plan a trekking program in the Alps for the Deaf and hard of hearing population, but for various reasons that never came about.

Miriam had asked me at various times during her High Points project, to guide her on one or more of the summits. Not having commercial permits to guide in the areas she was interested in, I was unable to help her. But when she contacted me about Denali, I agreed to see what, if anything, I could do. She really needed a custom, private trip, and wanted a guide she knew and trusted.

I was flattered and honored that she would ask me to guide her. Knowing some of the owners of guiding services with commercial permits on Denali, I contacted them, and both Mountain Trip and Alaska Mountaineering School were willing in principle to host us. The dates available through Mountain Trip did not work with my schedule, so we ended up being hosted, most warmly, by Colby Coombs of Alaska Mountaineering School.

Both Miriam and I knew that Denali would be the hardest of all the summits she has tried up to now, including Aconcagua. We discussed the challenges; the difficulties, the issues posed by her MS, and came up with some training and preparation plans. I met with her briefly in December to look at her gear, make recommendations for the purchases she still had to make, and talk some more about training and preparation.

Before we knew it, May was here, and we headed up to Talkeetna to meet and fly in to the mountain. We were joined by Alaska Mountaineering School guides Joel Geisendorfer and Mike Janes. These two made the trip complete, adding much-needed physical, technical and moral support. We made a great team, I think, all of us learning ASL as fast as our brains could take it in, and dealing with issues of weather and changes of plans as they arose. Surrounding teams, especially Joel and Mike's friends among the other AMS guides, were also very supportive and encouraging. Miriam drew the interest and admiration of various other groups around us, including three young women climbing to benefit breast cancer research funding. It was fun to visit with them in their mess tents on rest days, and to see Miriam's natural friendliness and sense of humor win her new friends and good wishes. Miriam has a gift of reaching out to others across the natural deaf/hearing communication barrier. I already knew this well, having benefited personally from that friendly open-heartedness myself.

We moved well in three days, to the camp at 11,000 feet. I was pleased to see that despite heavy packs and sleds, Miriam was able to move slowly but steadily, and needed only a few brief breaks. She has mountain experience enough to know the importance of keeping up momentum, even when one is tired or the hour is getting late. Her endurance and determination are remarkable.

We were stalled for a couple of days at 11,000 feet by heavy snow and poor visibility, but this was a good place to pause and consolidate acclimatization before moving up further.

Our day moving from 11,000 to 14,000 feet was very tough. It's a long day entailing 3,000 feet of altitude gain, and there is a long section near the top where rock-fall hazard dictates that the rope team not stop, but rather move as quickly and constantly as possible. Miriam persevered bravely, but I could see that this day had pushed her near her physical limits.

After a rest day in the 14,000 foot camp, Mike Janes and I carried a load to a cache at 16,200 feet, climbing the steep fixed lines that extend for about 600 feet up a headwall of snow and ice at an angle of about 50 to 55 degrees. I returned to report to Miriam that this would be much more difficult than the move from 11,000 feet had been.

After another rest day at 14,000 feet, Miriam suggested that we go as high as we could as a "day trip", with minimal gear, and see how that would go. I agreed that this was a sensible plan.

The following day was clear, warm and calm, with many parties moving up to a higher camp at 17,000 feet. We climbed among them to a big, comfortable snow ledge below an ice cliff at the base of the fixed lines, at about 15,500 feet. It was clear that this was as far as Miriam could safely go. A persistent cough due to the cold, dry air; the stress of living in the high and cold for two weeks; and possibly some effects of dealing with MS, added to her difficulties. She was serene and confident in the decision to turn back, showing grace and wisdom. We enjoyed the gorgeous view in perfect visibility, a short celebratory snack and photo or two, then headed back down to camp.

The next day, moving back down to the 11,000 foot camp in a gusty, bitterly cold wind, our decision to descend proved fortunate, as Miriam did suffer numbness and weakness which she attributed, based on her previous experience, to a possible MS flare-up. Her decision to take additional medication, as well as a good night's rest, had her feeling strong again the next morning, and we were able to descend all the way to Base Camp, arriving there at about 8 PM the following evening. The next afternoon we were able to fly out to Talkeetna, where we celebrated our return to green growing things, hot food served and dishes cleared away by other people, and running hot and cold water! We said good-bye at the Anchorage airport, and Miriam went on to visit with friends in Anchorage while I worked my way back home.

I truly enjoyed the chance to climb and spend time again with this warm and remarkable woman. I wish her well in all her future endeavors, which I'm sure will always be interesting and challenging ones.

Hilary White's Perspective

Upon her return to Oregon, Miriam's body was still recovering from her long ordeal on Denali and some MS symptoms remained. However, she could not pass up the opportunity to participate in World Deaf Timberfest XXV held in Stayton, Oregon. Although Miriam's health was not in top form, she could not afford to wait until the next WDT that would not be for another four years.

Miriam skipped the novice division and signed up for ten events, taking places in the following events:

Women's axe throwing	1st place
Women's "C" class chain saw	1st place
Women's "D" class chain saw	1st place
Julian Singleton's event (relay team event)	3rd place
Women's double bucking	1st place

Miriam was surprised to meet a deaf woman from back east also named Miriam so they teamed together for the womens double bucking and both Miriams won!

Miriam participated in three other events dominated by men. She competed in two other women's events. Although she did not place in the top three places for those events, she beat many men and women.

Word got around that Miriam had MS and the fans and fellow competitors were astounded. Some cried. Miriam received plaques as “Romeo Dare Memorial All Around Female Logger” and “Top Sportsmanship Female Award.”

Miriam, at home in Corvallis, Oregon, with Sierra. Photo courtesy of Jacob Blickenstaff

Epilogue

I often wear a T shirt that says:

> "Sometimes you conquer the mountain,
> Sometimes the mountain conquers you."
> (author unknown)

This has been my story and most likely will continue to be my story as it applies both to MS and to my climbing pursuits. I will never give up; I will never say *"I can't."* Life is out there to grab opportunities.

Following my MS presentations and motivational presentations, the question I am always asked is, *"What's next?"* You will have to wait for my next book (SMILE). My original dream was to conquer each of the 7 continents. Denali was and still remains at the top of my wish list. I hope that someday I will be dropped by helicopter onto Denali, enabling me to continue to the top after acclimatizing.

Climbing Denali would satisfy both my craving to complete all 50 state high points but also add to my list of continent high points. I have already summited Africa's highest point, Mt. Kilimanjaro in 2000 with Hilary. I came close to summitting Aconcagua, the highest mountain on the continent of South America. Mt. Elbrus, highest mountain in Europe is a strong possibility for me as well as Antarctica's highest summit, Mt. Vinson.

My plan is to return to teaching at Western Oregon University in the fall of 2007 as an adjunct instructor of American Sign Language (ASL). I will continue as an MS advocate and motivational speaker, as well as my odd jobs dog-walking, landscaping, forklift driver, fence building and repair.

Multiple Sclerosis research has been growing by leaps and bounds. My lesions in my brain actually shrunk as indicated by my most recent MRI. My most recent esophageal hernia surgery ended with the worst MS attack I have ever experienced. I was humbled by my experience of having become totally dependent on others to help me.

Following such a long MS aggravated recovery from my hernia surgery, I had cabin fever and was ready to get back to the outdoors. In July, 2007, my friend Lindy flew to Oregon to explore Crater Lake and the California Redwoods with me. It was wonderful!

Complications from my hernia surgery caused swelling from fluid around my heart. As Lindy and I were tent camping at Gold Beach on Oregon's coast, I began to experience intense chest pains. Lindy drove me six hours straight to Corvallis, where I was given emergency heart surgery on July 17, 2007, around 10:30 PM. Fluid surrounding my heart, Paracarditis, put pressure on my heart, giving me difficulty breathing. Three days later, I had to have a Paracardial Effusion, a procedure where a needle inserted into my back drew out fluid still remaining around my heart. With no stress having to await surgery this time, my MS villain had no time to react and I went home on July 20, 2007.

I feel that if I continue with my weekly Avonex injections without interruption, eat well, and exercise regularly, that I will return to good health and continue with my climbing. Keeping a positive outlook on life is the key; laughter is the best medicine.

My hope is that my story will inspire anyone who faces any type of adversity, whether physical or mental. I had to be aggressive to break down the barriers of others who thought I could not do what I set out to accomplish. Sometimes hard work is unbearably painful or arduous. With a goal in mind, your efforts will be rewarded.

Please check my website, www.climberm50.com for updates as I continue my goals. You are also free to contact me at miriam50@comcast.net. Thank you, again, for purchasing this book. Proceeds will go towards paying off my high point debt, and to my favorite charities as funds permit.

May God bless you and your loved ones.

.

About the Authors

Damara Paris was born in the Bay Area in California, but has lived in Oregon since age 13. She received her Master's in Rehabilitation Counseling in Deafness from Western Oregon University. Damara is deaf, and of mixed Native American descent. She has been in a number of leadership roles for Deaf Women United (Vice President, 1999-2001), Intertribal Deaf Council (President, 2002-2006), and Deaf Women of Oregon and SW Washington (Chair, 2005-06). She is the Chair of the National Deaf Women United Conference to take place in Portland, Oregonin July, 2009. Damara recently received the Randall McClleland Award from the National Association of the Deaf and Deaf Woman of the Year award from Oregon Association of the Deaf. A former manager for the State of Oregon's Telecommunications Assistance Programs (1998-2006), she currently works as a relay program manager for Sprint Relay.

Damara has always been an avid reader and enjoys writing, but put aside publishing her writing until she was in her early 30's. This is the 4th book she has written. Her other titles include *"Deaf Esprit," "You Might Be a Sign Language Interpreter If....", and "Step into the Circle: The Heartbeat of American Indian, Alaska Native and First Nations Deaf Communities."* She currently resides in Salem, Oregon, with her husband, Joe, and daughter, Sekoia.

Miriam Richards was born in Victoria, B.C. Canada and received her U.S. citizenship in 1995. Miriam is adjunct instructor of American Sign Language at Western Oregon University. She gives MS advocacy presentations and motivational speeches related to her climbing endeavors. At this time, Miriam is the 276th person to have summited the 48 US (lower 48) highpoints. She is currently the Chair of Deaf Women of Oregon and SW Washington (DWOW) and is on the committee for the Deaf Women United Conference for 2009. This is her first book.

Hilary White grew up playing in the hills with her two brothers.

After her ballet teacher rejected her for not being able to follow the music at age five, she was trained in ice-skating and school figures where music was not an issue. She competed in swimming and volleyball throughout high school and Cal State University Long Beach where she received her BA. She surfed many years in Santa Barbara. Her next sport was competitive tennis.

Although Miriam and Hilary were active in using different sports, she feels the overall variety of activities throughout their lifetimes gave them the strength for their tough climbs. Hilary feels that the toughness needed to climb some high mountains was the same type of true grit she endured when she chose to have a home birth.

Hilary teaches American Sign Language at a community college and volunteers as a well water tester. She has volunteered at deafblind retreats and at three American Association of the DeafBlind (AADB) conventions for 20 years. She hikes with Sierra Club and clears trails.

Hilary and her husband, Robert, have three athletic children of their own and helped raise a fourth, who is now a Gallaudet student. They have five grandchildren.